Dionysus Resurrected

BLACKWELL BRISTOL
LECTURES ON
GREECE, ROME
AND THE CLASSICAL
TRADITION

Blackwell Bristol Lectures on Greece, Rome and the Classical Tradition

Series Editors: Neville Morley, Charles A. Martindale and Robert L. Fowler

The Bristol Institute of Greece, Rome and the Classical Tradition promotes the study of Greco-Roman culture from antiquity to the present day, in the belief that classical culture remains a vital influence in the modern world. It embraces research and education in many fields, including history of all kinds, archaeology, literary studies, art history and philosophy, with particular emphasis on links between the ancient and modern worlds. The Blackwell Bristol lectures showcase the very best of modern scholarship in Classics and the Classical Tradition.

Publications

Why Plato Wrote
Danielle S. Allen

Tales of the Barbarians: Ethnography and Empire in the Roman West
Greg Woolf

Dionysus Resurrected: Performances of Euripides' The Bacchae *in a Globalizing World*
Erika Fischer-Lichte

Past Speakers and Lectures

2013 Mark Vessey, University of British Columbia "Writing before Literature: Later Latin Scriptures and the Memory of Rome"
2012 Bettina Bergmann, Mount Holyoke College "Worlds on the Wall: The Experience of Place in Roman Art"
2011 Colin Burrow, All Souls College, The University of Oxford "Imitation"
2010 Erika Fischer-Lichte, Free University of Berlin, "Dionysus Resurrected: Performances of Euripides' *The Bacchae* in a Globalizing World"
2009 Greg Woolf, St. Andrews University, "Barbarian Science: Ethnography and Imperialism in the Roman West"
2008 Danielle S. Allen, Institute for Advanced Study, Princeton University, "Philosophy and Politics in Ancient Athens"
2007 Ian Morris, Stanford University, "The Athenian Empire"

Future Speakers

2014 Andrew Feldherr, Princeton University
2015 Susan E. Alcock, Brown University
2016 Glenn W. Most, University of Chicago

BLACKWELL BRISTOL LECTURES ON GREECE, ROME AND THE CLASSICAL TRADITION

Dionysus Resurrected

Performances of Euripides' *The Bacchae* in a Globalizing World

Erika Fischer-Lichte

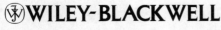

A John Wiley & Sons, Ltd., Publication

This edition first published 2014

© 2014 Erika Fischer-Lichte

Registered Office
John Wiley & Sons Ltd, The Atrium, Southern Gate, Chichester, West Sussex, PO19 8SQ, UK

Editorial Offices
350 Main Street, Malden, MA 02148-5020, USA
9600 Garsington Road, Oxford, OX4 2DQ, UK
The Atrium, Southern Gate, Chichester, West Sussex, PO19 8SQ, UK

For details of our global editorial offices, for customer services, and for information about how to apply for permission to reuse the copyright material in this book please see our website at www.wiley.com/wiley-blackwell.

The right of Erika Fischer-Lichte to be identified as the author of this work has been asserted in accordance with the UK Copyright, Designs and Patents Act 1988.

All rights reserved. No part of this publication may be reproduced, stored in a retrieval system, or transmitted, in any form or by any means, electronic, mechanical, photocopying, recording or otherwise, except as permitted by the UK Copyright, Designs and Patents Act 1988, without the prior permission of the publisher.

Wiley also publishes its books in a variety of electronic formats. Some content that appears in print may not be available in electronic books.

Designations used by companies to distinguish their products are often claimed as trademarks. All brand names and product names used in this book are trade names, service marks, trademarks or registered trademarks of their respective owners. The publisher is not associated with any product or vendor mentioned in this book.

Limit of Liability/Disclaimer of Warranty: While the publisher and author(s) have used their best efforts in preparing this book, they make no representations or warranties with respect to the accuracy or completeness of the contents of this book and specifically disclaim any implied warranties of merchantability or fitness for a particular purpose. It is sold on the understanding that the publisher is not engaged in rendering professional services and neither the publisher nor the author shall be liable for damages arising herefrom. If professional advice or other expert assistance is required, the services of a competent professional should be sought.

Library of Congress Cataloging-in-Publication Data

Fischer-Lichte, Erika, author.
  Dionysus resurrected : performances of Euripides' The Bacchae in a globalizing world / Erika Fischer-Lichte.
       pages cm
  Includes bibliographical references and index.
  ISBN 978-1-4051-7578-4 (cloth : alk. paper) – ISBN 978-1-118-60975-0 (epub) – ISBN 978-1-118-60977-4 (wol) – ISBN 978-1-118-60978-1 (epdf) – ISBN 978-1-118-60979-8 (mobi) 1. Euripides. Bacchae. 2. Greek drama–Modern presentation. I. Title.
  PA3973.B23F57 2014
  882'.01–dc23
                                                                              2013030057

A catalogue record for this book is available from the British Library.

Cover design by Nicki Averill Design

Set in 10/12pt, Sabon by Thomson Digital, Noida, India.
Printed in Malaysia by Ho Printing (M) Sdn Bhd

1 2014

Contents

Acknowledgments   vii

Preface   ix

Introduction   1
    –Rediscovering *The Bacchae* –

Part I: Festivals of Liberation: Celebrating Communality   25

Chapter 1:   The Birth Ritual of a New Theatre   27
               – Richard Schechner's *Dionysus in 69*
               in New York (1968) –

Chapter 2:   Celebrating a Communion Rite?   48
               – Wole Soyinka's *The Bacchae of Euripides*
               at London's National Theatre (1973) –

Chapter 3:   *Sparagmos* and *Omophagia*   72
               – Teat(r)o Oficina's *Bacantes* in São Paulo (1996) –

Part II: Renegotiating Cultural Identities   91

Chapter 4:   On the Strangeness and Inaccessibility of the Past   93
               – The Antiquity Project at the Schaubühne
               Berlin (1974) –

Chapter 5:   Performing or Contaminating Greekness?   116
               – Theodoros Terzopoulos' *The Bacchae* in
               Delphi (1986) –

Chapter 6:   In Search of New Identities   136
               – Krzysztof Warlikowski's *The Bacchae*
               in Warsaw (2001) –

Part III: Productive Encounter or Destructive Clash of Cultures?   157

Chapter 7: Dismemberment and the Quest for Wholeness   159
– Suzuki Tadashi's *The Bacchae* in Japan and on World Tour (1978–2008) –

Chapter 8: Transforming Kathakali   186
– *The Bacchae* by Guru Sadanam P. V. Balakrishnan in Delphi and New Delhi (1998) –

Chapter 9: Beijing Opera Dismembered   206
– Peter Steadman and Chen Shi-zheng's *The Bacchae* in Beijing (1996) –

Epilogue   225

Name Index   231

Subject Index   236

Acknowledgments

It is no secret that authors rely on the help of other people, without whom their books would not get written.

I would like to thank Charles Martindale for the invitation to Bristol and Pantelis Michelakis for taking such good care of me while I was there. At Wiley Blackwell, I am grateful to Alfred Bertrand for providing me with the initial guidance, to Haze Humbert and Ben Thatcher for seeing the project through from start to finish, and to Elizabeth Saucier for managing the public relations side of the book.

I am also indebted to the four respondents to my lectures, Martin White, David Wiles, Fiona Macintosh, and Oliver Taplin, whose insightful comments flowed into this book, as well as to the readers of the individual chapters, Susanne Klengel, Małgorzata Sugiera, Natassa Siouzouli, Georgios Sampatakakis, Eiichiro Hirata, Vasudha Dalmia, Phillip Zarrilli, and Shen Lin. I would also like to thank Fiona Macintosh and Maria Shevtsova for their helpful remarks after reading the full manuscript.

Dorith Budich and Konrad Bach provided invaluable assistance by formatting the manuscript in accordance with the stylesheet and taking care of the permissions for the images and the quotes. I am very thankful to Ursula Schinke for taking on the unenviable task of typing out my handwritten manuscript pages. Last but not least, I am very grateful to Saskya Jain for editing the manuscript.

Preface

This book seeks answers to the question of why Euripides' *The Bacchae*, which until the late 1960s had almost no performance record at all, has since been staged a number of times. This is true not just of Europe and the United States, which pride themselves on a long tradition of performing ancient Greek plays, but also of Africa, Latin America, and Asia.

During the time of late antiquity in Greece, *The Bacchae* was among the most popular tragedies. Plutarch (*De Gloria Ath.* 8) reports that it was performed in Athens frequently. Apart from performances of the whole play, actors also successfully toured with some of its solo arias. People referred to segments of the tragedy on a number of occasions – as for instance at an event that took place in the camp of the Parthians, as recorded by Plutarch (*Crassus* 33):

> Now when the head of Crassus was brought to the king's door, the tables had been removed, and a tragic actor, Jason by name, of Tralles, was singing the part of the "Bacchae" of Euripides where Agave is about to appear. While he was receiving his applause, Sillaces stood at the door of the banqueting-hall, and after a low obeisance, cast the head of Crassus into the centre of the company. The Parthians lifted it up with clapping of hands and shouts of joy, and at the king's bidding his servant gave Sillaces a seat at the banquet. Then Jason handed his costume of Pentheus to one of the chorus, seized the head of Crassus, and assuming the role of the frenzied Agave, sang these verses as if inspired (*anabakheusas . . . met' enthousiasmou*):
>
> > "We bring from the mountain
> > A tendril fresh-cut to the palace,
> > A wonderful prey."
> >   (1170–2)
>
> This delighted everybody.
>
>   (Perrin 1915: 421–422)

Plutarch also mentions that Alexander the Great frequently quoted from the tragedy at his banquets and that his mother Olympia, believed to have been a devotee of Dionysian cults, liked to play the role of Agave (Plutarch, *Alexander* 53).

In view of the tragedy's popularity during antiquity, its complete absence from European stages until 1908 and very rare reappearances after that until the end of the 1960s seems even more striking. This is not to say that *The Bacchae* had been forgotten. In the second half of the sixteenth century several translations into Latin and even one into Italian (in 1582) appeared. This more or less coincided with the inauguration of the newly built Teatro Olimpico in Vicenza, for which *Oedipus the King* was performed (1585). While many Greek tragedies were adapted or rewritten and performed during the seventeenth and eighteenth centuries, there is no record of a new version of *The Bacchae*. Interest in it was rekindled only in the first half of the nineteenth century, particularly in Germany. In 1799 Friedrich Hölderlin translated the first 24 verses of the 'Prologue', which inspired him to write his hymn "Wie wenn am Feiertage," in which Dionysus is likened to Christ. Goethe praised *The Bacchae* as his "favourite play by Euripides" and translated parts of it in 1821 (see Petersen 1974: 198). Despite his plaudits, however, the tragedy was not performed, and Goethe only staged Euripides' *Ion* (1802) in a version by August Wilhelm Schlegel and Sophocles' *Antigone* (1809) at his theatre in Weimar. Schlegel, who disliked Euripides' tragedies and set out to "correct" him in his version of *Ion*, excepted *The Bacchae* from his harsh verdict. In his *Lectures on Dramatic Art and Literature* held in Vienna in 1808, he states:

> In the composition of this piece, I cannot help admiring a harmony and unity, which we seldom meet in Euripides, as well as an abstinence from every foreign matter, so that all the motions and effects flow from one source, and concur towards a common end. After the Hippolytos, I should be inclined to assign to this play the first place among all the extant works of Euripides.
>
> (Schlegel 1965: 139)

Still, this did not encourage a theatre to stage the tragedy. It was not until the last three decades of the nineteenth century that *The Bacchae* and its protagonist Dionysus rose to prominence again, this time in the context of the quest for the origin of ancient Greek theatre, especially among classicists. The trigger was Friedrich Nietzsche's seminal treatise *The Birth of Tragedy out of the Spirit of Music* (1872), in which he states:

> Greek tragedy in its oldest form dealt with the sufferings of Dionysus . . . all the celebrated characters of the Greek stage – Prometheus, Oedipus and so on – are merely masks of that original hero . . . this hero is the suffering

Dionysus of the mysteries, the god who himself experiences the suffering of individuation.

(Nietzsche 1993: 51–52)

While Nietzsche identified the Dionysian chorus of satyrs as the origin of Greek theatre, the so-called Cambridge Ritualists some decades later believed to have found it in the so-called *eniautos daimon* ritual, the slaying and resurrection of the year-god. In her book, *Themis: A Study of the Social Origin of Greek Religion* (1912), Jane Ellen Harrison, a classics scholar and the leading spirit behind the Cambridge Ritualists, set out to prove that ancient Greek theatre originated as such a ritual. Gilbert Murray contributed a chapter entitled 'Excursus on the Ritual Forms Preserved in Tragedy' to the book. In it he attempted to show that the elements identified by Harrison as constitutive of the *eniautos daimon* ritual had survived in *The Bacchae*, where, so he argues, they fulfill similar functions as in this ritual. Murray's enthusiasm for the tragedy grew to the extent that he translated it into English, but, rather than spurring a series of performances in England, this led to only one: in 1908 the stage director William Poel, famous for his Shakespeare productions, used Murray's translation for staging the play at London's Court Theatre. Instead, in England as in the United States, *The Bacchae* was relegated to university campuses, particularly at women's colleges.

Yet the tragedy and its protagonist remained a favorite subject of classical scholarship, as demonstrated impressively by, amongst others, Walter F. Otto's study, *Dionysus: Myth and Cult* (1933), and Eric Robertson Dodds' edition of and commentary on *The Bacchae* (1944).

Despite the classicists' fascination with the play, it remained more or less absent from the stage. Two performances are known to have taken place at the ancient theatre of Syracuse (in 1922 and in 1950, the latter starring Vittorio Gassman as Dionysus) and one was recorded at the Teatr Wielki in Lwów in Poland in 1933. In 1950 Linos Karzis staged *The Bacchae* at the Odeon of Herodes Atticus in Athens, and in the early 1960s the tragedy was performed at the National Theatre of Greece, directed by Alexis Minotis (1962).

Against this backdrop of the rather meager performance history of the tragedy until the late 1960s, the sudden abundance of productions from 1968 onwards begs for an explanation. The worldwide spread of *The Bacchae* coincided with the dissemination of ancient Greek plays in general. As Edith Hall has stated in *Dionysus Since 69*, "more Greek tragedy has been performed in the last thirty years than at any point in history since Greco-Roman antiquity" (Hall, Macintosh, and Wrigley 2004: 2). Hall, Macintosh, and Wrigley (2004) focus on the question, which is also the title of their introduction, "Why Greek Tragedy in the Late Twentieth Century?" By restricting their examples to performances in Western countries (with one notable exception: Lorna Hardwick's contribution on "Greek Drama and Anti-Colonialism") and discussing them in the context of issues such as the sex war, politics, aesthetics of performance, and "the life of the mind," the performances are related to more recent social, political, aesthetic, and scientific developments in that part of the world, serving as a kind of missing link in terms of an explanation.

Other classicists often discuss the fascination with and subsequent spread of performances of Greek tragedies, especially when including those of non-Western countries, in terms of an ideology of universalism. The tragedies can be performed in cultures that lie outside of the purview of the Greek heritage, so the argument goes, because they embody universal truths and values (e.g., McDonald 1992). The same argument also frequently appears in Western theatre reviews when such performances are presented at international theatre festivals in Europe.

This argument is unacceptable for at least two reasons. First, during the colonial period, it was generally used to back up the colonizers' claim to superiority. The dichotomy between the universalism of Western cultures and the particularism of colonized cultures, constructed and upheld by the colonial masters, suggested that the only way in which the people they ruled over could enjoy universally valid cultural goods was to adopt Western ones. This means that, even today, performing a Greek tragedy enables them to experience the universal truths and values embodied in it. The concept of universalism must therefore not only be questioned but also abandoned altogether.

Second, the argument of universalism fails to answer the question of why Greek tragedies were not performed between the sixteenth and nineteenth centuries. Once translated or performed, they ought to have revealed their universal truths and values and spread like wildfire – right? The fact that this did not happen and the plays remained neglected until fairly recently highlights that the argument of universalism simply makes no sense.

Moreover, two other ideas I do not believe in often go hand in hand with universalism – that of ownership and that of the text as the primary authority controlling the performance. Often, an author's birthplace or passport is used to justify a nationalistic claim. Shakespeare is thus believed to be "owned" by the British, Ibsen by the Norwegians, Brecht by the Germans, and so on. This becomes more complicated in the case of the ancient Greek tragedies. Undeniably, the Greeks claim the exclusive right to ownership. However, most European nations but also the United States, Canada, and Australia have appropriated these plays, asserting that they also form an essential part of their cultural heritage. But if ownership can be extended from one nation to include another, as has clearly been the case, why not extend it to all without claiming universalism? The claim to ownership usually serves the purpose of awarding oneself greater competence in interpreting, understanding, and staging the plays and of rebuking "misinterpretations" committed by others.

The debate on the relationship between text and performance is not new. The idea that the written text of a play serves as an authority that controls the process of staging or that a performance acts as "concretion" or "realization" of the meanings hidden inside the text has long been superseded. Yet it is still reproduced by Western critics and sometimes even scholars with regard to Greek tragedies performed by artists from non-Western cultures. It was Brecht who already argued with respect to *Antigone* that the text of a play is nothing but a raw material to be changed at will to serve the most diverse purposes. Greek tragedies are usually translated in order to be performed. All translations are by their very nature "adaptations" and should be seen as a first step in the process of appropriation culminating in a stage production. The creative use of the main materials – the space, the actors' bodies, the translation, light, sound, etc. – and their combination, synchronization, or opposition is what constitutes the production. In addition, it is the special relationship between stage/auditorium and actors/spectators that, each night, determines the success and impact of a performance. The text is just one enabling factor among others and by no means the determining one.

This understanding of ownership and of the text as a controlling authority ultimately serves the same purpose as the ideology of universalism – to maintain the superiority of Western artists, critics, and scholars over everyone else. It does not offer any clues concerning our question.

The subtitle of this study, "Performances of Euripides' *The Bacchae* in a Globalizing World," might suggest some kind of a connection between the renewed interest in the play and globalization, even though the beginning of globalization has been a subject of some debate. Some date it to after the fall of communism, others to the 1960s, when societal shifts, e.g. due to the emergence of postcolonialism, the passage from industrialism to post-industrialism (such as in Japan and in the Western countries) and the rise and spread of novel communication technologies, provided new conditions and possibilities for politics, the economy, the market and financial flows, the production and circulation of commodities and knowledge, services, information, lifestyles, etc. As such, the above-mentioned time frame does more or less coincide with the period during which *The Bacchae* began to be revived on the world's stages.

The concept of globalization has also been defined in many different ways, which, mostly, are not mutually exclusive but simply bring one or more aspects of it into sharper focus (e.g., Appadurai 1996; Beck 2000; Ellwood 2001; Held and McGrew 2003; Lechner and Boli 2007; Steger 2003; Waters 2001). For our purposes its consequences rather than definitions are of interest, which the above-mentioned authors also discuss at great length. In summary, they seem to agree on three interrelated consequences:

1. Globalization has led to the fragmentation, indeed dissolution, of communities, giving rise to the need to find new ways of bonding. The dissolution was experienced both as a threat but also as a liberation from different kinds of oppression. In the latter case, this meant enabling a new form of bonding, allowing for the experience of a fair and equal communality. In the first case, attempts were made to restore the lost community, which ultimately turned out to be impossible. In this scenario, the new community was often only temporary and/or unstable.
2. The second consequence is the process of dedifferentiation, resulting in the loss of clear-cut, fixed and stable collective and individual identities. Instead, identities have and continue to become flexible, fluid, and ever-changing – they are identities in limbo that can no longer be described through dichotomies, which subsequently collapse.
3. The third concerns the increased number of encounters between members of different cultures and/or social classes and milieus, religions, linguistic communities, etc. They either happen as productive encounters, in which the "border" that separates them is redefined as a threshold that invites transgression, or as a destructive clash, when any attempt to transgress the "border" is seen as a hostile attack to be dealt with accordingly.

It is striking that the three most influential scholarly interpretations of *The Bacchae* in the early 1970s – i.e., at the beginning of the process of globalization – by the Swiss and German (respectively) classicists Walter Burkert and Bernd Seidensticker, the Polish theatre scholar Jan Kott and the French literary scholar and anthropologist René Girard, each focus on one of these three consequences, as will be explained in the introduction. Similarly, the performances discussed in this book all highlight one of these aspects while also considering the others. This is not to say that the reference to the process of globalization will fully answer our question. The performances discussed here all came into being in different countries between 1968 and 2008 and often under very different circumstances – in other words, global processes encountered very specific local conditions.

In this context I would like to define "local" as the given frameworks and particular circumstances prevalent at the place in which the production came into being. These include specific social and political conditions as well as cultural and theatrical traditions. The latter, for example, refers to the artists' and spectators' knowledge of various theatre forms, performance traditions and conventions, acting, dance and music styles, the actors of the company, their repertoire of plays, and their performance history, as well as many other aspects.

These conditions are important for any process of staging without, however, determining it. They form a sort of enabling structure allowing for a number of possibilities to be tried out and realized without imposing one. That is to say that the local is not necessarily or exclusively to be identified with the traditional but with the sum total of the factors and conditions prevalent at that place. The particular performance aesthetic can therefore not be predicted on the basis of a detailed description and thorough analysis of all the local conditions informing the process. The local, with all its specific conditions, does not act as a determining but as an enabling factor.

This scenario renders any kind of generalizing or homogenizing approach counterproductive, which is why I will base my arguments on individual case studies instead, taking into consideration the specific conditions of each production and its particular ways and purposes of appropriating and localizing the tragedy.

The present book is not a reception study in the classical sense. It does not consider all performances of the tragedy during this time span or investigate the different readings of the tragedy highlighted by each performance. Rather, this is a study centered on why and how the play is put to productive use and whose needs it is meant to satisfy.

This is also not a study on intercultural theatre. It is true that my case studies include performances from the United States, Great Britain, Germany, Greece, and Poland, as well as from Nigeria, Brazil, Japan, India, and China. Yet the mere fact that a text usually regarded as constitutive of the Western tradition is performed in a non-Western cultural context does not make it "intercultural theatre," especially not if we truly are to abandon the ideology of universalism, dismiss such concepts as ownership or authority of the text, and focus instead on the practices of localization. With regard to the guiding question of this study, I cannot identify a single fundamental difference between performances in so-called Western and so-called non-Western cultures that would suggest the use of the term "intercultural theatre" as a useful heuristic tool.

Lastly, I would like to define more positively what kind of a study this is. My analysis of the carefully selected performances examines how each of them dealt with and related to the three consequences of the globalizing process outlined above in terms of what they chose to show, how they showed it, and what its effect might have been. The assumption of such a link to the globalizing process serves as the point of departure. The performances in this book were chosen on the basis of whether they suggested a certain, even if not as yet apparent, affinity to this process at an early stage of my research. In order to avoid the risk of a premature and altogether misleading tendency to generalize and homogenize, I do not discuss the general link to the process of globalization in my chapters, of which each one is devoted to a different production. Instead, I relate each production to one of the consequences of globalization outlined above. It is in the epilogue that the overall process of globalization is addressed.

The situation regarding the availability of sources and other documents on the productions varies greatly in each case. Some of the performances I have seen myself. Others are documented in detail, while in some cases only a number of photographs, very few reviews, and an interview with the director, stage designer, and/or the actors exist. A note at the beginning of each chapter indicates what kind of material was available for that production. Since the material is rather scarce in some cases, it cannot be avoided that some conclusions are drawn as a result of my argument without any further evidence at hand. These cases are clearly marked, so that the reader will not mistake an assumption for the statement of an evidenced fact.

This book is intended for a broad readership. It primarily addresses theatre as well as classics scholars and students with an interest in the performance history of Greek tragedy. It is also meant for a wider public interested in theatre and its relationship to overarching political, social, and cultural developments. Moreover, those researching such developments and the impact they may have had on cultural institutions in different societies hopefully will also find some stimulating ideas in this book. Lastly, it might offer some food for thought to readers working on or interested in problems of cultural comparison – a vast and still deeply contested field. Since this book addresses not only specialists but also a broad readership, it is inevitable that, depending on their field of interest, some readers might wish that this or that argument or aspect had been included or elaborated on in more detail. However, it is my hope that the overarching line of argument is drawn clearly enough that it might spark a fruitful discussion.

References

Appadurai, Arjun. 1996. *Modernity at Large: Cultural Dimensions of Globalization.* Minneapolis: University of Minnesota Press.
Beck, Ulrich. 2000. German 1997. *What is Globalization?* Cambridge: Polity.
Dodds, Eric R. ed. 1960. *Euripides' Bacchae.* Oxford: Oxford University Press.
Ellwood, Wayne. 2001. *No-Nonsense Guide to Globalization.* London: Verso–New Internationalist.
Hall, Edith, Fiona Macintosh, and Amanda Wrigley, eds. 2004. *Dionysus Since 69: Greek Tragedy at the Dawn of the Third Millennium.* Oxford: Oxford University Press.

Harrison, Jane Ellen. 1962. *Themis: A Study of the Social Origin of Greek Religion (1912)*. New York: Meridian Books.
Held, David, and Anthony McGrew, eds. 2003. *The Global Transformations Reader: An Introduction to the Globalization Debate*, 2nd ed. Cambridge: Polity.
Lechner, Frank J., and John Boli, eds. 2007. *The Globalization Reader*, 3rd ed. Oxford: Blackwell.
McDonald, Marianne. 1992. *Ancient Sun, Modern Light: Greek Drama on the Modern Stage*. New York: Columbia University Press.
Murray, Gilbert. 1962. "Excursus on the Ritual Forms Preserved in Greek Tragedy." In *Themis: A Study of the Social Origins of Greek Religion*. Edited by Jane Ellen Harrison, 341–363. New York: Meridian Books.
Nietzsche, Friedrich. 1993. *The Birth of Tragedy out of the Spirit of Music (1872)*. Translated by Shaun Whiteside, edited by Michael Tanner. London: Penguin.
Otto, Walter F. 1965. German 1933. *Dionysus: Myth and Cult*. Translated by Robert B. Palmer. Bloomington: Indiana University Press.
Perrin, Bernadotte. 1915. *Plutarch's Lives*. London: William Heinemann; Cambridge, MA: Harvard University Press.
Petersen, Uwe. 1974. *Goethe and Euripides: Untersuchungen zur Euripides-Rezeption in der Goethezeit*. Heidelberg: Winter.
Schlegel, August Wilhelm. 1965. German 1808. *Courses of Lectures on Dramatic Art and Literature*. Translated by John Black. New York: AMS Press.
Steger, Manfred B. 2003. *Globalization: A Very Short Introduction*. Oxford: Oxford University Press.
Waters, Malcolm. 2001. *Globalization*. London: Routledge.

Further Reading

Fischer-Lichte, Erika, and Rustom Bharucha. 2011. "Dialogue on Intercultural Theatre." At http://www.textures-platform.com/?p=1667. Accessed June 12, 2013. On my rejection of the term "intercultural theatre."
Rebellato, Dan. 2009. *Theatre and Globalization*. New York: Palgrave Macmillan. Some more aspects of the relationship between theatre and globalization.

Introduction
Rediscovering *The Bacchae*

FIGURE 0.1 Bronze sculpture of Dionysus. Photo: bpk/Antikensammlung, SMB/Johannes Laurentius.

Dionysus Resurrected: Performances of Euripides' The Bacchae in a Globalizing World, First Edition. Erika Fischer-Lichte.
© 2014 Erika Fischer-Lichte. Published 2014 by John Wiley & Sons, Ltd.

Re-enter Dionysus

Dionysus, the ancient god of wine, of communal celebration, of the mysteries and of theatre, is dead. He was ousted centuries ago by Jesus Christ and passed away. But is he really gone from us? As the myth tells us, Dionysus, son of Zeus and Semele, the daughter of King Cadmus of Thebes, was dismembered and devoured by the Titans. However, Zeus destroyed them with a throw of his thunderbolt, reassembled the parts of Dionysus' body and restored his son to life. What happened once could happen again.

And it did. On June 7, 1968, at the Performing Garage on Wooster Street in New York, a slender young man with glasses addressed the audience with the following words:

> Good evening, I see you found your seats. My name is William Finley, son of William Finley. I was born twenty-seven years ago and two months after my birth the hospital in which I was born burned to the ground. I've come here tonight for three important reasons. The first and most important of these is to announce my divinity. The second is to establish my rites and my rituals. And the third is to be born, if you'll excuse me.
>
> (Schechner 1970: n.p.)

After having undergone the ritual of his rebirth the man continued:

> Here I am. Dionysus once again. Now for those of you who believe what I just told you, that I am a god, you are going to have a terrific evening. The rest of you are in trouble. It's going to be an hour and a half of being up against the wall. Those of you who do believe can join us in what we do next. It's a celebration, a ritual, an ordeal, an ecstasy. An ordeal is something you go through. An ecstasy is what happens to you when you get there.
>
> (Schechner 1970)

This was clearly Dionysus resurrected, making his reappearance in the United States of America. He came back to life in a place that had genuinely belonged to him at least from the sixth century BCE onwards: the theatre. He did so through a performance of Euripides' *The Bacchae* entitled *Dionysus in 69*, but he did not stay long. A few years later he left again and continued his journey through the modern globalizing world. Where he went immediately after his departure from the United States is unknown. Some years later he popped up again in Jamaica, England, Germany, Austria, France, Italy, and later on back home in Greece, from where he set out on a long journey to Japan, India, China, Brazil, Cameroon, and Nigeria, to name just a few countries which he honored with his divine presence. He is still roaming the five continents.

The Bacchae was Euripides' final tragedy. He wrote it in the last years of his life in Macedonia, where he had been exiled from Athens. It was performed after his death (406 BCE) in Athens, along with *Iphigenia in Aulis* and *Alcmaeon at Corinth*, which were also written abroad. *The Bacchae* is the only extant tragedy in which the god Dionysus himself appears, not just as a character but as the protagonist. The tragedy tells the gruesome story of revenge by the god against his mother's family for not believing in his divinity and spreading the rumor that he was fathered by a mortal lover of his mother. Arriving in Thebes as a stranger in the guise of a mortal human being and accompanied by a band of women from Lydia, he strikes the women of Thebes with madness so that they leave their households and ecstatically celebrate the god in the Cithaeron mountains. Pentheus, ruler of Thebes and son of Agave, one of Semele's sisters, confronts Dionysus and throws him in jail. The god frees himself by causing an earthquake that destroys the palace. Pentheus wants to spy on the women in the mountains, suspecting acts of immorality. Dionysus convinces him to dress in women's clothes in order to watch them unrecognized. He guides him to the mountains, places him on a tall fir tree and announces his presence to the women of Thebes. They get Pentheus down and tear him apart, the first blow dealt by his own mother, Agave. She impales his head on a thyrsus – a long stick twined with ivy branches and tipped with a pine cone – believing in her frenzy that it is the head of a young lion. At Thebes she awakens from her madness and falls into a state of desperation. Dionysus reveals himself and his revenge, granted to him by his father Zeus. He bans Agave, her sisters, and her parents from Thebes and the chorus sings in praise of the god.

While other Greek tragedies in the 1960s, in particular *King Oedipus*, *Antigone*, and *Medea*, had been part of a roughly 200-year-long performance history on modern European stages, *The Bacchae* had almost no performance record at all until that point. Hans Werner Henze's opera *The Bassarides*, directed by Gustav Rudolf Sellner, premiered in 1966 at the Salzburg Festival. It was a new version of *The Bacchae*. After the festival, the production was transferred to the Deutsche Oper Berlin, where it remained in the repertoire for quite a while. It constitutes a prelude of sorts to a series of performances starting in 1968 with *Dionysus in 69* (directed by Richard Schechner) and continuing throughout the 1970s. The most famous and widely discussed among them were the productions by Hansgünther Heyme at the Cologne Theatre (1973); by Luca Ronconi at Vienna's Burgtheater (1973); an adaptation by Wole Soyinka, later a Nobel laureate, commissioned by the London National Theatre, where it premiered (1973); a production of this version by Carol Dawes in Kingston, Jamaica (1975); the performance staged by Klaus Michael Grüber at the Berlin Schaubühne (1974); another one by Luca Ronconi in Prato, Italy (1977); productions by Michael Cacoyannis at the Comédie Française in Paris (1977), by Karolos

Koun at the Theatro Technis in Athens (1977), and by Tadashi Suzuki in Tokyo (1978). This impressive record would justify labeling the years between 1968 and 1978 the decade of *The Bacchae*. However, this was just the beginning. The tragedy not only entered the repertoire of European theatres and was henceforth performed on a more or less regular basis. Until recently in Japan, Tadashi Suzuki restaged it several times and encouraged other directors to do the same. Moreover, *The Bacchae* has been performed in other parts of Asia and in Africa and Latin America since the 1990s. Its recurring presence on the stages of the world over the last forty years, contradicting its almost complete absence until the late 1960s, is remarkable. With it, Dionysus returned to the theatre, raising the question of why this happened. Did staging *The Bacchae* seem an adequate response to the issues and developments that were on people's minds? Was it understood as a topical play?

The Topicality of *The Bacchae*

Dionysus' return to the theatre was not entirely coincidental. It responded to certain events and developments within the societies in which he made his appearance. The plot of *The Bacchae* seemed somehow to have resonated with these societies. *The Bacchae* was performed because its protagonist, Dionysus, in whatever manifestation, was about to appear to the community or had already done so. The play became topical because it was interpreted differently in each cultural context, depending on the local situation.

However, the tragedy is ambiguous and so is its protagonist Dionysus. The tragedy continuously emphasizes two of the god's attributes. Firstly, he is a "democratic" god because "To rich and poor he gives/the simple gift of wine,/the gladness of the grape" (Euripides 1960; v. 423–5). Secondly, he has no fixed physical form, but rather takes on different appearances at will (v. 478), his favorite embodiments being three aggressive and dangerous animals – the bull, the snake, and the lion.

The first characteristic offers comfort and gives joy to all: "by inventing liquid wine/as his gift to man,/For filled with that good gift/suffering mankind forgets its grief; from it/comes sleep; with it oblivion of the troubles/of the day" (v. 280–3). Wine releases man from the burdens of social pressures and needs and induces a state of physical satisfaction and well-being.

The second characteristic incites man's urge to commit acts of violence:

> O Dionysus, reveal yourself a bull! Be manifest
> A snake with darting heads, a lion breathing fire!
> O Bacchus, come! Come with your smile!
> Cast your noose about this man who hunts your Bacchae! Bring him down, trampled underfoot by the murderous herd of your Maenads!
>
> (v. 1017–23)

Through this second characteristic the god stokes man's drive to overpower the opponent through aggressive and brutal acts of violence. He invokes the wild beast in man.

These are only two of the many ambiguous characteristics of Dionysus as well as of the tragedy. A single reading cannot possibly account for its topical relevance in so many different places and over such a long stretch of time. Rather, each case brought into focus specific aspects and elements of the tragedy.

In this respect, the analogy between the events of the tragedy and phenomena emerging in the 1960s in the United States, Europe, and other parts of the world is striking. As happened in Thebes after the appearance of Dionysus, many countries faced serious challenges to the political, social, cultural, and moral order established or reestablished after World War II. It was a time of transition and transformation, a time of politically motivated violence – a time of crisis. In November 1963 the US President John F. Kennedy was assassinated. One year later Congress authorized President Johnson to greatly increase US involvement in Vietnam. The 1960s will always be remembered as the years of the Vietnam War and of the fierce protests against it. It was also the era of the Civil Rights Movement. Riots took place in New York, Newark, Chicago, Detroit, Washington, and Los Angeles. Martin Luther King, Jr. was assassinated in May 1968, which resulted in another outburst of riots. In 1968 the Civil Rights Movement and the protests against the Vietnam War reached a peak. Robert Kennedy was killed in June 1968 – and with him, the last hope of a speedy end to the war. A colossal anti-war demonstration was held at the Democratic Convention in Chicago in August but it was brutally put down by the police.

The year 1968 also saw various rebellious movements peak across Europe. In May, millions of French students and workers erected barricades and demanded significant changes to the French educational system. In Germany, riots had already begun in 1967. In June, when the Shah of Persia visited Berlin, students at the Free University organized a large-scale demonstration against his dictatorial reign. When the police tried to control the protest, one student was shot – we know today that the bullet was fired by a policeman who worked for the Stasi, the secret service of the GDR. This was the beginning of the student rebellion led by Rudi Dutschke, who later survived an attempt on his life but suffered from its consequences until his untimely death. The Baader-Meinhof gang, which later developed into the Red Army Faction terrorist movement, was born, first targeting huge department stores with arson, later robbing banks and kidnapping important business and finance figures, humiliating them in public and killing them.

In August 1968 Catholic civil rights marches took place in Derry, Northern Ireland. These marches are usually regarded as the beginning of a new outbreak of violence between the Protestants and the Catholics, between the British occupying forces and the Irish people, a kind of civil war that lasted about thirty years. The same month, the Prague Spring, which seemed to bring Czechoslovakia closer to democracy, was crushed by Soviet tanks. One year earlier, Greece saw the establishment of a brutal dictatorship, which lasted until 1974.

The situation was equally disastrous in other countries in which *The Bacchae* was performed. After Nigeria gained independence in 1960 and drafted its constitution in 1963, a military dictatorship was established in 1966 following several coups. In 1967 the Biafran War broke out. The region of Biafra, mainly inhabited by Christian-Catholic Ibos, declared itself an independent republic. The bloody war, notorious for its cruel hunger blockades, ended in 1970 with the reintegration of Biafra into Nigeria. This meant the end of the war but not of the instability of the political situation.

In Brazil the military coup of 1964 led to a wave of oppression and persecution. People were arrested on the most unlikely charges and tortured by the military police. Freedom of speech and expression in the arts was abolished. The military regime lasted for more than twenty years. It began to crumble from 1982 onwards and finally came to an end in 1985.

The 1960s in Japan were marked as much by rebellion, upheavals, and changes as in Europe and the United States. The protests against the US occupation and the Westernization of all strands of Japanese life first erupted in 1960 and were directed at the planned US–Japan Mutual Security Treaty. They intensified when the USA entered the Vietnam War and continued for fifteen years, i.e., even after the treaty had been signed and implemented by both parties. At the end of the 1980s and the beginning of the 1990s a new religious sect, Asahara Shôkô's AUM Supreme Truth Cult, plagued Japanese society, splitting up families and other groups, if not the society as a whole.

In the early 1990s, India was faced with renewed clashes between Hindu and Muslim communities. In December 1992 the Babri Masjid, a sixteenth-century mosque located in the town of Ayodhya, was destroyed by a mob of Hindu fanatics who believed that the mosque had been erected after the destruction of a Hindu temple marking the birth place of Lord Rama on the same site. Hundreds of people were killed as the tensions between Hindus and Muslims escalated in the aftermath of the demolition. Riots broke out, leading to many more deaths and horrendous destruction.

With the fall of communism at the end of the 1980s and beginning of the 1990s, the world order as established after World War II dissolved. All central European countries underwent a period of transformation. The German Democratic Republic (GDR) ceased to exist – Germany was reunified. The others, liberated from Soviet dominance and oppression, regained national autonomy. In Poland the process of transformation had already begun on July 1, 1980, when the Union Solidarity called a strike because of rising meat prices. This triggered a huge wave of other strikes. Although the union was outlawed under martial law on December 13, 1981, and Jerzy Popiełuszko, a Catholic priest and supporter of the Solidarity movement was murdered by the Polish secret service, it continued its work towards bringing about change from the underground or exile. The first, partly free, elections on June 4, 1989 were won by Solidarity. Tadeusz Mazowiecki from the movement became the first non-communist prime minister of Poland after World War II. Lech Wałęsa, the icon of the 1980 strike of Gdańsk, was elected president in December 1990. From the very beginning the new government turned towards Western Europe. As early as September 1989, Poland entered into an economic contract with the European Economic Community. In 1994 Poland applied for membership of the European Union.

Meanwhile, the United States found it necessary to redefine its status and role in the face of radical changes going on around the world. It claimed to be and act as the only superpower, as emphasized by George H. W. Bush in his "Address on the State of the Union" on January 28, 1992, when he declared that "the leader of the West . . . has become the leader of the world." China set out to rival this claim. After the end of the cultural revolution (1966–1976) and, even more so, after the death of Mao Zedong, who had fiercely opposed all Western influence, Deng Xiaoping inaugurated a policy of opening up to the West. The economic reforms beginning in the 1980s enabled a broader and deeper engagement with Western cultures, resulting in, among other things, the first performance of a Greek tragedy in China: *Oedipus the King* was directed by Luo Jinlin in 1986. The claim of the United States as expressed by Bush was met with reflections on how to compete in the field of culture, especially how to respond to the "invasion" of US popular culture. Attempts were made to succeed with one's own cultural productions in the worldwide markets.

Most of these cases speak to a particular kind of violence – violence by individuals against others who represent the state; violence by the government against the people of another state or against their own people; violence by groups of people against the representatives of the state or different groups fighting each other. In general terms, the authority of the state or government was challenged, to which its representatives responded with violence. This led to power struggles of many different kinds.

The same scenario can be found in *The Bacchae*. Pentheus, the ruler and representative of the State of Thebes, is introduced as a tyrant who reigns by spreading fear and terror. He has abolished free speech, as the shepherd's words confirm:

> But may I speak freely
> in my own way and words, or make it short?
> I fear the harsh impatience of your nature, sire,
> too kingly and too quick to anger.
> (v. 668–71)

His subjects also fear his uncontrolled, despotic whims because, once challenged, he maintains his control as king solely through violence. He orders Tiresias' abode to be demolished with "crowbars" (v. 346); he sends out soldiers to "catch" (v. 433) the Stranger (Dionysus) and bring him "in chains" (v. 355); he threatens to execute him, later to stone him, and orders him to be locked up in the "stables" (v. 509). He intends to fetch the women who escaped from Thebes to Cithaeron "out of the mountains" and have them trapped in "iron nets" (v. 288/9); later, to "march against them" with "all heavy armoured infantry" and the "finest troops among our cavalry" (v. 781–2, 784), and be rid of them through "a great slaughter in the woods of Cithaeron" (v. 796). After being confronted with disorder, he confirms his identity as ruler of Thebes exclusively through acts of crude military power. Anyone who refuses to comply with his will or who opposes him in any way – such as the Stranger, the Lydian Bacchae, the Theban women, or Tiresias – is accused of "mocking me and Thebes" (v. 503), of being "unruly" (v. 247) and is brutally hunted down. Pentheus is, in fact, nothing more than a wild beast which only knows how to assert itself through physical violence:

> With fury, with fury, he rages,
> Pentheus, son of Echion,
> born of the breed of Earth,
> spawned by the dragon, whelped by Earth!
> Inhuman, a rabid beast.
> A giant in wildness raging,
> storming, defying the children of heaven.
> (v. 537–44)

However, he seems to be convinced that he alone defends the integrity of the state and works for the common good. All those who do not follow him are denounced, charged with the pursuit of egotistical or amoral goals. Thus Pentheus accuses Tiresias of self-serving profit-seeking in following Dionysus: "Yes you want still another god revealed to men/so you can pocket the profits from burnt-offerings/and bird-watching" (v. 255–7). He believes he can prosecute the women of Thebes who have left "home" (v. 217) because the cult of the new god is being used solely as an excuse for immoral behavior:

> And then, one by one, the women wander off
> to hidden nooks where they serve the lusts of men.
> Priestesses of Bacchus they claim they are,
> but it's really Aphrodite they adore.
> . . . When once you see
> the glint of wine shining at the feasts of women,
> then you may be sure the festival is rotten.
> (v. 222–5, 260–2)

When Pentheus learns from the messenger that his suspicions are unfounded, he quickly finds a new excuse for violent action against the women: "Like a blazing fire/this Bacchic violence spreads. It comes too close. We are disgraced, humiliated in the eyes/of Hellas/ . . . Affairs are out of hand/ when we tamely endure such conduct in our women" (v. 778–9, 785–6).

Pentheus believes he must take action against the Stranger because "His days and nights he spends/with women and girls, dangling before them the joys/of initiation in his mysteries" (v. 235–6) and, thus, is "mocking me and Thebes" (v. 503). He rationalizes and legitimizes his brutal acts of violence with carefully chosen words, so that Tiresias justly accuses him of being "The man whose glibness flows/from his conceit of speech declares the thing he is:/a worthless and stupid citizen" (v. 269–71).

However, politically motivated violence, challenging an authority that has lost its legitimacy and entering into power struggles, were not the only issues faced by many countries in the 1960s and later. Deeper cultural changes were taking place. For instance, the 1960s saw the feminist movement grow and witnessed the emergence of a new youth culture. Young people were not only committed to political causes such as anti-war demonstrations and civil rights marches. They also experimented with new lifestyles and cultural expressions that undermined the social and moral order of the establishment. These were realized through rock music and ecstatic dances; they used psychedelic drugs; they grew their hair long and wore patchwork clothing. In Germany the student movement also meant living together in groups, so-called communes, replacing family and university dormitories, and practicing sexual freedom. Wilhelm Reich became the most popular author among German students. The students' movement also resulted in a far-reaching generational conflict. Young people attacked their parents for not having resisted the Nazis or for having contributed to their crimes in one way or another.

In some respects, the feminist movement, the hippies, the flower power movement and, generally, the new youth culture found an analogy in the women of Thebes leaving their households in order to realize a radical alternative to their former lives. After leaving their homes and their town (v. 217), they take on another way of life in the mountainous forests of Cithaeron.

> First they let their hair fall loose, down
> over their shoulders, and those whose straps had slipped
> fastened their skins of fawn with writhing snakes
> that licked their cheeks. Breasts swollen with milk,
> new mothers who had left their babies behind at home
> nestled gazelles and young wolves in their arms
> suckling them. Then they crowned their hair with leaves
> ivy and oak and flowering bryony. One woman
> struck her thyrsus against a rock and a fountain
> of cool water came bubbling up. Another drove
> her fennel in the ground, and where it struck the earth,
> at the touch of god, a spring of wine poured out.
> Those who wanted milk scratched at the soil
> with bare fingers and the white milk came welling up.
> (v. 696–712)

After giving up their social duties as defined by the men, the women have become one with nature. Not only do they dress in animal skins, living snakes, and plants, they also adopt wild animals by feeding them. In return, they themselves are nurtured by nature's juices – water, wine, milk, honey. The boundaries of the ego are lifted and any kind of identity of the self is extinguished. Its place is taken by a collective identity with nature, φύσις.

The crumbling of obsolete forms of authority and these new, alternative ways of living seem generally to justify labeling the 1960s and 1970s in the Western world and Japan as well as the 1990s in other parts of the world as a time of transition and transformation. Focusing on the cultural changes, one might subsume them under the term "cultural revolution" as it was coined by the philosopher Herbert Marcuse:

> In the West, this term first suggests ideological developments which rush ahead of the development of the social basis. Cultural revolution – but not (yet) political or economical revolution. Whilst changes have occurred in art, literature and music, in forms of communication, in morals and customs, which cause new experiences, a radical reevaluation of values does not seem to alter the social structure and its political forms of expression very much, or at least lags behind cultural changes. "Cultural revolution" implies at the same time that radical opposition today extends in a new way to the region beyond material needs and aims towards wholly reorganizing traditional culture in general.
> (Marcuse 1973: 95)

The term "cultural revolution" in our context foregrounds the radical transformation and, indeed, total break with traditional culture. Revolutionary times – including those of a cultural revolution – are liminal times. The term "liminality" was coined by the anthropologist Victor Turner in the 1960s with reference to the work of Arnold van Gennep. In his study *The Rites of Passage* (1909), van Gennep compiled a vast array of ethnological material demonstrating that rituals are linked to liminal and transitional experiences loaded with symbolic meaning. He divided rites of passage into three phases:

1. the phase of separation, in which the subjects partaking in the ritual are taken from their daily contexts and removed from their social milieu;
2. the liminal or transformational phase, in which the subjects partaking in the ritual are put into an extraordinary state, allowing for entirely new and partly disturbing experiences;
3. the incorporation phase, in which the transformed subjects are incorporated into society and accepted in their new statuses and altered identities.

According to van Gennep, this structure can be observed in a wide range of cultures. The content alone distinguishes its variants from culture to culture. Victor Turner labeled the state induced during the second phase the state of liminality (from Latin *limen* – threshold) and defined it as a state of a labile existence, "betwixt and between the positions assigned and arrayed by law, custom, convention and ceremonial" (Turner 1969: 65). He elaborates that the liminal phase creates an experimental and innovative sphere for cultures insofar as "in liminality, new ways of acting, new combinations of symbols are tried out, to be discarded or accepted" (Turner 1977: 40). According to Turner, the changes brought about by the liminal phase usually affect the social status of the participants in the ritual and extends to the entire society.

Even if taken out of the context of ritual theory, Turner's definition of liminality still applies to the state of many societies in the 1960s and 1970s and later on in the 1990s. It also applies to the plot of *The Bacchae*. In all of these cases we are confronted with new forms of behavior, in which "new ways of acting, new combinations of symbols are tried out" – be it by challenging an authority that seems to have lost its legitimacy, be it in the acts of violence ordered or committed by the state and its representatives, be it in the new ways of life adopted by members of the feminist movement or the new youth culture or in the new life the women of Thebes lead in the mountains. Although one has to be careful not to generalize, it appears that the societies in which *The Bacchae* has been performed from the late 1960s onwards can be regarded as societies in transition, experiencing a liminal state and partly even deep crisis, which will be described and defined in greater detail later on. The above sketch of the political, social, and cultural situation in the countries concerned has undeniably been executed with a very broad brush that allows only for the most obvious similarities to emerge. The specific political, social, or cultural factors and analogies between elements of the tragedy and the societies in which it was performed will be considered and discussed in the following chapters that will each focus on a particular performance.

Theories of Sacrificial Ritual in the 1970s

At the end of the 1960s and in the early 1970s *The Bacchae* was rediscovered not only by theatres, but also by classicists and other theoreticians once again dealing with the question of the origin of Greek tragic theatre. Despite key differences between their theories, they all agreed on the importance of focusing on the ancient sacrificial ritual as the most likely origin. In his essay "Greek Tragedy and Sacrificial Ritual," which appeared in 1966, Walter Burkert argues that tragedy grew from the sacrificial ritual: "The τραγῳδοί are originally a troop of masked men who have to perform the sacrifice of the τράγος which falls due in spring." Later on, "τραγῳδία emancipated itself from the τράγος, and yet the essence of the sacrifice still pervades tragedy even in its maturity. In Aeschylus, Sophocles and Euripides there still stands in the background, if not in the centre, the pattern of the sacrifice, the ritual slaying, θύειν" (Burkert 1966: 115, 116). Burkert took Aeschylus' *Agamemnon*, Sophocles' *Trachiniae*, and Euripides' *Medea* as examples for his main argument. Bernd Seidensticker (1979) argues that, in fact, *The Bacchae* provides the most convincing example. As he demonstrates, the second half of the tragedy follows exactly the order of the sacrificial ritual as described by Burkert,[1] although it does not mirror or even perform a sacrificial ritual but rather perverts it.

It begins with the decoration of the victim, which in the tragedy corresponds to Pentheus being dressed up. Then the victim is led in a procession to the place where the actual sacrifice will happen – as Dionysus leads Pentheus into the Cithaeron mountains. As in the case of the sacrifice, everything is prepared for its performance before the arrival of the sacrificial animal; in the case of the tragedy the bacchants are assembled, singing holy songs in praise of Dionysus. In the next step, the sacrificial animal "was supposed to express its consent by bowing its head" (Burkert 1966: 107). In *The Bacchae* it is Pentheus himself who asks to be placed on top of the fir tree, which is sacred to Dionysus. The god does as requested, places him on the tree, and disappears. Now, the sacrifice proper begins: "There is a prayer, a moment of silence and concentration; then all participants throw the οὐλαί (the barley) 'forward' at the victim and the altar" (Burkert 1966: 107).

Accordingly, Dionysus speaks a "prayer": "Women, I bring you the man who has mocked/at you and me and at our holy mysteries./Take vengeance upon him" (v. 1078.18). It is followed by a "moment of silence" – "The high air hushed, and along the forest glen/the leaves hung still, you could hear no cry of beasts" (v. 1084–5) – as well as by a "moment of concentration": "The Bacchae heard that voice but missed its words,/and leaping up they stared, peering everywhere" (v. 1086–7). Then the women run towards the tree and begin to throw stones, branches, and their thyrsoi at Pentheus. As described by Burkert, all participants are involved.

According to Burkert, the participants form a sacred circle around the victim and the priest steps forward to begin the sacrifice as it is here done by Agave. "Now the fatal stroke follows. At this moment the women scream, ὀλολύγουσιν . . . ; this marks the emotional climax of the θυσία" (Burkert 1966: 108). Agave is the first to "wrench away the arm at the shoulder" (v. 1126/7), immediately afterwards accompanied by her two sisters Ino and Autonoe and then the rest of the women of Thebes, who are "shrieking in triumph" (v. 1133).

After being killed, the sacrificial animal is dismembered, the inedible parts are burned on the altar, and the rest is prepared in a sacrificial bowl for a common meal. In *The Bacchae* the dismemberment of the victim, the *sparagmos*, is performed as a tearing apart, thus recalling Dionysus' dismemberment by the Titans.

> One tore off an arm,
> another a foot still warm in its shoes. His ribs
> were clawed clean of flesh and every hand
> was smeared with blood as they played ball with scraps
> of Pentheus' body.
>
> (v. 1133–6)

Agave puts Pentheus' head on her thyrsus and invites the chorus to a feast, a common meal. Later she asks Cadmus also to invite his friends to the meal.

Even the expulsion of Agave and her family from Thebes finds its model in a custom reported by Burkert. Since there might be a feeling of guilt towards the sacrificial animal, this is enacted as a kind of punishment or mock-punishment of the priest who did the killing. In some cases the sacrificial meal is followed by a trial in which the knife is found guilty and sentenced to be thrown into the sea; in others, the priest is expelled (Seidensticker 1979: 188).

As Seidensticker emphasizes, the analogy between a sacrificial ritual and the second half of *The Bacchae* is further strengthened by the particular choice of expressions used by the messenger to report the events and by Cadmus to respond to Agave's invitation to the meal (v. 124–5). They either point back to the context of such a sacrificial ritual or address it directly.

Not in spite of but because of the ritual being perverted here, the analogy between the two, in our context, is of particular interest. Burkert attributes an important social function to sacrifices:

> In a sacrifice the circle of participants is segregated from the outside world. Complicated social structures find expression in the diverse roles the participants assume in the course of the ritual, from the various 'beginnings', through prayer, slaughter, skinning, and cutting up, to roasting and, above all, distributing the meat. There is a 'lord of sacrifice' . . . And as for the rest, each participant has a set function and acts according to a precisely fixed order. The sacrificial community is thus a model of society as a whole divided according to occupation and rank. Hence, the hierarchies manifested in the ceremony are given great social importance and are taken very seriously. The sacrificial meal is particularly subject to sacred laws that regulate social interaction in distributing, giving and taking.
>
> (Burkert 1983: 37–38)

The sacrifice has the power to strengthen or renew the communal bond between the different members of a society. The ritual and, in particular, the common meal of the sacrificial animal affirms the community as such and enhances in its members the sense of *communitas*. The assumption that tragic theatre originated in sacrificial rituals seems to imply the idea that it may serve more or less the same purpose – to strengthen the bond between the citizens of the state of Athens, of the polis. Accordingly, Seidensticker calls *The Bacchae* "a tragedy about tragedy" (Seidensticker 1979: 182), i.e., a tragedy reflecting on and questioning the replacement of the sacrificial ritual by the tragedy as regards its function of communal bonding, of reaffirming a community by perverting it so that the tragedy instead deals with the dissolution of the community.

As we shall see later in a number of performances discussed in this book, the analogies between sacrificial ritual and *The Bacchae* are highlighted and laid bare with regard to the question of how to build, affirm, or even split up communities.

The same year as Burkert's *Homo Necans* (1972) another book on sacrificial ritual and the origin of theatre was published – René Girard's *Violence and the Sacred*. Girard not only deals with Greek sacrificial ritual. Rather, his is also a cross-cultural study that intends to identify features and functions of sacrifice that can be observed in different cultures. However, he uses prominent examples from ancient Greece and relates the origin of ancient Greek theatre to a crisis in the sacrificial cult. Drawing on a wealth of examples from different cultures, Girard explains that situations with a drastically growing potential for violence, which exists more or less latently in all societies, trigger an odd mechanism: a victim is found. Thus, the violence of all members of a community against each other turns into a common force directed against one victim. The "guilty" party has to be annihilated. The mob action on an allegedly guilty victim brings unity; social peace is reinstated. Girard calls this violence cathartic. It prevents the "unclean" violence of members of the community aimed at each other. This is why Girard argues that the sacrifice protects the whole community from its inherent violence. For it directs the community to specific victims beyond itself. The sacrifice relates the first sign of conflict to the victim and, at the same time, dissipates it by temporarily appeasing the members of the society. In sacrificial rituals in which an animal replaces the original, reconciling victim, this ur-scene of founding violence is repeated and reenacted. It is not only the original sacrifice but also the symbolically reenacted sacrifice that is endowed with an almost magical power to bring about a community and sustain it.

As Girard goes on to argue, the symbolic sacrifice loses this power in times of crisis in the sacrificial cult. In its place, other phenomena and institutions may step in temporarily. This is how Girard explains the emergence of Greek tragic theatre. According to him, theatre was an attempt to overcome a crisis in the sacrificial cult by symbolically representing the mechanism which underlies the reconciling sacrifice. Through its symbolic representation, theatre succeeded in serving the purpose of the reconciling sacrifice at least temporarily, i.e., in preventing a relapse into mutual violence.

Girard demonstrates this with reference to *Oedipus the King* and *The Bacchae*. He argues that *The Bacchae* is to be understood as "a festival that goes wrong" (Girard 1977: 127), for the sacrificial crisis manifests itself in the bacchanalia celebrated here. The tragedy "traces the festival back to its violent beginnings, back to its origins in reciprocal violence" (Girard 1977: 127). It emphasizes an important aspect of the crisis, namely the cancellation of difference. At first, the Dionysian annulment of difference seems peaceful. However, very quickly, it turns into an excessively violent dedifferentiation. Any and all difference is abolished: the women adopt the most violent activities of men: to hunt and go to war. The men, in turn, become effeminate. Pentheus, too, dresses up as a woman. Even the difference between man and beast is erased. The women ambush a herd of cattle because they mistake them for men trying to spy on them. Alternately, they mistake Pentheus for an animal. The difference between gods and humans, too, seems to have vanished – that between Dionysus and Pentheus. They seem to swap roles in their two confrontations. In the second half of the tragedy Pentheus appears as a kind of doppelgänger of Dionysus, suffering dismemberment as the god himself did at the hands of the Titans.

While in sacrificial rituals as described by Burkert the differences and social hierarchies among the participants remain intact even while the whole community is involved, here the differences are abolished. Thus, the sacrificial cult, according to Girard, enters a crisis. However, since in this case the crisis is brought about by the god himself, the sacrificial ritual performed with Pentheus as the victim once more is able to overcome it. The killing of Pentheus, in the reading of Girard, is the "culmination and resolution" (Girard 1977: 130) of this crisis. After the god has caused his death and chased away the ruling Cadmus family from the city, peace and order return to Thebes where, from now on, the new god will be worshipped in accordance to his wishes. Girard concludes that Dionysus turns out to be "the god of decisive mob action" (Girard 1977: 134).

Girard's theory, thus, corresponds to the situation of his own time, i.e., the outbursts of violence in modern Western societies, which went hand in hand with the transition from industrial to post-industrial societies. Social identities that constituted difference had been believed to be stable once successfully adopted. The transformations undergone by Western societies since the 1960s questioned, even shattered, such a stability. When seemingly fixed identities are destabilized, the differences between them vanish. This marks the outbreak of a crisis. Will Dionysus reappear as the "god of decisive mob action" and bring about peace and order to the societies haunted by crisis? With respect to this question, too, *The Bacchae* seemed to have been highly topical.

Another rather influential study linking Greek tragedy, specifically *The Bacchae*, to sacrificial rituals appeared in the early 1970s – Jan Kott's *The Eating of the Gods* (1974).[2] The chapter on *The Bacchae* focuses on the subject of religion and on the oscillating dichotomy between the sacred and the profane that it entails. Kott argues that the first part of the tragedy deals with a sacred ritual of sacrifice which results in the resurrection of the god; the second half, however, relates to a profanation of this ritual resulting in ritual murder.

Regarding the first half of the tragedy, Kott underlines his argument by drawing analogies between the songs sung by the chorus – a chorus of believers (Kott 1974: 201) – and the prophecies by Isaiah as well as the medieval hymns sung in Christian churches during Holy Week, and also between the tragedy and the Easter liturgy as well as the medieval Easter and Passion plays. The imprisonment of Dionysus in the dark as symbolic death is likened to Christ's crucifixion and burial and the bacchants of Lydia standing in front of the palace to the three Marys from the *Visitatio Sepulcri*:

> The symbolic sign of god's resurrection is the same in *The Bacchae* as in all medieval passion plays: emerging from the darkness of the tomb. The ritual death and resurrection of the god is accompanied by the same archetypal signs: earthquake, eclipse and thunder.
>
> (Kott 1974: 217)

Kott not only sees a strong parallel between the first half of the tragedy and the medieval Easter or Passion plays. He also remarks that the ritual elements, which Gilbert Murray in his "Excursus on the Ritual Forms Preserved in Greek Tragedy" identified as elements of the ritual of the *eniautos daimon*, the year-god, as well as of Greek tragedy, are all included in the first half of the tragedy:

> ... the clash between the god and his earthly antagonist, the suffering and symbolic death of the god, the lament, the climactic reversal of the situation, and the joyous theophany. The drama develops from tristia to gaudium and ends as in a medieval play: 'The Lord has arisen from the sepulcher.' The bacchants cry the same hallelujah: 'He has brought the high house low!/He comes, our god, the son of Zeus!' (601/2) Theophany, which closes the first part of *The Bacchae*, is the same sacred renewal of the alliance between heaven and earth.
>
> (Kott 1974: 218)

In contrast to this "sacred ritual" performed in the first half of the tragedy, the ritual sacrifice performed in the second half must be seen as profane, albeit perverted. The similarity between Dionysus and Pentheus, so central to Girard's argument, serves, according to Kott, as a precondition for the scapegoat ritual that is about to happen. He argues that the scapegoat is a surrogate who must be made to resemble the one whom he has replaced. Although the killing of Pentheus is performed as a reenactment of a divine sacrifice, it does not lead to unity and prosperity for the city. While Dionysus' dismemberment happened in *illo tempore*, in cosmic time, Pentheus is torn apart in historical time. While the god is restored to wholeness and to life, the human corpse remains torn to pieces that might be reassembled but will never be restored to life. Kott comes to the following conclusion:

> Eating of the gods – the Dionysian ritual and the Easter rite – is the victory of life over death, a triumphant feast of rebirth, fertility and abundance. *The Bacchae* ends with the defeat of order and life by sterility, negation and decay. Theophany turns into antitheophany. God has departed. Thebes is empty. All that remains is the unburied body of the King.
>
> (Kott 1974: 222)

All of Thebes' life forces have dried up. Seemingly paradoxically, "the arrival of Dionysus, god of fertility, is the destruction of procreation." Although *The Bacchae* is pervaded by eroticism,

> Eros is perverted in the Thebes of law and order, as on the green slopes of Mount Cithaeron where Dionysus rules. Eros suppressed and Eros liberated are

equally barren. In a tyrannical system Eros is always suspect. The Puritan tyrant is a voyeur.

(Kott 1974: 224–225)

On the one hand Kott historicizes the tragedy by pointing out that it was written in the third decade of the Peloponnesian War, two years before Athens fell. He states: "*The Bacchae* is the tragedy of the madness of Greece, the madness of rulers and of people" (Kott 1974: 229). On the other he topicalizes it by talking about the Puritan tyrant. Here, he not only alludes to a situation far away in the West when writing: "Pentheus looks at the Stranger the way a sheriff in Arizona would at a bearded guru who has invaded the town with a gang of tattered girls" (Kott 1974: 188). It also applies to the communist rulers in his own country, Poland, at that time.

As in the last quotation, Kott labels Dionysus a Stranger over and over again – a term used repeatedly by Pentheus (as for instance in v. 233, 353, 453, 644). He confronts Dionysus and Pentheus as "the god and the man, the King and the Stranger" (Kott 1974: 187). He stresses the intrusion of the god and his cult as the intrusion of a Stranger, who infects the city with a strange disease (v. 354) and exerts a strange new magic (v. 677) over it. Accordingly, he describes the switched roles of Dionysus and Pentheus, their reversal, as follows: "Dionysus comes to Thebes as a stranger, Pentheus leaves Thebes as a stranger . . . The godlike King had thrown the Stranger into the palace stable; now the Stranger, transformed into a god, looks in his glory from the tall stage roof at the royal body" (Kott 1974: 192–193). It is the unwise, arrogant encounter, the clash of the city's representative with the Stranger – the new god, the new cult, the new religion – that ultimately causes his own cruel death as well as that of the city.

The three readings of the tragedy, all focusing on the sacrificial ritual performed in it, are very different and partly even contradict each other. While Girard interprets the ending as a return to peace and order and a devotion to the god who will benefit the city, Kott has the horror-vision of an empty city, as dismembered as the body of Pentheus. In the context of this study there is no reason to choose one interpretation over another, or to favor one over the many others that preceded or followed them. Neither are they discussed because in the program notes to a performance one or two of them are mentioned (as in the case of Grüber's production, where the program notes include excerpts from Burkert and Kott) or because a director openly relates to one – as Warlikowski did to Kott. Rather, they are introduced here at some length because they each address one of the consequences of globalization as summarized in the preface. While Burkert/Seidensticker focus on the problem of communality and bonding, the affirmation as well as the splitting up and dissolution of a community, Girard highlights the process of dedifferentiation that results in the loss of previously given identities. Kott finally emphasizes the confrontation between the King and the Stranger, the political order and a new religious cult resulting in the destruction of the polis. These three interpretations, which all refer to the sacrificial ritual, are thus not of interest to us because they are thought of as more valid than others or even have stood the test of time – Girard's, in particular, has been quite controversial and was/is not accepted by many classicists. Rather, they form a promising point of departure because, when the process of globalization had only just begun, they already recognized in this tragedy the mechanisms and problems that theoreticians of globalization identified as resulting from this process in the 1990s. These mechanisms and problems are highlighted by the performances under discussion.

From "Text" to "Performance": A New Theatre Aesthetics

It was also in the 1960s that theatre underwent significant transformations. The focus shifted from the dramatic text to the performance itself. Performance no longer was understood and defined by the text to which it referred, but by the relationship between actors/performers and spectators. Experimental theatre and action and performance artists such as Joseph Beuys, Wolf Vostell, the FLUXUS group, or the Viennese Actionists involved the spectators in new ways, encouraging so-called audience participation or challenging them to intervene in the performance. It was stressed that a performance takes place in and through the bodily co-presence of actors/performers and spectators. Whatever the performers do affects the participating spectators; and whatever the spectators do affects the performers and other spectators. Thus, a performance comes into being only during its course. It arises from the encounter, the interaction of performers and spectators.

Hence it follows that its course cannot be entirely planned or predicted. Performances rely on autopoietic processes involving all participants, performers and spectators alike, and are characterized by a high degree of contingency. The exact course of a performance cannot be foreseen at its beginning. Even if performers set the decisive preconditions for the progression of a performance – preconditions that are determined by a set of rules or the process of the mise en scène – they are not in a position fully to control the course of the performance. Many elements emerge during a performance as a consequence of certain interactions.

In other words, over its course a performance creates the possibility for all participants to experience themselves as a subject that can co-determine the actions and behavior of others and whose own actions and behavior are similarly determined by others. The individual participants – be they performers or spectators – experience themselves as subjects that are neither fully autonomous nor fully determined by others; subjects that accept responsibility for a situation which not all of them have created but which all participate in.

This demonstrates that any performance is also to be regarded as a social process, in which different groups encounter, negotiate, and regulate their relationships in different ways. Such a social process can take different directions. It can turn into a power struggle between performers and spectators or between different groups of spectators, when one group attempts to force certain definitions of the situation or the relationship between the participants, certain ideas, values, convictions, or modes of behavior on the other(s). Since all individual participants – even if to varying degrees – co-determine the course of the performance as well as let themselves be determined by it, there are no "passive" participants. However, instead of a power struggle, some kind of a union may just as well come about among the spectators or even between performers and spectators. It is even possible that for the whole duration of the performance or at least for certain stretches of time a community among the spectators or even between actors and spectators may come into being – a community which is not necessarily based on common beliefs, ideologies, or convictions but on shared experiences (cf. Fischer-Lichte 2008).

In this respect, the performance is able to bring about what the sacrifice was supposed to accomplish – to create a bond uniting the individual participants in one community, even if it does not last. It comes as no surprise, then, that this potential of performance was stressed in the 1960s and early 1970s. The performances under investigation show that it is often the transfer of this function from sacrificial ritual to theatre that comes to the fore.

The new understanding of performance also alludes to the sacrificial ritual in another way. Given that performances arise out of the encounter of different groups of people who negotiate and regulate their relationship in different ways, it cannot be assumed that performances transmit given meanings – the meanings of a particular text or of an interpretation of it. There are the unforeseen and unplanned elements that emerge in the interaction between performers and spectators during the performances, which disturb the planned process of meaning generation. Moreover, focusing the attention on the particular phenomenality of bodies, objects, atmospheres, runs counter to the procedure of such an interpretation. Rather, it is the performance which brings forth meaning. The given text is incapable of controlling the meanings that come into being during its course. Therefore the performance cannot be seen to convey the meanings of the text or a particular interpretation of it. How then can we describe the relationship between text and performance?

On the one hand, the text can be regarded as one of the materials out of which the performance comes into being – a material just as the bodies of the performers and the particular space of the performance. It is a material that will change in the process of its usage. For the text as it stands in the book can never appear as a whole in the performance even if all lines are spoken. For one, they are spoken and, secondly, they are spoken by different actors, with breaks and silences and ruptures. On the other hand, the text is a very particular material, which, in contrast to the actors' bodies and the space, has to undergo a complete transformation in order to be performed. It has to be dismembered: the artists, actors, musicians, stage director, and designer have to tear it apart in order to be able to incorporate it into a performance piece by piece. They proceed in a manner similar to that described by Burkert. For they use and internalize that which they, a "priest" or some ruling "Zeitgeist," deem edible. That which appears to them as "bones," "inedible innards," or even "fatty vapour" is burned on the "altar" for the "gods" of the time, i.e., will not be considered in the instance of this particular production. The dismemberment of the text, its *sparagmos*, is followed by the "the common meal," the *omophagia*. The remaining pieces are put together and incorporated into the performance. The text has to be sacrificed in order to let the performance come into being. Without *sparagmos* and *omophagia* there would be no performance. In this respect, staging a play always means performing a sacrificial ritual.

In the 1960s, theatre artists in different Western countries believed that theatre needed to develop from a "hermeneutic," interpretive institution, which claims to convey timeless values formulated in the texts of the classics, into an unmistakably "political" institution. The primacy of the text was thus refuted. The classical texts were now read in terms of their potential topicality and staged accordingly. That is to say, the dismemberment of the text was no longer hidden but performed demonstratively by different means which, however, were all intended to establish a new relationship between actors and spectators and to open up possibilities for all participants to undergo new, maybe even irritating, experiences.

In light of these deliberations, it makes little sense to begin our analysis and discussion of the nine different performances of *The Bacchae*, which took place in different cultures at different times within the last forty years, with a single reading of the play. Even if a particular reading was intended, it can be safely assumed that it was different in each case. However, we can never be sure that such a reading played any role at all. Each time, the focus was on different aspects and elements which, while referring to the play, did not necessarily articulate a particular reading of it. Considering the correspondence of the three focal points identified by Burkert/Seidensticker, Girard, and Kott with the three consequences of the globalization process as identified by its theoreticians, the idea suggests itself to group the performances accordingly. That is to say that the three parts of this study will each relate to one of these three focal points or problems. This does not mean that they are mutually exclusive. Rather, the performances grouped together in this way simply emphasize and highlight that particular aspect considerably more than the others, although how this is done differs significantly in each case. While in the brief introductions to each of the three parts Dionysus is described as a liberating and community oriented god (Part I), as a god who destabilizes identities (Part II), and as the god who appears as a stranger to bring about a productive encounter or a destructive clash of cultures (Part III), this is not to say that he was intended to represent such a god in the productions discussed. Rather, it simply means that the performances achieved what the title of each part describes – they celebrated liberation and communality, destabilized the cultural identity of their spectators, and performed a productive encounter or destructive clash of cultures.

Notes

1. Burkert makes this argument first in the quoted essay and later in a much more detailed form (Burkert 1983). In the subsequent paragraphs I will sketch the analogies between the sacrificial ritual as described by Burkert and the events in the second half of *The Bacchae*, where I shall mainly follow Seidensticker's (1979) argument.
2. The book appeared first in Polish in 1970.

References

Burkert, Walter. 1966. "Greek Tragedy and Sacrificial Ritual." *Greek, Roman, and Byzantine Studies* 7: 87–121.
Burkert, Walter. 1983. German 1972. *Homo Necans: The Anthropology of Ancient Greek Sacrificial and Myth*. Translated by Peter Bing. Berkeley: University of California Press.
Euripides. 1960. *The Bacchae*. Translated by William Arrowsmith. In *The Complete Greek Tragedies*, Vol. 3. Edited by David Grene and Richmond Lattimore, 189–261. Chicago: University of Chicago Press.
Fischer-Lichte, Erika. 2008. *The Transformative Power of Performance: A New Aesthetics*. New York: Routledge.
Girard, René. 1977. French 1972. *Violence and the Sacred*. Translated by Patrick Gregory. Baltimore: Johns Hopkins University Press.

Kott, Jan. 1974. Polish 1970. *The Eating of the Gods: An Interpretation of Greek Tragedy*. Translated by Boleslaw Taborski and Edward J. Czerwinski. London: Eyre Methuen.

Marcuse, Herbert. 1973. "Art and Revolution." In Marcuse, Herbert. *Counterrevolution and Revolt*, 79–128. Boston: Beacon Press.

Schechner, Richard, ed. 1970. *Dionysus in 69*. New York: Farrar, Straus and Giroux.

Seidensticker, Bernd. 1979. "Sacrificial Ritual in *The Bacchae*." *Arktouros (FSB.M. W. Knox)*: 181–190.

Turner, Victor. 1969. *The Ritual Process: Structure and Anti-Structure*. New York: Routledge.

Turner, Victor. 1977. "Variations on a Theme of Liminality." In *Secular Rites*. Edited by S. F. Moore and B. C. Myertoff, 36–57. Assen: Van Gorcum.

van Gennep, Arnold. 1960. (1909). *The Rites of Passage*. Translated by Monika B. Vizedom and Gabrielle L. Caffee. Chicago: University of Chicago Press.

Further Reading

Schlesier, Renate, ed. 2011. *A Different God? Dionysos and Ancient Polytheism*. Berlin: De Gruyter. Provides an extensive presentation of the newest research results about Dionysus.

Seaford, Richard. 2006. *Dionysus*. New York: Routledge. Regarding the god Dionysus and his later fate in Christianity.

BLACKWELL BRISTOL LECTURES ON GREECE, ROME AND THE CLASSICAL TRADITION

Part I

Festivals of Liberation: Celebrating Communality

In antiquity, Dionysus was worshipped first and foremost as the god of liberation and communality. Even slaves were included in the festive communities at the Anthesteria and the rural Dionysia. According to Seaford, there is overwhelming evidence that Dionysus was regarded as a liberating god:

> We are told that for the duration of the City Dionysia prisoners were released from gaol and that at the same festival the freeing of slaves was announced in the theatre (Aeschines 3.41). Dionysus releases from imprisonment (. . . Pausanias 9.16.6) and in the dreams of slaves cult for Dionysus signifies freedom (Artemidorus 2.37). Even to chained slaves he brings rest (Tibullus 1.7.41–2). Plutarch (*Moralia* 613c) and Aelius Aristides (2.331 Keil) state that he releases from everything.
>
> (Seaford 2006: 29)

Dionysus Resurrected: Performances of Euripides' The Bacchae in a Globalizing World, First Edition. Erika Fischer-Lichte.
© 2014 Erika Fischer-Lichte. Published 2014 by John Wiley & Sons, Ltd.

On the one hand, Dionysus "releases from everything," while on the other, he has the power to unite people in an ecstatic community. The Dionysiac festivals served to express and affirm the unity of the polis, exhibiting it to its citizens as well as to outsiders. They continued to serve this function even in late antiquity. "For instance, St. Augustinus (AD 354–430) writes about the public nature of bacchic cult (in North Africa), with leading men of the city 'moving in a bacchic frenzy through the streets of the city' (Ep. 17.4)" (Seaford 2006: 28).

The productions of *The Bacchae* discussed in the first part of this book served seemingly similar purposes as the Dionysiac festivals by striving to bring about what in the above-quoted passages the god is said to have stood for – liberation from all kinds of barriers and pressures, be they political, social, moral, or psychological, and either the affirmation of an existing community or the uniting of the participants into a new one. Even if such a community was formed only between the performers or the spectators or a combination of both groups, and even if it didn't outlast the performance or came about only for stretches of time within the performance, it gave rise to the experience of communality, which these performances celebrated in different ways.

This happened irrespective of the ways in which Dionysus was characterized as the protagonist of the tragedy, i.e., whether or not he acted in accordance with these goals. The resurrection of Dionysus did not so much point to the protagonist and his embodiment. Rather, it pointed to functions said to have once been fulfilled by Dionysus and realized here in the – in each case very different – performances of *The Bacchae* from the United States, Nigeria, Great Britain, and Brazil. They brought to life – or at least tried to bring to life – in our times what Dionysus was believed to have accomplished in antiquity.

Reference

Seaford, Richard. 2006. *Dionysus*. New York: Routledge.

1

The Birth Ritual of a New Theatre
Richard Schechner's *Dionysus in 69* in New York (1968)

Richard Schechner and the Performance Group's adaptation of *The Bacchae* entitled *Dionysus in 69* premiered in June 1968, the day after Robert Kennedy was assassinated in Los Angeles. It closed in July 1969 after a total run of 163 performances and one month before the Woodstock Festival, one of the first major events of the hippie movement. Suspended between the manifestations of politically motivated violence and a new youth culture, the production responded to both by placing itself within this new context.

In his essay "The Politics of Ecstasy," written for an anthology about revolution and completed in March 1968 while the rehearsals of the Performance Group were still under way, Schechner deals with the question of whether and how art, particularly theatre, can contribute to revolutionary changes – especially of a cultural kind. He proceeds from the assumption that "our culture is presently in transition. It is not simply the movement from one base to another, but a process of dislocation and rearticulation" (Schechner 1969: 214). According to Schechner, this state of liminality, as Turner would call it, is caused by the inability of modern societies, particularly in the US, to reconcile individualism with communality, because, as he writes, even "Western art is individualized" (Schechner 1969: 218). Theatre, however, by its very nature as a collective art "can be celebratory, even orgiastic, and communal . . . In its communal forms, theatre is both socially constructive

---

Dionysus Resurrected: Performances of Euripides' The Bacchae in a Globalizing World, First Edition. Erika Fischer-Lichte.
© 2014 Erika Fischer-Lichte. Published 2014 by John Wiley & Sons, Ltd.

and personally 'transcendent' or ecstatic" (Schechner 1969: 213, 218). However, Western theatre has "emphasized story and character at the expense of dance, spectacle, ritual and communal celebration" (Schechner 1969: 213). If modern theatre in the United States were able to regain these lost qualities, it would be in a position to bring about a cultural revolution, to reconcile individualism and communality. This is what the Performance Group's adaptation of *The Bacchae* was meant to accomplish:

> The event will be dance, an ecstasy, and the audience will perform along with members of the Group. Our Bacchanale will not be completely celebratory: that would not be true to our social context. We hope to explore the 'politics of ecstasy', which is so important to many young people today.
> (Schechner 1969: 228)

The production remained a work-in-progress throughout its run of over one year, constantly undergoing changes. It was not intended to conjure up Dionysus' presence in the United States but paid tribute to the fact that he had arrived there already. "Dionysus' presence," which could no longer be ignored,

> can be beautiful or ugly or both. It seems quite clear that he is present in today's America – showing himself in the hippies, in the 'carnival spirit' of black insurrectionists, on campuses; and even in disguise, on the patios and in the living-rooms of suburbia. There is a qualitative link between the Orokolo Fire Fight, the Greek chorus, and our own folk-rock discothèques. LSD is contemporary chemistry, but freaking out is ancient. I take this special, ecstatic quality to be essentially theatrical.
> (Schechner 1969: 217–218)

Clearly, it is Dionysus, the god of wine – or LSD – of ecstasy, of communality and the theatre, who is being addressed here. Is this the god who is worshipped in the performance and expected to bring about social and individual change in US society? The following passage from a review might suggest such an idea:

> Finley is the play's catalyst. Around Dionysus in his near nudity and pulsating rhythm the frenzy grows. Playing music and dancing both in front of and among the audience, the actors respond to their god, Dionysus. The beat quickens. Some of the audience clap their hands, some get up and dance . . . Everyone worships Finley, even to the extent of a few actresses disrobing until they are nude from the waist up. At this point there are no actors, there is no audience, there are only Orphics.
> (DeBroske 1968: 10)

The review seems to suggest the realization of a hippie utopia, i.e., of the god of ecstasy "personally transcendent" and of the worshipping of communality. However, a few paragraphs further down we read:

> The climax of this Euripides–Schechner play leaves a horrifying imprint. The final scene, the dismemberment of Pentheus by his own mother and sisters [sic], is carried out with such precision and such emotion that parts of the audience and even one of the players objected.
> While the degenerated Bill "Pentheus" Shephard . . . is being chased by the Bacchants, fearful gasps escape from the spectators. One man who had previously danced and revelled in the cult of Dionysus, sprang into the midst of the violence shrieking: "Don't kill him! Don't kill him! Animals, you're all animals!"
>
> (DeBroske 1968: 13)

Here, the "ugly" Dionysus seems to have appeared – the god who encourages the human drive to overpower the opponent with aggressive and brutal acts of violence, invoking their beastly side. What some spectators experienced in this moment might have been the very phenomenon against which Schechner warns at the end of his essay when he writes: "Are we ready for the liberty we have grasped? Can we cope with Dionysus' dances and not end up – as Agave did – with our sons' heads on our dancing sticks?" In this scene, the "hidden fear about the new expression . . . that its forms come perilously close to ecstatic fascism" (Schechner 1969: 228) had, at least for some spectators, come true.

In the following, the abundant material on the production[1] will be analyzed with regard to three closely interrelated questions:

1. What kind of cultural revolution did *Dionysus in 69* intend to bring about?
2. What artistic means and strategies were employed to create the conditions for this cultural revolution to come about, at least for the duration of the performance?
3. What impact did participating in the performance have on the spectators?

Lastly, I wish to explore how the ambiguity of Dionysus' "beautiful" and "ugly" presence, of liberating ecstasy and "ecstatic fascism," worked.

In his essay, Schechner emphasizes that theatre is capable of contributing to a cultural revolution when it becomes communal. Then it will be both "socially constructive and personally 'transcendent' or ecstatic" (Schechner 1969: 218). As long as it continues to be individualistic, however, it will even be unable to contribute to the unfolding of an individual's potential. In his later writings Schechner elaborates on how people in industrial, individualistic societies lack essential dimensions, which define humanity as such: "Wholeness, process/organic growth, concreteness, religious, transcendental experience" (Schechner 1973: 197). Such dimensions can only be regained by reconciling individualism with communality:

> Links must be discovered or forged between industrial societies and non-industrial ones, between individualistic and communal cultures. And a vast reform in the direction of communality – or at least a revision of individualism – is necessary. This reform and revision will leave no aspect of our modern society untouched: not economics, government, social life, personal life, aesthetics, or anything else. Theatre takes a pivotal position in these movements because these movements are histrionic: a way of focusing attention and demanding change. The marches, demonstrations, street and guerrilla theatres, arrests of well-known and unknown people were for show: symbolic gestures.
>
> (Schechner 1973: 197–198)

If theatre is to bring about or at least contribute to such "a vast reform in the direction of communality," it must "discover" and realize two such "links." The first is entailed by a turn from "verbal stories" to the "event" (Schechner 1969: 227), from texts by individuals about individuals to performance. In Schechner's view, the extreme individualism of modern Western societies that robs people of dimensions defining their humanity is closely related to textual culture in general: "Because our tradition is written, it has become a burden. An oral tradition quite naturally takes its shape from the changing culture, which transmits it. A written tradition, however, tends to solidify and becomes reactionary" (Schechner 1969: 227). Schechner was here advocating a performative turn to transform the solid and fixed textual culture of the past into a fluid, ever-changing performative culture of the present and the future, which would provide the missing dimensions. Theatre could contribute to this performative turn when it set out "to treat the text as if it were part of an oral tradition" (Schechner 1969: 227). The fixed text had to be dismembered in order to allow the ever-changing performance to emerge.

The second "link" is provided by the transference or invention of particular ritualistic structures. This is why Schechner describes in detail the ritual of the Fire Fight of the Orokolo and the adoption ritual of the Asmat tribe, the first living in South and the latter in Western New Guinea.

Elaborating that such rituals bring forth communality by reaffirming the community in each repetition, he concludes "that the structure of performance is universal, that differences between 'ritual' and 'theatre' are of social function, not of performance credibility or repeatability"

(Schechner 1969: 227). If theatre is intended to bring about a reconciliation of individualism and communality, it must adopt a ritualistic form.

These two guidelines did, in fact, serve as the basis for *Dionysus in 69* to redefine individualism and to create communities of a special kind, as personal growth and communality are interdependent.

The first guideline – treating "the text as if it were part of an oral tradition" – was realized in a unique way. Schechner felt a close affinity to Jerzy Grotowski's ideas of the relationship between the textual role and the actor/performer. In Grotowski's view, the actor cannot serve the purpose of portraying and thus embodying a dramatic character. Rather, he sees the role created by the playwright as a tool: "[the actor] must learn to use his role as if it were a surgeon's scalpel, to dissect himself" (Grotowksi 1968: 37). Thus, the relationship between role and actor is reversed. The role serves as a tool to help the actor "grow," to restore "wholeness" and, thus, to be transformed. "It is a serious and solemn act of revelation – it is like a step towards the summit of the actor's organism in which consciousness and instinct are united" (Grotowksi 1968: 210).

In line with Grotowski's thinking, Schechner rejected the tacit assumption underlying realistic psychological acting, i.e., that the actor has to represent the role and, in this sense, embody it. "Rather, there is the role and the person of the performer; both role and performer are plainly perceivable by the spectator. The feelings are those of the performer as stimulated by the actions of the role at the moment of performance" (Schechner 1973: 166). This distinction does not allude to the Brechtian alienation effect. In contrast also to Grotowski's ideas, the performers should instead use the role in order to incorporate their own, wholly personal, problems and feelings into the acting. One of the performers described the process as follows:

> I am not interested in acting. I am involved in the life process of becoming whole. I do many technical exercises, which organically suit that process. They act as a catalyst for my ability to let essence flow, to let my soul speak through my mind and body . . . I am acting out my disease, the disease that plagues my inner being, that stops the flow . . . Dionysus is not a play to me. I do not act in Dionysus. Dionysus is my ritual.
>
> (Schechner 1970: n.p.)

Here, performing meant undergoing a rite of passage that might lead to a new individual identity which could encompass all the dimensions Schechner listed as lacking in people living in industrial societies. In order to make this happen, the text had to be dismembered. Of the over 1,300 lines in Arrowsmith's translation of *The Bacchae* only 600 were used, some more than once. Sixteen lines from Elizabeth Wyoff's translation of *Antigone* as well as six lines from David Grene's translation of *Hippolytus* were included.

The rest of the text – i.e., most of it – was written by the performers, either at home or in workshops. The focus was on the performers' individuality, their personal problems and expression, in order to enable the release of personal energy.

One might ask why, then, was it necessary to refer to a given text at all, especially one so far removed as an ancient Greek tragedy? Why not just use one's own texts? In his essay Schechner emphasizes that the theatre of fifth century BCE Athens – as was the case later with medieval theatre – was "community expression. We understand now that nothing the Greeks did in their arts was separate from the fabric of city life" (Schechner 1969: 219). This came close to Schechner's ideal of communal theatre. Moreover, following in the footsteps of the Cambridge Ritualists, the classics scholars of the 1960s were discovering and elaborating the ritual structure of Greek tragedy, in particular of *The Bacchae*. Ritualistic structures were needed in order to channel the enactment of personal problems and emotions should individualism and communality ever be reconciled.

On the other hand, long before staging the production, Schechner had expressed his fascination with *The Bacchae*. In his reading of the tragedy he comes to the following conclusion: "The analogues between the situation in *The Bacchae* and our own times are obvious" (Schechner 1967: 107). All members of the Performance Group responded to the tragedy more or less in the same way, as Shephard reports:

> When we first read *The Bacchae* together out loud, we were amazed how well it suited the Group. To begin with, the basic themes of the play – violence, madness, ecstasy, challenge of authority, moral choice – were all issues of great concern in American society at the time, and they seemed particularly suited to the Group's extremely physical, impulse oriented way of working. Moreover, the basic conflict in the play (in Nietzschean terms, the Appollonian [sic]/Dionysian conflict) seemed remarkably similar to the Group dynamic which fluctuated between precision and order on one hand and impulsive abandon on the other. In both, the play and the structure of the Group, the dramatic tension between social order and anarchy, discipline and impulse, created a highly charged atmosphere of social instability poised between change into a new society and self-destruction.
>
> (Shephard 1991: 52)

As Schechner did in his essays from 1967/1968, so Shephard emphasizes the Dionysian ambiguity which, on the one hand, bears the potential to create a new society while, on the other, can lead to self-destruction. As such, the text of *The Bacchae* was not perceived as being historically so far removed that a huge distance had to be overcome or bridged. Rather, it could easily be appropriated and adapted. In fact, it seemed to set free and channel personal as well as social energy.

In order to allow the performers not only to incorporate their own issues and emotions into the text but also to mark them as their own, they introduced themselves to the audience by using their proper names. As William Finley had done in the passage quoted in the introduction to this book, so did all the others. When Jason Bosseau took over the part of Dionysus, his first words were:

> My name is Jason Bosseau. I am the son of Damar Bosseau and Jessie Bartoletti. I was born twenty-seven years ago in a small boring, typical Midwestern town in south eastern Kansas called Pittsburgh . . . I've come here tonight for three very important reasons. Number one is to announce my divinity. I mean: I am a god. Number two is to establish my rites and rituals . . . And number three is to be born – in this, my birth ritual, if you'll excuse me.
>
> (Schechner 1970)

Although the performers wrote their own dialogues, there was a formal pattern underlying the creation of the text. While those taking over the part of Dionysus were free to work with their own texts right from the beginning and, over the course of the performance, moved closer and closer to Arrowsmith's translation, Pentheus had to stick to it from the start until the scene in which he is seduced/threatened by Dionysus. From then on he was allowed to speak his own lines. In both cases, the relationship between the performer and his role changed over time, allowing for ever-new identity factors to emerge or to disappear.

During the performance the performers called each other by their proper names as well as by the names of the dramatic figures they portrayed. This brought about a particular shift in their identities. The audience no longer perceived the people on stage as the actors perhaps familiar to them from before, nor could they see them as the dramatic characters alone. They had adopted another identity through the process of performing – an in-between identity that was neither clearly one nor the other. It had elements from both. It came into being by permanently crisscrossing the boundaries between the person and the dramatic character without ever completely identifying one with the other, but leaving them blurred. In addition, the performers exchanged parts over the thirteen-month run of the production, thus also swapping their in-between identities. The transformations they underwent during this time did not proceed in a linear fashion from identity A to identity B, as would have been the case in a traditional rite of passage. Rather, it was a permanent process of being transformed from one in-between identity into another. The in-between identity that emerged and disappeared in a continuous loop was the result of the performative acts carried out over the course of the performance, which suspended the actors in a liminal state and rendered the idea of the individual's stable, fixed identity and that of a definite, unambiguous text obsolete. This could potentially lead to an identity that would be individual as well as communal, thus providing the prerequisite, the *conditio sine qua non*, for a new society. However, it could just as well end up in the total loss of any kind of individual identity and pave the way for self-destruction and "ecstatic fascism."

The second guideline, the realization of given ritualistic structures – those of the play and the inclusion of certain rituals derived from other cultures, e.g., from the Asmat tribe – was applied in order to bring about a sense of communality while also minimizing the risk of self-destruction and ecstatic fascism.

The performance as a whole was structured according to the three phases of a rite of passage as elaborated by van Gennep, thus indicating that some kind of a transformation was going to take place. The first phase, determining a separation, was realized in such a way that each spectator had to enter the performance space individually. One of the performers announced to the waiting crowd:

> Ladies and gentlemen! May I have your attention, please. We are going to start letting you in now. You will be admitted to the theatre one at a time, and if you're with someone you may be split up. But you can find each other again once you're inside. Take your time to explore the environment. It's a very interesting space, and there are all different kinds of places you can sit. We recommend going up high on the towers and platforms, or down underneath them.
>
> (Schechner 1970)

The performance itself can be regarded as the liminal or transformational phase. It was structured by a sequence of rituals and ritualized events that, later on, will be analyzed more closely.

The incorporation phase began when the doors of the Performance Garage opened and the performers began to march out into the streets, often followed by a large number of spectators. Were all of those participating in the incorporation phase actually transformed during the liminal or transformational phase, so that they had to be accepted by and incorporated into society with their new identities? And, if so, what kind of transformation did they undergo?

The most important rituals, in which the performers and some of the spectators were involved, were the birth ritual of Dionysus in the beginning (which corresponded to the death ritual Pentheus underwent in the end); the so-called Dionysus Game which replaced the scene after Dionysus was arrested by Pentheus' guards, when the king's palace collapsed because of an earthquake; and the "Total Caress," which took place towards the end of the play (and after Pentheus and Dionysus had left the scene for a homoerotic encounter inside the palace). All these rituals were meant to establish a community or strengthen the sense of communality either among the members of the Group only or among all participants, including the spectators.

Although not in agreement with David Cooper's overall description of communes (Cooper 1970: 44–45), Schechner uses his definition of communal groups as "a viable dialectic between solitude and being with others" (Cooper 1970: 44). This definition may serve us as a yardstick for trying to assess whether communities were established and whether communality was actually celebrated over the course of the performance.

Among the rituals mentioned above the only one clearly involving only members of the Group was the Dionysus Game:

> We turned to exercises from the workshop. We had been playing an encounter game in which one performer challenges another. A question or statement is made which, according to the rule of the exercise, must 'cost something'. An answer is given which is equally revealing and difficult. And so on, until every one has contributed at least once . . . After every one in the group had participated in the encounter, people could turn on Shephard, who was playing Pentheus at this time. Shephard had to answer the questions, but could not ask any. The game continued until Shephard's opacity was sufficiently pierced so that he could not respond to the question. Then he said, 'This is mortifying', and the game was over. Once the questioning went on for more than an hour.
>
> (Schechner 1970)

At first glance, it may seem that the conditions were the same for all the participants. The question-and-answer game challenged everybody taking part in it equally, for it must always "cost something." Each member of the group became vulnerable. Secondly, it was officially declared a game, which meant that whoever was intended as the victim, so to speak, only took over that role for the duration of the game. Thirdly, the game was part of a fictitious story. The chosen victim played the role of Pentheus, the ruler and man of law and order who brutally suppressed the others. In this scenario the game oscillated and blurred the boundaries between the social reality of the Group, the reality of the game, and the fictitious reality of the play. Everyone involved in the game permanently transgressed the boundaries between different realities and found themselves poised in between.

However, this in-betweenness did allow for varied perceptions regarding individual participants. While most members might have focused their attention on the ludic aspect or the storyline of the play, Bill Shephard experienced it as something like Girard's ur-scene: a victim is identified in order to be expelled from the community (of the Group) and sacrificed. Despite the rule that everyone at least once take on the role of the victim,

Shephard–Pentheus experienced the situation as a kind of exclusion from the Group. More than twenty years later, he still states:

> I believe that I was the only person in the Group . . . who had misgivings about the performance strategy we had adopted . . . I began to feel more and more separated from the rest of the Group in my role as Pentheus.
> (Shephard 1991: 114, 116)

In this sense, Shephard/Pentheus was "sacrificed" for the sake of the rest of the Group so that they could see themselves and act as a community. Even here, the ambiguity of the performance strategy comes to the fore.

This experience might have prompted Shephard to change his role (Shephard 1991: 181). The critic Stefan Brecht, who went to see the production several times in the spring of 1968, the fall of 1968, and in the winter of 1968/69, writes about a change he witnessed in the fall:

> The story of Pentheus has become central to the production. Bill Shephard from being no actor has become a good one; his experiences over the summer led him to reject his initial authoritarian interpretation of Pentheus. He now starts out playing him as a reasonable, responsible, mildly conservative ruler. His counsellors Cadmus & Teiresias have become strident rebels. This sets Pentheus as a juvenile victim. Thus, the play has become apolitical. The theme of resistance to authority has been dropped. (Brecht 1969: 166)[2]

This change seems also to have affected the Dionysus Game, turning it from a kind of sacrificial ritual into a playful game.

All the other ritualistic structures were meant as opportunities for the performers and spectators to experience themselves as members of a community and to celebrate communality. Of great importance was the birth ritual as the beginning of the performance. It was modeled after the adoption ritual of the Asmat people of New Guinea, which Schechner describes at some length in his essay "The Politics of Ecstasy." Its main features were kept. Five men lay side by side on the floor, while four women stood over them with splayed legs, leaning forward slightly so that their bodies formed a tunnel representing the birth canal.

At the beginning of the performance, the performer playing Dionysus was reborn as a god – he was pushed through the "birth canal" by the rhythmic gyrations of the men. As Shephard reports, the birth ritual was essential "not only in our work but also in our collective existence because it gave us the opportunity of experiencing and expressing our common bonds in non-rational symbolic forms." Shephard states that because of the "highly charged libidinal bonds between members of the group . . . the birth ritual became a symbolic expression of the Group dynamic" (Shephard 1991: 88).

FIGURE 1.1 Birth ritual from *Dionysus in 69*. Adaptation: Richard Schechner from *The Bacchae* of Euripides. Director: Richard Schechner. Production: The Performance Group. Performed by: The Performance Group. Photo: © Max Waldman, New York, 1969. All rights reserved.

In May 1968 a critic wrote about the Group's performances of the birth ritual and the opening speeches of Finley/Dionysus and of Shephard/Pentheus at a festival of short theatre pieces in New York:

> Schechner's ritual is perhaps more Greek than tribal in inspiration, and more erotic than natal. But that is really beside the point, for Schechner . . . is primarily concerned with breaking down the barriers between art and life, symbol and event, through the techniques of environmental theatre, confrontation and ritual . . . The reality of the moment is living flesh touching living flesh as a deeply felt experience, quite apart from the symbol. Community is thus experienced and affirmed, though at what level of consciousness is uncertain. The actors, and perhaps the audience, are liberated, but of what? If we do not know the answer, can we say there has been a liberation?
> (Velde 1968)

According to the review, the "cultural revolution" brought about here was, in fact, the "revolution in the flesh" (Schechner 1969: 219) which

Schechner advocated and celebrated so passionately in his quoted essay. The critic also establishes that "community is experienced and affirmed" in the birth ritual. However, the question of liberation remains open for him – not only with regard to the spectators but also concerning the performers.

In the performance, the birth ritual was followed by a dance. The spectators were expressly asked to join in:

> You shall have an extraordinary experience tonight. Something you won't forget. Together we can make one community. We can celebrate together. Reach ecstasy together. So join us in what we do next. It's a circle dance around the sacred spot of my birth. It's a celebration of me, of my nativity.
> (Joan MacIntosh as Dionysus in Schechner 1970)

In order to allow, indeed enable and encourage, the audience to participate, the space of the Performance Garage was designed so that all divisions between the stage and the auditorium were abolished. This turned the whole theatre into a performance space – into an "environment." The spectators could choose their own spots to sit – high up on a tower, at a relative distance on the scaffolding surrounding the walls, or close to the action on the carpeted floor, either near the center or hiding behind the scaffolding. All these places could be and were used by the performers as well. The audience could change their seats during the two-hour performance, which always also meant a shift in perspective and in the relationship to the performers and the other spectators. It was up to the individual spectator, for example, whether to join the circle dance or other actions.

In Brian de Palma's film version of this production, the dance scene, accompanied by live music played by members of the Group, takes more than ten minutes. Many spectators join in – performers and spectators alike disrobe until they are dancing naked. This kind of audience participation was new and uncommon at the time. According to Schechner and the Group, enabling the spectators to carry out the same actions alongside the performers would be conducive to letting a community emerge out of actors and spectators, which could be defined as a "viable dialectic between solitude and being with others." It was for this reason that audience participation was encouraged. According to Schechner, it was dependent on two conditions:

> First, participation occurred at those points where the play stopped being a play and became a social event – when spectators felt that they were free to enter the performance as equals . . . The second point is that most of the participation in Dionysus was according to the democratic model: letting people into the play to do as the performers were doing, to 'join the story'.
> (Schechner 1973: 44)

This would at least answer the question of liberation with regard to the spectators: they were free "to do as the performers were doing." Judging by the film version, it seems that for the Group and for at least a few members of the audience a kind of community as described by Schechner did come into being. However, this performative opportunity was not seen as a liberation by everybody, and several critics took up the issue. Walter Kerr in his *New York Times* review, for instance, objected that

> it is only the actors who are liberated in this sort of meeting, and there is something arrogant, condescending, and self-indulgent about that. Clearly, they enjoy the unleashing of their own inhibitions. During an impromptu aside on the opening night, an actress was asked by another how she felt about dancing on the night of Senator Kennedy's death. She thought intensely for a moment, then answered, 'I have to. It's my statement.' But it is her statement, not ours. She and her colleagues are in control of the master plan. They are free to do what they wish to do. We are only free to do what they wish us to do or invite us to do. That is not engagement. It is surrender. I'm still uptight.
>
> (Kerr 1968)

He was not the only one who felt manipulated. While Kerr blamed the performers, Stefan Brecht directed his critique at Schechner. He saw his mise en scène as

> a staging of the whole theatrical event, the reactions or rather predicaments of the audience included. He has directed the Group with view to controlling the audience ... The audience can only be responsive & that only feebly & making a fool of itself. No stimuli for audience initiative, no opportunities for creative participation or spontaneous interference.
>
> (Brecht 1969: 162)

By the fall performance, however, Brecht appreciated that "the hold of the show has increased considerably," but he was still unable to see any participatory or even liberating effect with reference to the spectators. The performers themselves would

> destroy the illusion of participation they create. Presupposed: the willingness of an American audience to actively cooperate in producing an appearance of participation. This willingness to take co-managerial status is indispensable to the democratic process & corporate economy of this country. The production's calling on them is not fascist but simply modern America.
>
> (Brecht 1969: 164)

Thus, Brecht concludes: "The only free reaction & thus the only genuine participation possible is a gesture of refusal to participate. If genuine audience participation is excluded, is a liberation effect possible?" (Brecht 1969: 164).

Another ritual segment which called for audience participation was the so-called Total Caress. It was meant as a substitute for the peaceful unification of the women of Thebes with nature as reported by the messenger (v. 696–712). While the chorus began to sing "When shall I dance once more with bare feet all night dances/tossing my head for joy in the damp air, in the dew?" (v. 862–5), the performers moved slowly into the audience, sometimes individually, mostly in groups of two, three, or four. They were supposed to select audience members at random, avoiding anyone they knew, selecting strangers who seemed responsive.

> The caress began with touching, erotic but not passionate . . . It is an exquisitely polymorphous experience, full of smells and difficult sensations. But soon resistances fell away, a basic animal-comfort trust arises, and one flows with the touching.
> (Schechner 1970)

The spectators' reactions varied strongly. Some, mostly female, simply put up with it. Most, if not all, men reciprocated the caresses and extended them to body parts which the performers had deliberately avoided. These spectators ignored the implicit rules that aimed at a playful "dialogue" and redefined them as a real situation of intimacy beyond the pretense of "play." The performers, for their part, understood the breakdown of rules as an indecent infringement and an unseemly definition of the situation, which degraded them to objects of lust.

In his fall 1968 review, Stefan Brecht characterized this scene as a "sex show":

> The lovemaking is now intimate & passionate, muscular and to the point. Except for Finley–Dionysus' seduction of Shephard–Pentheus, it is neither tender nor personal . . . The choreography of these anonymous couplings suggests the impersonality of street prostitution . . . The play . . . has become a simulated enactment/glorification of erotic passion . . . telling the spectator to free himself "as a person" by fucking – fucking freely . . . The spectators, of course, are unfree and fuck unfreely.
> (Brecht 1969: 163–164)

In November 1968 Grotowski attended the performance. His criticism centered mainly on two points. The first concerned the acting, which he deemed hysterical. He felt that it confused the touching of skin with psychic contact. The second referred to the costumes. In his view, the red chitons and black underpants of the women and the black jockstraps of the men smacked too much of striptease. He suggested either performing naked as "a sacred act" or letting the nakedness be revealed through everyday clothes. A few days later Schechner decided that the performers would do sections of the performance naked. This, however, only led to more problems with the Total Caress scene, as the female performers felt prostituted. In December it was decided to take it out and to replace it with the so-called moiety dance.

On the one hand, the critics complained that the spectators were not "free," that they could only take part in certain actions at the performers' invitation or behest. On the other hand, the performers complained that the spectators did not respond to them according to their rules and instead abused the situation by imposing their own ideas of "liberation" on them. Both parties blamed the other for robbing them of their freedom and self-determination. The concept of freedom underlying and nurturing the perception of the situation as well as the problems connected to it are closely related to the dichotomy between the idea of an autonomous subject and that of a subject determined by others. Both parties overlooked that within a performance or any other kind of communal gathering as well as in society as a whole the idea of an autonomous subject is delusive. Our actions in such situations are always co-determined by others just as they co-determine the actions and the behavior of others. Therefore, it is not so much the question of "a viable dialectic between solitude and being with others" but rather of a viable dialectic between co-determining the actions and the behavior of others and letting one's own actions and behavior be co-determined by others (Seel 2002a; 2002b).

A performance is never constituted by one person alone and always requires at least one member of each group – performers and spectators – to be present. The performance comes into being out of their encounter and interaction – whatever its nature may be (Fischer-Lichte 2008: 38–74). The audience always participates in one form or another. This new and explicit kind of audience participation developed in the 1960s, however, shifted the focus to the fact that in a performance they have to negotiate their relationship, which indicates that the rules cannot be set up by one party alone. When Schechner and his performers set out to "liberate" the spectators from the tired theatrical conventions which seemed to offer certain possibilities of behavior and action while excluding many others (even though theatre scandals demonstrate that spectators were always also "free" to break these rules), they went no further than simply to replace one set of rules by another. Ultimately, the spectators were expected to follow and so it comes as no surprise that they tried to set up their own rules whenever the opportunity presented itself.

At least some spectators experienced the performers' effort to "liberate" them as manipulation, which reduced them to objects. On the other hand, the reifying attempts by some spectators – for instance, during the Total Caress – to "liberate" themselves and live out their sexual drive made the performers feel degraded as objects of lust. In both cases the so-called liberation meant exerting power over others against their own will. There was no balance between co-determining the actions and the behavior of others and letting one's own actions and behavior be co-determined by others. What was proclaimed as liberation was, in many cases, experienced as violence – as was the liberation through Dionysus by the women of Thebes.

This violence was openly acted out in the killing of Pentheus. It was performed as a mob action, as later described by Girard. After the Caress, Dionysus and Pentheus reappeared from the pit and Dionysus pulled the two Agaves – played by Joan MacIntosh and Ciel Smith during the first months – from the body piles formed in the preceding scene and handed Pentheus over to them: "Agave! Joan! Ciel! There's a boy in the woods. A young boy. I've marked him for you. I want you to find him, and caress him and kiss him, and love him, and kill him for me!" (quoted from Shephard 1991: 127). When the tender caresses turned into clawing and biting, Pentheus broke away and the chase began. It was spread out all over the entire space and involved loud screaming, biting, and scratching. As Schechner reports, the women learnt to make their "bodies into those of animals, especially big cats" for the "animal chase." This had the effect that "pandemonium filled the room, with screams of the audience joining our own" (Schechner 1970). Finally, Pentheus was tracked down and mortally wounded by being gouged in the gut.

Now the death ritual began. The dismemberment of Pentheus was performed in slow motion as a reversal of the birth ritual. Before assembling in the ritual formation, the women dipped their hands and forearms into a marble basin filled with stage blood, so that everyone in the formation became smeared with "blood." There were other small changes – during the scene the women held up their bloodstained hands, this time facing the opposite direction so that they could see Pentheus as he entered the death canal. In this manner, Pentheus was symbolically swallowed by the community that, as an individual, he had tried to dominate.

The death ritual thus accomplished several different goals simultaneously. On the one hand, by closely mimicking the birth ritual and thus allowing for very similar physiological, affective, motoric, and energetic experiences, it affirmed the communal nature of the Performance Group, including Shephard. On the other hand, it performed the sacrifice of Pentheus not as an expulsion from and dismemberment of the community, but as a symbolic act of incorporation as he physically became one with the community he had terrorized. It could be said, then, that the Performance Group was not confirmed as a community through the sacrifice but by performing particular bodily actions together and by sharing the same experiences. The sacrifice was of a theatrical nature – it was a symbolic gesture.

However, such a conclusion does not do justice to the cruelty with which the scene was performed. Because of it, Brecht interpreted the vicious hunting and the death ritual according to the model later elaborated by Girard:

> An intruder is killed, a man is dealt with as an animal, there is gang action, blind passion. Crime in the streets, riot, lynch justice, the slaying of lovers in boiler rooms, the stabbing of a pusher, ghetto pogroms – all that's as American as cherry pie.
>
> (Brecht 1969: 161)

However, the scene did not end with Pentheus' death. After killing him, the women attacked all the men in the formation and slew them, too.

> The staging & acting hardly prepares us for this: the slaying is a shocking surprise & as allegory a puzzle. In any case, a passionate visceral a- & anti-social (though intensely communal) violence is shown & though the spectators are supposed to empathize they are not to sympathize with the maenads.
>
> (Brecht 1969: 161)

In my view, this scene enacted the "ecstatic fascism" of the followers of Dionysus, i.e., the women, and was directed at all those who did not belong to their group, i.e., the men in the formation. Here, the performance made a political statement. During the following recognition scene between Cadmus and the Agaves, Dionysus/Finley wiped the blood from his hands, combed his hair, and dressed in a blue suit and tie. He carried a red, white, and blue bag filled with *Dionysus in 69* buttons. Delivering his curse from the top of one of the towers, he threw the buttons down to the spectators, many of whom scrambled to get one. As the performance was taking place during the pre-presidential elections of 1968, the curse clearly alluded to the ongoing election speeches. Even if he brought the members of the Group on the mats below him back to life and onto their feet by calling their names (Shephard 1991: 129), the curse could clearly be identified as a "Dionysus for President" campaign. This was highlighted when Finley opened the doors of the Performance Garage to reveal a poster with his picture on it. Thus, Dionysus, who was responsible for the slaying of all those who did not "believe" in him through his own hysteric followers, was revealed as a tyrant and fascist. In this context, the slaying of the men, which happened without any preparation or warning, made perfect sense, intimating the Group's anticipation of fascism taking over in the United States.

According to Brecht, however, the end had become "meaningless, but humorous" in the fall. Dionysus' "jolly speech to the audience" and his scattering of the campaign buttons now "suggests only that platform: 'let's make this country free – sexually'" (Brecht 1969: 163). In the fall performance Brecht identifies the theme of gynophobia in the slaying "as this production's latent content."

> The theme of gynophobia is carried by the slaying. Though the love-making has now become passionate rather than gentle, the transformation of passionate caresses into castrating gestures of dismemberment is a purely visual device. The scene does not so much project the wildness of women as the fear of the victims . . . we respond to it but weakly. Weakly, because mise-en-scène & acting, being hopelessly concerned with making the women seem predatory, fail to compel either a dominant mood of terror or an evolution of mood from passion to terror.
>
> (Brecht 1969: 165)

The production, Brecht claims, thus also lost its political meaning and relevance over the course of its thirteen-month run: "The Group transformed what had turned out a manual for (hip) civil disobedience into a sex manual: a retreat from politics into the personal. But personal life is also a place of fear & violence – particularly for those fleeing to it from the aggressions of institutional repression (parental, economic or political)." Moreover, he accuses the Group of "a desperate thrashing about in search of authenticity that the Group so far has denied itself, settling instead for a socially & commercially successful appealingness" (Brecht 1969: 168).

Brecht's review and, if to a lesser degree and only implicitly, the history of the production's run as told and interpreted by Shephard, allow for the conclusion that the changes which it underwent over the thirteen months were essential. They not only concern details but also its overall meaning and impact. The initial goal had been to reflect on and trigger a cultural revolution that would reconcile individualism and communalism. Such a reconciliation was to be realized by liberating the individual participants, performers and spectators alike, from all kinds of institutional repression, in particular those inherent in politics and in society at large, and by allowing them to experience themselves as members of a community, especially through states of ecstasy. This was to be made possible mostly through audience participation. As a number of reviews suggest, this goal was not achieved, mainly because spectators did not feel liberated but manipulated, even repressed, by the "demand" for a specific kind of participation. With regard to the ambiguity of Dionysus' ecstasy as communal ecstasy, the possibility of turning it into ecstatic fascism was enacted in the killing of Pentheus and the men. With the changes in Pentheus, the determination to challenge political authority disappeared over the course of the production's run; moreover, the reflection on fascism as an imminent threat was reduced to the acting out of gynophobic fantasies comparable to that of the *vagina dentata*. Initially a critically refined production, *Dionysus in 69* ended up as a pleasing and entertaining performance that was socially and commercially successful. The cultural revolution it proclaimed and to which it wanted to contribute turned out to be a sexual revolution only, epitomized in the invitation, the mandate even, "to fuck freely."

While there are other views on the production, mostly by critics and other spectators who participated in the early performances, all agree on the ambiguity of the performance itself. It allowed everyone, actors and spectators alike, to attribute meaning to their individual experiences. It is almost impossible to assess now whether or not the performance contributed to a cultural revolution and, if so, what kind of a cultural revolution this was. However, when it comes to the question of the historical significance of *Dionysus in 69*, we are in a better position to determine that it considerably contributed to, indeed initiated, a theatrical revolution. *Dionysus in 69* is a landmark in the establishment of US neo-avant-garde theatre.

It may seem strange that an adaptation of *The Bacchae* – Euripides' last tragedy which, in a way, marked the end of the Greek polis and thus of Athenian democracy, and, as a tragedy on tragedy, also marked the end of Greek tragic theatre – also indicated the spread, if not the beginning, of a new theatre in the United States. With theatre always embedded in society in many different ways, the production also heralded the beginning of a new era in US society. The Performance Group was by no means the first experimental theatre group in the United States. Apart from happenings, dance groups such as Merce Cunningham's, or John Cage's pioneering music performances from the 1950s, there were experimental theatre groups such as the Living Theatre, founded in 1947 by Julian Beck and Judith Malina. However, after their arrest in 1965, they performed mostly in Europe. Key productions such as *Antigone* (Krefeld, Germany 1967) or *Paradise Now!* (Festival d'Avignon, France 1968) aimed at a "transformation of the demonic forces into the celestial" (program notes to *Paradise Now!* quoted in Innes 1981: 187) by a particular use of ritualistic group actions, nudity, and audience participation.

Nonetheless, the Performance Group and, in particular, *Dionysus in 69* stand out in the landscape of the US avant-garde movements. Its impact on the collective memory was stronger and lasted longer because of its long run, the fact that it was shown not only in New York but also in other parts of the country (where it caused an even greater sensation – in Ann Arbor in January 1969, the Group was arrested and put into prison for a night on the charge of "corrupting the morals of the good people of the State of Michigan" (Shephard 1991: 201)) and, not least, because of its excellent documentation. Through this production a broader public was made aware of a new era in US theatre that seriously questioned its accepted "essential" characteristics: the rigid spatial division between actors and spectators, precluding any physical contact; the primacy of the dramatic text that was regarded as the controlling instance and authority; the body of the actor as a sign for a single dramatic figure – as a semiotic body. Instead, here was an environment which was shared by actors and spectators and allowed for audience participation, perhaps even for a temporary community between actors and spectators; the text was merely a tool to be used by the actors in order to fulfill specific tasks; the phenomenal bodies of the performers – in particular, their naked bodies – emanated an energy; they had to be touched and experienced, not interpreted.

While performances of traditional theatre had until that point always been regarded primarily as works of art that had to be analyzed with regard to the particular meanings they conveyed, avant-garde performances were seen as aesthetic and, at the same time, social processes that had an impact on the spectators and bore the potential to transform them, even if not for the entire duration of the performance but only temporarily. Theatre turned into a site where communality was not represented but negotiated and new forms of community building were tried out. In *Dionysus in 69* Dionysus, the god of theatre, performed the dismemberment of the theatre in its old, traditional form so that it could be reborn in a new shape and function.

Notes

1. The performances, which I did not see myself, are very well documented. Besides the reviews and Schechner's (1973) long deliberations, see also Schechner (1970: n.p. – approx. 350 pages and many photographs), as well as the film by Brian de Palma, available on video. The film was made from the recording of two different performances appearing on a split screen, so that the differences between the two stand out quite clearly. Bill (W. H.) Shephard, who played Pentheus most of the time, wrote his Ph.D. dissertation (Shephard 1991) on the performance. See also Puchner (2006); Van den Heuvel (2006); and Zeitlin (2004).
2. Quotations from Stefan Brecht, "Dionysus in 69, from Euripides' *The Bacchae*: The Performance Group," *TDR/The Drama Review*, 13: 3 (Spring 1969), pp. 156–168. © 1969 by New York University and the Massachusetts Institute of Technology. Used by permission of the publisher.

References

Brecht, Stefan. 1969. "Dionysus in 69, from Euripides' *The Bacchae*: The Performance Group." *Drama Review* 13 (3): 156–168.
Cooper, David. 1970. *The Death of the Family*. New York: Pantheon.
DeBroske, Su. 1968. "Dionysus 69: Nudity, Guts and Truth." *Washington Square Journal*, November 21.

Fischer-Lichte, Erika. 2008. *The Transformative Power of Performance: A New Aesthetics*. New York: Routledge.
Grotowski, Jerzy. 1968. *Towards a Poor Theatre*. New York: Simon and Schuster.
Innes, Christopher. 1981. *Holy Theatre, Ritual and the Avantgarde*. Cambridge: Cambridge University Press.
Kerr, Walter. 1968. "'Come Dance With Me'. 'Who, Me?': Review of Dionysus in 69." *New York Times*, June 16.
Puchner, Martin. 2006. "The Performance Group between Theatre and Theory." In *Restaging the Sixties: Radical Theaters and their Legacies*. Edited by James M. Harding and Cindy Rosenthal, 313–331. Ann Arbor: University of Michigan Press.
Schechner, Richard. 1967. "In Warm Blood: The Bacchae." In Schechner, Richard. *Public Domain: Essays on the Theater*, 93–108. New York: Avon 1970.
Schechner, Richard. 1969. "The Politics of Ecstasy." In *Public Domain; Essays on the Theatre*. Edited by Richard Schechner, 209–228. Indianapolis: Bobbs Merrill.
Schechner, Richard, ed. 1970. *Dionysus in 69*. New York: Farrar, Strauss and Giroux.
Schechner, Richard. 1973. *Environmental Theatre*. New York: Hawthorne Books.
Seel, Martin. 2002a. "Bestimmen und Bestimmen lassen." In Seel, Martin.*Sich bestimmen lassen: Studien zur theoretischen und praktischen Philosophie*, 146–166. Frankfurt am Main: Suhrkamp.
Seel, Martin. 2002b. "Sich bestimmen lassen. Ein revidierter Begriff der Selbstbestimmung." In Seel, Martin. *Sich bestimmen lassen: Studien zur theoretischen und praktischen Philosophie*, 179–298. Frankfurt am Main: Suhrkamp.
Shephard, William Hunter. 1991. *The Dionysus Group*. American University Studies, Series 26. Theatre Arts vol. 5. New York: Peter Lang.
Van den Heuvel, Mike. 2006. "A Different Kind of Pomo: The Performance Group and the Mixed Legacy of Authentic Performance." In *Restaging the Sixties: Radical Theaters and their Legacies*. Edited by James M. Harding and Cindy Rosenthal, 332–352. Ann Arbor: University of Michigan Press.
Velde, Paul. 1968. "Review of the First American Radical Theatre Festival at the Washington Square Methodist Church." *Commonweal*, May 24.
Zeitlin, Froma I. 2004. "Dionysus in 69." In *Dionysus in 69: Greek Tragedy at the Dawn of the Third Millennium*. Edited by Edith Hall, Fiona Macintosh, and Amanda Wrigley, 49–75. Oxford: Oxford University Press.

Further Reading

O'Gorman, Ned, ed. 1968. *Revolution*. New York: Random House.
van Gennep, Arnold. 1960. (1909). *The Rites of Passage*. Translated by Monika B. Vizedom and Gabrielle L. Caffee. Chicago: University of Chicago Press. Regarding the three phases of a rite of passage.

2

Celebrating a Communion Rite?
Wole Soyinka's *The Bacchae of Euripides* at London's National Theatre (1973)

> I see *The Bacchae* ... as a prodigious, barbaric banquet, an insightful manifestation of the universal need of man to match himself against Nature. The more than hinted-at cannibalism corresponds to the periodic needs of humans to swill, gorge and copulate on a scale as huge as Nature's on her monstrous cycle of regeneration. The ritual, sublimated or expressive, is both social therapy and reaffirmation of group solidarity, a hankering back to the origins and formation of guilds and phratries. Man reaffirms his indebtedness to earth, dedicates himself anew to the demands of continuity and evokes the energies of productivity. Reabsorbed within the communal psyche he provokes the resources of Nature; he is in turn replenished for the cyclic drain in his fragile individual potency. This version of *The Bacchae* has been conceived as a communal feast, a tumultuous celebration of life. It must be staged as such. (Soyinka 1988: 70)[1]

At the center of Wole Soyinka's understanding of *The Bacchae*, as sketched in his "adaptor's note," clearly is the particular relationship between the collective life of a human community and Nature's cycle of regeneration. It is the ritual, the communal feast, celebrating life, that connects the one with the other. In this note not only Soyinka's earlier writings on African drama resonate but also the Cambridge Ritualists' view on the origin of Greek theatre.

Dionysus Resurrected: Performances of Euripides' The Bacchae in a Globalizing World, First Edition. Erika Fischer-Lichte.
© 2014 Erika Fischer-Lichte. Published 2014 by John Wiley & Sons, Ltd.

The rewriting of *The Bacchae* was commissioned by the National Theatre in London and its newly appointed director, Peter Hall. At that time, Hall was greatly acclaimed for his experimental work in collaboration with Peter Brook at the Royal Shakespeare Company. Here, the two directors had explored the possibilities that Antonin Artaud's theatre of cruelty seemed to offer. The National Theatre, at that time, therefore, was regarded as open to new approaches to the canon. What such openness entailed and whether it was interpreted by the artists and the spectators – mostly from the educated middle classes – in the same way, is not certain – nor how both would respond to the adaptor's note.

Wole Soyinka wrote his version of *The Bacchae* during his exile in Britain. It was not his first stay in the United Kingdom. In the 1950s (1954–1957) he had studied at the University of Leeds, and later, while holding the post of Reader at the Royal Court Theatre in London, he had produced, directed, and acted in his own plays, *The Swamp Dwellers* and *The Invention*. He had returned to Nigeria on January 1, 1960, the first day of independence celebrated by a performance of his play *A Dance of the Forests*. From August 1967 to October 1969, Soyinka was held in prison, for some time in solitary confinement. He was accused of supporting secessionist Biafra against the federal government at the outset of the civil war in Biafra. This means he was in jail almost exactly the same time that Richard Schechner wrote about a cultural revolution in the United States, formed his Performance Group, prepared and rehearsed *Dionysus in 69*, and had it performed. In 1973, when Soyinka rewrote *The Bacchae*, he was quite informed about that production, which drew "among other sources, upon an Asmat New Guinea ritual in its search for the tragic soul of twentieth-century white bourgeois-hippie American culture" (Soyinka 1976: 7). No doubt he was determined to demarcate sharply his own version from that of Richard Schechner in particular, since the question "of the supposed dividing line between ritual and theatre should not concern us much in Africa, the line being one that was largely drawn by the European analyst" (Soyinka 1976: 7).

As can be guessed, not least from the above quoted sentence, the dilemma of the envisaged new version of the tragedy lay in the claim to serve two different purposes. Since it was commissioned by the National Theatre in order to be performed there, it must consider this context, i.e., the tradition of the house and the special expectations and background of the spectators; the situation of contemporary Britain at the time of the performance as well as certain older English traditions, still alive and prevalent or at least known. On the other hand, the writer intended to deal with the tragedy from the perspective set by his own Yoruba culture and to enable the British audience to accept and adopt it.

In colonial times, Greek tragedy was taught at schools in Nigeria and other African countries as the epitome of European culture – one of the tools of the colonizers to justify their claims to superiority. After independence many African playwrights turned to Greek tragedy in order to rewrite it, transferring it to an African context. John Pepper Clark's *Song of a Goat* (τραγωδία) draws on Aeschylus' *Agamemnon*, reworking important aspects. In 1962 it was first performed at the Mbari Centre, directed by Wole Soyinka. In 1965 it was staged at the Commonwealth Festival of the Arts in London. It is not unlikely that some of the spectators at the National Theatre saw it.[2] Also in 1962, Kamau Brathwaite's *Odale's Choice*, a new version of Sophocles' *Antigone*, premiered at the Mfantisman Secondary School, Saltpond, in Ghana. Brathwaite, after independence, had returned to Ghana from the Caribbean. Efua Sutherland's *Edufa* took up themes from Euripides' *Alcestis*. It was performed at the Drama Studio, University of Ghana, in 1962. Ola Rotimi's *The Gods are Not to Blame* was performed by Rotimi's own company, the Olukuin Acting Company. It draws on Sophocles' *Oedipus the King* and includes lines spoken or sung in Yoruba and seems to provide an allegory for the Biafra war.[3]

This process of rewriting and thus decolonizing and appropriating Greek tragedy was accompanied by a lively discussion about the relationship between Greek and African drama. In particular in Nigeria, the striking kinship between the pantheon of Yoruba and Greek gods, so important for drama in both cultures, was often noted, even if interpreted differently. In his early essay "The Fourth Stage," the first version of which was written before Soyinka's imprisonment,[4] the author contributes to this discussion by highlighting the correspondences as well as the fundamental differences between the Greek and Yoruba gods and in particular between Dionysus and Ogun. Since in his *Bacchae* Soyinka replaces Dionysus with Ogun, even though he keeps the name of the Greek god, this comparison is crucial in our context. No doubt there are striking parallels. Dionysus' thyrsus is paralleled by the *opa*, a willowy pole bedecked with palm fronds, carried by his male devotees; the rites of Dionysus culminate in the *sparagmos*, the tearing apart of a sacrificial animal. At the climax of Ogun's rites a sacrificial dog is slaughtered and dismembered in a mock-struggle of the head priest and his acolytes for the carcass. Apart from these correspondences there are fundamental differences. For Ogun "is best understood in Hellenic values as a totality of the Dionysian, Apollonian and Promethean virtues" (Soyinka 1988: 22). Soyinka describes him as god of iron, whose powers include war, revolution, liberation, and creativity. He appears as the first actor in the battle fought in "the fourth area of experience, the immeasurable gulf of transition" (Soyinka 1988: 26). And since "Yoruba drama is the reenactment of the cosmic conflict" (Soyinka 1988: 27) he is, so to speak, also the god of Yoruba theatre. Soyinka goes on to explain that the state of transition in Yoruba culture is regarded as "the vortex of archetypes and home of the tragic spirit."

Accordingly, Yoruba drama comes into existence out of this fourth stage:

> The stage of transition is, however, the metaphysical abyss both of god and man, . . . nothing rescues man (ancestral, living, or unborn) from loss of self within this abyss but a titanic resolution of the will whose ritual summons, response, and expression is the strange alien sound to which we give the name of music. On the arena of the living, when man is stripped of excrescences, when disasters and conflicts (the material of drama) have crushed and robbed him of self-consciousness and pretensions, he stands in present reality at the spiritual edge of this gulf, he has nothing left in physical existence which successfully impresses upon his spiritual or psychic perception. It is at such moments that transitional memory takes over and intimations rack him of that intense parallel of his progress through the gulf of transition, of the dissolution of his self and his struggle and triumph over subsumation through the agency of will. It is this experience that the modern tragic dramatist recreates through the medium of physical contemporary action, reflecting emotions of the first active battle of the will through the abyss of dissolution.
>
> (Soyinka 1988: 27)

Evidently, in Soyinka's notion of the tragic as necessitating a radically liminal state, there resonates Nietzsche's notion of the tragic, as developed in *The Birth of Tragedy out of the Spirit of Music*, without being identical. It is to be assumed that in rewriting *The Bacchae* this "gulf of transition," this extreme mode of liminality which, in some way, is characteristic of the tragedy anyway, will be highlighted.

In this process, Soyinka also paid tribute to the Cambridge Ritualists, in particular Gilbert Murray. In the acknowledgments of his version he writes:

> A twenty-year rust on my acquaintanceship with classical Greek made it necessary for me to rely heavily on previous translations in this adaptation of *The Bacchae*. Two versions, which deserve especial mention in that I have not hesitated to borrow phrases and even lines from them are those by Gilbert Murray . . . and by William Arrowsmith.
>
> (Soyinka 1973: 234)

By declaring his indebtedness to Murray's translation of *The Bacchae*, Soyinka, at least implicitly, points back to the first production of the tragedy on an English stage, done by William Poel in 1908 at the Court Theatre in London. This production was ill-fated. Poel had agreed on the project only on the condition that he was allowed to make some changes to the text, which, in his view, was too poetical to be staged. Dionysus was played by the actress Lillah McCarthy. She seems to have modeled her appearance on

Caravaggio's famous painting *Bacchus*, as can be guessed from a review in *The Times* on November 19, 1908:

> It can be imagined how compelling a figure Miss Lillah McCarthy looks with the ivy and grapes in her hair, and the flame-coloured tunic under her tiger-skin, a strange Eastern god full of grace and beauty, and of subtle perfume-like charm.
> (Quoted from Sampatakakis 2005: 141)

Her acting, however, seems not to have quite matched her appearance. Two weeks before the premiere, Poel wrote to Murray, who had demanded a quiet Dionysus:

> If gods can do what the Bacchus can do, they don't want to mess about the stage . . . as wizards and show how clever they are. This cleverness is what they do. Miss Baker (her husband's name) has not yet (prompted) that.
> (Quoted from Sampatakakis 2005: 142)

It was not only Lillah McCarthy's Dionysus who caused such dismay. The chorus

> consisted of four 'stately' Maenads, who moved only once from the sides of the proscenium during the two-hour production, and whose function was to chant the 'more solemn passages and to strike the note of the inevitable fate'. They were matched by three coryphées, who danced and sang 'the gayer chorus speeches'.
> (Macintosh 2007: 157–158)

However, this was not the only, nor even the greatest concern of Murray. It related primarily to Poel's "reading of the play which had led to the removal of all mysticism surrounding Dionysus (what Poel felt were the Euripidean 'digressions') and had reduced Euripides' 'Mystery Play' . . . to a 'rational' satire *tout court*" (Macintosh 2007: 158). Although Murray and Poel had an extensive correspondence on the tragedy, in the course of which Murray agreed on some slight changes, on attending the performance he was very upset to find the tragedy robbed of what in his reading and translation was essential to it. He refused to allow the production to continue after the first two matinees. How the audience in these two performances responded is not known. However, it is to be assumed that if it had been enthusiastic or shown any signs of deeper involvement, Murray would not have insisted on the end of its run. Apparently, it was a failure even in this respect – which would explain why on professional stages almost no other production followed over the next sixty years.[5]

It is difficult to assess whether and to what extent the audience at the National Theatre in 1973 was familiar with Murray's ideas on Greek tragedy's relationship to ritual, with his translation and reading of *The Bacchae*, and with the fate of Poel's production. Since the spectators belonged to the educated middle classes, some knowledge can be assumed. How it may have informed perceptions of the production of Soyinka's version by Roland Joffe is not even to be guessed.

Soyinka understood his adaptation of the tragedy as ritual theatre – which of course meant something completely different from what the term entailed in Schechner's usage. Soyinka's procedure of rewriting the tragedy explicitly opposed the way and means employed by Schechner. While Schechner and the Performance Group dealt with Euripides' text "as if it were part of an oral tradition," cutting it considerably and mixing its remains with personal statements, Soyinka linked his adaptation to actual oral traditions like the *egungun* festival and the worship of the god Ogun, proceeding from one of the striking affinities between Dionysus and Ogun, as explained in the "The Fourth Stage":

> He [Ogun, F.-L.] had first to experience, to surrender his individuation once again (the first time, as a part of the original Orisa-nla Oneness) to the fragmenting process; to be reabsorbed within universal Oneness, the Unconscious, the deep black whirlpool of mythopoetic forces, to immerse himself thoroughly within it, understand its nature and yet by the combative value of the will to rescue and reassemble himself and emerge wiser, powerful from the draught of cosmic secrets, organizing the mystic and the technical forces of earth and cosmos to forge a bridge for his companions to follow.
>
> (Soyinka 1988: 29f)

Such an affinity not only allows for the substitution of one by the other, it also makes this substitution meaningful. Indeed, both underwent dismemberment and rebirth:

> Ripped in pieces at the hands of the titans for the (by him) unwilled acts of hubris, a divine birth, Dionysus–Zagreus commences divine existence by this experience of the destruction of the self, the transitional horror. For it is an act of hubris not only to dare the gulf of transition but to mingle essences for extra measure. We approach, it seems, the ultimate pessimism of existence as pronounced by Nietzsche's sage Silenus: it is an act of hubris to be born. It is a challenge to the jealous chthonic powers, to *be*. The answer of the Yoruba to this is just as clear: it is no less an act of hubris to *die*. And the whirlpool of transition requires both hubristic complements as catalyst to its continuous regeneration. This is the serene wisdom and essential art of Obatala. All acts are subordinate to these ultimates of the human condition and recreative will.

> To dare transition is the ultimate test of the human spirit, and Ogun is the first protagonist of the abyss.
>
> (Soyinka 1988: 32)

This is why the Dionysus drama can be rewritten and staged as an Ogun drama, why Greek tragedy can merge with Yoruba rituals.

Soyinka also accomplished this transformation by including in the chorus songs passages from his own poem on Ogun, *Idanre*, which incorporates material from oral tradition, and by inserting orally transmitted so-called *oriki* verses which praise Ogun in his various qualities, such as "shield of orphans" or "gore-drunk hunter." Unlike Dionysus, however, Ogun is a decidedly masculine god, the god of war and fire. There is no oscillation in him between the sexes, no androgyny. Rather, Dionysus is a "being of calm rugged strength, of a rugged beauty, not of effeminate prettiness. Relaxed, as becomes divine self-assurance but equally tensed as if for action, an arrow drawn in readiness for flight" (Soyinka 1973: 235).

Quite in agreement with Schechner, Soyinka holds the view that the spectators must also enter the state of liminality – plunge into the gulf of transition, even if not quite as radically as the protagonist. However, quite in opposition to Schechner, he does not believe that the kind of audience participation as encouraged, even demanded, by *Dionysus in 69* would be able to induce this state. Soyinka rejects this kind of audience participation on principle.

> A commonly mistaken notion . . . exists in this movement, which, because of the opposition of communalism to individualism . . . has turned into a fetish that is called audience participation . . . This is the burden of my statement – that audience participation is not really necessarily tactile, however much that becomes the vogue, nor is the frenetic effort to equate a contempt for the human body on stage with the liberation of his social personality anything but a blasphemy of the culturally depraved . . . I see nothing significantly anti-bourgeois in a bare arse clambering over the audience and flipping ugly tits between me and the main body of action on stage . . . When I go to the theatre it is not to suffer drooling morons translate audience participation into a license to maul me with their bodies simply because they are incapable of reaching me with their minds.
>
> (Soyinka 1988: 54–57)

For Soyinka the relationship between actors and spectators should be modeled after the traditional mask–drama *egungun*. For the transformation of the spectator cannot be achieved by letting him join in the play and act himself, but only by making him understand the protagonist's actions as performed on his (the spectator's) behalf and therefore fear for him (the protagonist): "Will this protagonist survive confrontation with forces that exist within the dangerous area of transformation? Entering that *microcosmos* involves a loss of individuation, a self-submergence in universal essence. It is an act undertaken on behalf of the community and the welfare of that protagonist is inseparable from that of the total community" (Soyinka 1976: 42). That is to say that in order to open up the possibility for spectators to experience a liminal situation, a state of transition, precisely such a liminal situation must be represented on stage. This means that the relationship between actors and spectators is fundamentally different from that in Schechner's *Dionysus in 69*. The traditional mask–drama of the *egungun* festival provides the model on which Soyinka wants this relationship to be based:

> Any individual within the 'audience' knows better than to add his voice *arbitrarily* even to the most seductive passages of an invocatory song, or to contribute a refrain to the familiar sequence of liturgical exchanges among the protagonists. The moment for choric participation is well-defined, but this does not imply that until such moment, participation ceases. The so-called audience is itself an integral part of that arena of conflict, it contributes spiritual strength to the protagonist through its choric reality which must first be conjured up and established, defining and investing the arena through the protagonist's incantations. Overt participation when it comes is channelled through a formalized repertoire of gestures and liturgical responses.
>
> (Soyinka 1976: 38f)

In this context, "spontaneous" audience participation would be regarded as an "aberration, which may imperil the eudaemonic goals of that representation."

Rewriting *The Bacchae* and adapting it to the context of Yoruba culture thus meant representing meaningful liminal situations, states of transition, on stage. Identifying Dionysus with Ogun and referring to the model of the *egungun* mask festival strongly and evidently connects the Greek tragedy with Yoruba culture, without completely transposing it. In Soyinka's version the tragedy itself remains in a state of in-betweenness – it is located in the "immeasurable gulf of transition." Indeed, it not only refers to ancient Greek and traditional Yoruba culture, but also to modern Western culture, incorporating elements of slapstick, rock concerts, gospel singing, and night club stunts as well as traditional elements of English culture like the Jacobean masks in the dressing scene, or the Maypole dance of the Maenads before Agave's recognition. Such elements, no doubt, were supposed to help the audience get involved in a manner similar to that described above (cf. Nouryeh 2001).

In his adaptation Soyinka relies on the ritualistic structure of Euripides' tragedy emphasized by Murray and then by scholars in the late 1960s and early 1970s.[6] It can be described as a sequence of liminal situations. Within this structure he introduced some changes, which mainly refer to the question of political revolution, a liberation of the oppressed, as well as to the problem of establishing a new political order as a particular community brought about by ritual sacrifice.

The most important changes made by Soyinka are the addition of the slaves and their leader, the inclusion of the mysteries of Eleusis, and the transformation of Pentheus' brutal killing into a scapegoat ritual. By introducing the figures of the slaves the motif of spiritual liberation through Dionysus is related to that of political liberation from the very beginning. A herdsman offers a jug of wine – the essence of Dionysus – to the slaves, who share it as in a communion rite. The leader of the slaves comments:

> There is heaven in this juice. It flows through my lips and I say, now I roll the sun upon my tongue and it neither burns nor scorches. A scent-laden breeze fills the cavern of my mouth pressing for release. I know this scent. I mean, I knew it once. I live to know it once again . . . A scent of freedom is not easily forgotten.
> (Soyinka 1973: 236)

The advent of Dionysus is to be understood as a signal of revolution. As Soyinka explains in *Myth, Literature and the African World*:

> Ogun for his part becomes not merely the god of war but the god of revolution in the most contemporary context – and this is not merely in Africa, but in the Americas, where his worship has spread.
> (Soyinka 1976: 54 n.7)

This way of inscribing Yoruba culture into Euripides' text can be regarded as a political act.[7]

Soyinka's version of *The Bacchae* deals with the meaningfulness of rituals, with their ability to bring about a state of transition, to open up the space for new identities to emerge. The mysteries of Eleusis demonstrate under which conditions a ritual loses its meaning and transformative power. Usually, an old slave is chosen for the scapegoat role of the Old Year, which has to be expelled with violence in order to allow the new one to arrive.[8]

Leader:	Suppose the old man dies?
Herdsman:	We all have to die sometime.
Leader:	Flogged to death? In the name of some unspeakable rites?
Herdsman:	Someone must clean the new year of the rot of the old or the world will die. Have you ever known famine?
Leader:	Why us? Why always us?
Herdsman:	Why not?

| Leader: | Because the rites bring us nothing! Let those who profit bear the burden of the old year dying. |

(237)

The slave is not a member of the community on behalf of which and for whose welfare the rite is performed. The rite thus becomes ineffective. Moreover, the corruption of the ritual creates a revolutionary situation, as recognized by the seer Tiresias: "And Thebes – well, let's just say, the situation is touch and go. If one more slave had been killed at the cleansing rites, or sacrificed to that insatiable altar of nationbuilding . . . " This passage quite openly alludes to Nigeria's civil war and its aftermath.[9] In view of this situation, Tiresias is willing to take on the role of the scapegoat, partly because he wants to experience the state of liminality, partly in order to prevent a revolution – as Dionysus remarks, "Quite a politician, eh, Tiresias?":

> In this job one lives half a life, neither priest nor man. Neither man nor woman. I have longed to know what flesh is made of. What suffering is. Feel the taste of blood instead of merely foreseeing it. Taste the ecstasy of rejuvenation after long organizing its ritual. When the slaves began to rumble I saw myself again playing the futile role, pouring my warnings on deaf ears. An uprising would come, bloodshed, and I would watch, untouched, merely indicated as before – as prophet. I approach death and dissolution, without having felt life . . . its force.

(243f)

It is Dionysus who prevents him from offering himself up for sacrifice, promising however: "Thebes shall have its full sacrifice. And Tiresias will know ecstasy" (244).

And it is Pentheus, the king, who has to sacrifice himself on behalf of the community, thus also liberating it from his despotic rule. Pentheus, in this version, may be associated with the British colonizers as well as with Nigeria's new rulers. By making him drink wine, Dionysus leads him into a state of transition that allows him to transgress the boundaries of his ruler-self, to experience liminality and to take on the role of the scapegoat. In this context, and by contrast to Euripides' original text, the words with which Dionysus accompanies Pentheus to Mount Cithaeron are only partly to be understood as ironic:

> Yes, you alone
> Make sacrifices for your people, you alone.
> The role belongs to a king. Like those gods who yearly
> Must be rent to spring anew, that also is the fate of heroes.

(293)

The killing of Pentheus is thus performed as a scapegoat ritual that brings about a new communal identity. The king must be sacrificed in order to let a community emerge – a new political order, in which all are liberated although the liberated slaves do not appear any more; instead, the members of the royal family take up the words of the slaves.

> *Kadmus*: [The cry is wrung from him] Why us?
> *Agave*: [Her hands are on Pentheus' head, about to lift it. Quietly] Why not?
> [The theme music of Dionysus begins, welling up and filling the stage with the god's presence. A powerful red glow shines suddenly as if from within the head of Pentheus, rendering it near-luminous. The stage is bathed in it and, instantly, from every orifice of the impaled head spring red jets, spurting in every direction. Reactions of horror and panic . . .]
> *Kadmus*: Again blood Tiresias. Nothing but blood.
> *Tiresias*: [He feels his way nearer the fount. A spray hits him and he holds out a hand, catches some of the fluid and sniffs. Tastes it] No. It's wine.
> [Slowly, dreamlike, they all move towards the fountain, cup their hands and drink.]
>
> (307)

Through his death and dismemberment, Pentheus the tyrannical ruler and oppressor has become one with the force he had fought. Like the slaves at the beginning, at the end all soak up energy from the wine, a source of strength that now springs from Pentheus' head. Such a fundamental transformation of Euripides' text is announced by the subtitle of Soyinka's adaptation: "A communion rite."[10]

This "communion rite" was supposed to be performed also on behalf of the spectators, by involving them emotionally. Throughout the tragedy this is aimed at not only by referring to well-known elements from traditional English and modern Western culture but also, if not in the first place, by the music. The "music of Dionysus" for the first time is to be heard when Dionysus watches the procession of the slaves before his words: "Sing Death of the Old Year and – welcome the new – god" (238). During the dialogue between the bacchants and the leader of the slaves it swells up several times and usually sets some or all of the *dramatis personae* present on stage in dance-like motion. The music is described as having

> the strange quality – the nearest familiar example is the theme-song of *Zorba the Greek* – with its strange mixture of nostalgia, violence and death. The scene which follows needs the following quality: extracting the emotional colour and temperature of a European pop scene without degenerating into that tawdry commercial manipulation of teenage mindlessness. The lines are chanted, not sung, to musical accompaniment. The Slave Leader is *not* a gyrating pop drip.

His control emanates from the self-contained force of his person, a progressively deepening spiritual presence. His style is based on the lilt and energy of the black hot gospellers who themselves are often first to become physically possessed. The effect on his crowd is, however, the same – physically – as would be in a teenage pop audience. From orgasmic moans the surrogate climax is achieved. A scream finds its electric response in others and a rush begins for the person of the preacher. Handfuls of his clothes are torn, his person is endangered but he never 'loses his cool'.

(248f)

A kind of music is intended that not only leads the chorus of bacchants into a state of ecstasy but also is supposed to work on the senses of the spectators and to let them tune in rhythmically. Gospel music "might prompt a loss of sense for both singer and audience" (Baker-White 1993: 386). It is meant to elicit the kind of audience participation that Soyinka described when he referred to the *egungun* festival.

However, it did not accomplish this in the production at the National Theatre, as can be gathered from the reviews. The critic Albert Hunt wrote:

Soyinka has come into direct collision with the unyielding amateurism of the British professional theatre. The company that presents Soyinka's play contains a drummer who can't drum, dancers who can't dance, and actors whose only concept of narrative acting is to begin every speech in the flat clipped tones that used to characterize British war movies, and then to rise in a gradual crescendo towards uncontrolled emotional wallowing. Where the play calls for ecstasy, the girls in the chorus offer a well-bred imitation of a hop at the local disco; and where the play calls for horror, we're given a crude imitation of a Madame Tussaud head, out of which spurts pink paint. The strength of Soyinka's final assertion is frittered away in a grotesque attempt, by this production, to express release.

(Hunt 1980: 114–115)

Another critic, Harold H. Hobson, summarized the production in similar terms:

Without ecstasy and without order *The Bacchae* of Euripides is nothing. In Roland Joffe's production of Wole Soyinka's adaptation at the Old Vic there is neither. No amount of rushing about, clothed or naked, in a Greek city or an African village, will produce an authentic fever in the blood. An unidentifiable Maenad, with kissing bells on her exciting wrists, comes nearest to it; Constance Cummings is a brief fine Agave, and Martin Shaw a serene Dionysus. The rest is sweating thighs, wobbling bottoms, and the propaganda of barbarism.

(Hobson 1973)

Other reviews are no more appreciative of the production. It seems that it was unable to transpose the dramatic figures or the actors and spectators into a liminal state. The production was a failure. As the reviews suggest, the reasons for this failure are to be found in bad acting and a lack of technical competence. But is it really a likely assumption that the National Theatre did not have good actors and technicians at its disposal?

Ten months after the production's first night, on the occasion of a Symposium of Artists, Sociologists, Critics at the Aspen Foundation in Colorado, Soyinka delivered a speech on the state of Euro-American theatre and its so-called idiom of revolution. Referring to the production of *The Bacchae* he recalls the rehearsal process – which took eight weeks – and the discussions he had with the director as well as with Peter Hall and Kenneth Tynan, the literary adviser of the National Theatre, after almost all of his rehearsal attendances. He also quotes quite extensively from his follow-up notes and letters to the theatre.

One of the aspects Soyinka was troubled about relates to the music. He had described at some length in the script what kind of music he thought suitable. And what happened here?

> Where I had called for some kind of recognizably Aegean music, specifying some composition by Theodorakis as example, the composer had given a mélange of Indian and Japanese music. Hare Krishna silver bells, operated by an admittedly nubile nude, tinkled like demented fairies, drowning every spurt by the actors towards audibility. Bamboo percussions and cymbals seemed to promise the eruption of the fierce ghost of a samurai from beneath the causeway, which ran the whole length of the theatre – another oriental pseudism. But the bias came down decidedly on the side of India. Our Dionysus introduced himself onto the stage with the sign of the namaste and the lotus posture; the gestures which accompanied the recitation of his rout of Pentheus were a mixture of the dance of Shiva and Lord Krishna narrating the battle of Arjuna. Plus a touch of Kung Fu.
>
> (Soyinka 1988: 73)

Quite obviously, there was nothing African – or Greek – in this music or in the acting. However, in one of his rehearsal attendances Soyinka noticed a Yoruba talking drum "sitting among the usual debris of stage props." It was used only to announce the entrance of Pentheus, beating a two-tone rhythm. "A Yoruba talking-drum in the heart of Thebes, a two-tone march from an octave-plus capacity instrument which is actually designed to imitate the complex nuances of Yoruba speech" (Soyinka 1988: 73).

Another concern of Soyinka's was the nudity of the bacchants (which no doubt was indebted to Schechner). It was troubling because the actresses obviously did not feel comfortable about stripping. Soyinka suggested that "a more convincing performance would be obtained if the actresses were permitted clothing or non-clothing in which they felt comfortable." For "to berate the Puritanic principles of society, then legislate an inverse censorship that leads to expressive unease in an artistic interpretation, seems perverse and fundamentally anti-liberating" (Soyinka 1988: 74f).

The "crude imitation of a Madame Tussaud head, out of which spurts pink paint", as described in Hunt's review, is also addressed. After seeing one of the first week's performances, Soyinka wrote to the theatre:

> Paint, viscous paint flowed from Pentheus' head on Tuesday! Roland promised after the run-through that he would get some wine. Instead we get obvious, viscous paint. Is this a school production? We get realistic, grisly innards and a mangled head but not a convincing wine fluid. Aren't the actors supposed to *drink* the stuff? Why invite the audience into titters when that mixture flows out after the line, 'It's wine?'
>
> (Soyinka 1988: 76)

Soyinka provides these examples in order to substantiate his argument that "a celebration of Dionysus becomes, truthfully, a celebration of theatre: theatre as community, as idiom of liberation and renewal," but that it is "the deep malaise of Euroamerican theatre" that it is unable "to celebrate its roots because the idiom of that celebration has been appropriated and trivialized by the activities of faddism." Referring to what "one easily ecstatic critic in America has termed 'The Decade of Dionysus'" he concludes:

> Because theatre was indeed the medium of that mono-thematic consciousness called 'The Decade of Dionysus', it proved ironically impossible to achieve the tiniest shred of ecstatic liberation on a subject that had supposedly provided the idiom for the theme of the decade.
>
> (Soyinka 1988: 69)

This might be true. However, it does not explain the failure of the production. Why were music and gestures chosen from Indian and Japanese but not from African theatre? Why were all the principal actors among the slaves and the followers of Dionysus black, although Soyinka stated that

> the Slaves and the Bacchants should be as mixed a cast as is possible, testifying to their varied origins. Solely because of the 'hollering' style suggested for the Slave Leader's solo in the play it is recommended that this character be fully negroid?
>
> (Soyinka 1973: 234)

It is most likely that there was more at stake than sheer incompetence. In a note following an early rehearsal attendance, Soyinka complained that Roland is crippled by a narrow appreciation of the 'classic' mould – all this continuous reversion to the reappearance of Dionysus and some form of literary summation! ... Roland's ability to accept, on the one hand that the social (slave) reality of Greek society can be suggested in production without my iterative bias while on the other insisting on his double iterative message of the Dionysian a-moral truths at the end, when this is more than symbolically realized in my version, seems to me, a contradiction which can only be explained by an enslavement to the original. So, why did you ask me, a playwright, in on the job in the first place?

(Soyinka 1988: 71f)

One could extend this question by asking why Soyinka was not invited to stage the production of his own version himself. He was an experienced director, having staged plays in Nigeria as well as in London's Royal Court Theatre. He would have been the perfect choice if one actually wanted to have an African version of Euripides' *The Bacchae* at the National Theatre.

In the National Theatre version, elements from three different cultural strands were linked to each other – from ancient Greece, from African (especially Yoruba) culture, and from the West – establishing particular relationships. In the production the African was almost completely left out – instead, Indian and Japanese cultures are plundered. Only the black leading slaves and bacchants – and the abused Yoruba talking drum – remind the spectators of Africa – i.e., those dramatic characters who are regarded as "barbarians." In Euripides' original the idea of the Greek as civilized people and the others, the foreigners, as barbarians, is questioned:

Dionysus: Foreigners everywhere now dance for Dionysus.
Pentheus: They are more ignorant than Greeks.
Dionysus: In this matter they are not. Customs differ.

(v. 482–4)

In Soyinka's version the relationship between Greek and barbarian is more strongly destabilized, if not reversed:

Pentheus: We have more sense than barbarians.
Greece has a culture.
Dionysus: Just how much have you travelled Pentheus?
I have seen even among your so-called
Barbarian slaves, natives of lands whose cultures
Beggars yours.

(Soyinka 1973: 268)

This destabilization is foreshadowed when Pentheus knocks the old slave flat and threatens to overthrow Tiresias' place:

Various: Age is holy,
To hit an old man
Or demolish the roof of a sage?
Yet we are the barbarians
and Greece the boast of civilization.
We are slaves and have no souls.
(Soyinka 1973: 264)

Greece, as here represented by Pentheus, is as barbarous as the colonizing West. On the other hand, the liberating god is the Greek *and* "foreign" god Dionysus as well as the African and foreign god Ogun. Thus, the relationship between ancient Greece, the West, and Africa, which for the West had seemed to be stable and fixed, is set in motion. This seems to have troubled the production of the play. Its history "suggests a struggle, between two of the terms, over ownership of the third" (Goff 2005: 79). The colonial powers of the West brought Greek tragedy to the colonized Africans as their own cultural heritage in order to demonstrate their cultural superiority, emphasizing their identification with ancient Greek culture. Quite in opposition to that, in his version of *The Bacchae* – not only in the introduction and other writings on the tragedy, but also in the play itself – Soyinka links Greek culture to Yoruba culture and elaborates their affinities, even kinship. The tragedy meant to be performed at the National Theatre in London, the capital of the former British Empire, invites the British and other Western spectators to change their perspective and look at Greek culture through the lens provided by an African culture, thus questioning the sense of ownership as well as cultural superiority. Moreover, by denying the former colonizers this ownership and the claim of superiority that went with it, and instead merging Greek and Yoruba culture, Soyinka's version performed a political act – liberation from a seemingly fixed system of cultural coordinates that justified colonialism and the oppression, exploitation, and violence entailed by it. This meant, in fact, performing a cultural revolution.

With the production itself, the Empire struck back. By plundering diverse cultures in a way that makes no sense at all it demonstrated that the former colonizers still had the power and claimed their right to appropriate whatever elements they want, if only for the purpose of demonstrating this power and this claim. As for the spectators, such a procedure did not allow any transfer of energy from the actors, any rhythmic tuning in, let alone any empathy with the dramatic characters – it blocked off all kinds of positive response. The nudity of the bacchants in a still-Puritan culture made them appear as barbarians – "sweating thighs, wobbling bottoms, and the propaganda of barbarism," as Harold Hobson put it. Thus, the equation of foreign bacchants with barbarians, and of Greeks – as well as modern colonizers – with civilized people, which Euripides himself had questioned, was once more confirmed. Soyinka's third point, the ruining of the ending by ridiculing it and inviting the spectators to laugh at it – thus demonstrating their own superiority over such a barbaric communion rite – can be regarded as openly waging war on Soyinka's appropriation of Greek culture, whether or not this was consciously intended. It was achieved through the particular strategies and measures of staging that were chosen.

Thus, the failure cannot be fully explained by artistic and technical shortcomings. Rather, it was due to the uneasiness, even indignation with which the director Roland Joffe – with the tacit agreement of Peter Hall and Kenneth Tynan – encountered Soyinka's claim to ownership of Greek culture. The cultural revolution brought about by the play itself provoked a counter-revolution performed by the production. It denounced the transformative, liberatory, and communal feast celebrated in the play as a barbaric ritual of some "primitive tribes" to be laughed at with a mixture of amusement and disdain. Thus, the spectators' sense of superiority was confirmed; they could feel as a community, bonded by the exclusion of the "barbarians" represented on stage. Here, once more, the colonial situation was reestablished. The cultural revolution realized in and by Soyinka's version did not take place in the theatre. The counter-revolution won.

Many critics took a negative stance not only towards the production, but also towards the play, unable to distinguish between the two. Only a few of them who had obviously read the play made a distinction in favor of the play (e.g., Hobson, Hunter, and John Barber of the *Daily Telegraph*). After making fun of the music as "rub-a-dub jungle percussion" and of the maenads "represented by half-a-dozen bare-breasted and bare-bottomed actresses, dancing around banging drums and bearing good will" who reminded him of "the drilled hysteria of Bradfield College's chorus last June," Barber concedes:

> More interesting is the new adaptation by the distinguished Nigerian writer Wole Soyinka. The language is plain, vivid and humorous, even colloquial ("Gets in your blood, that rhythm, it really does.") And it has a central thesis.
> (Barber 1972)

The spectators, most of whom had certainly not read the play, identified the production with the text and related what they found ridiculous or barbaric to Soyinka's adaptation. Thus, they did not even obtain a glimpse of the cultural revolution that it performed. As a result they could feel as a community, bonded by the exclusion of the "barbarians" represented on stage.

In order to be able to unfold its revolutionary potential, the play had to be staged in another cultural context. This happened eighteen months later when it was staged by Carol Dawes in Kingston, Jamaica. First, the topicality of the tragedy was highlighted. In 1972, ten years after gaining independence from Great Britain and becoming a free member of the Commonwealth, Jamaica experienced a dramatic change. The People's National Party won the general election. The party's aim was to establish democratic socialism. While Jamaica's foreign policies were previously oriented toward Western countries – mainly Great Britain and the United States – it now turned to the socialist countries – principally Cuba and the Soviet Union – while itself remaining a democratic state. Thus, the performance took place in times of transformation. It is quite telling that Soyinka's version of the tragedy was performed. One critic, discussing the reason for the play's popularity in the mid-1970s, found the answer in its "relevance to a world in transition to a new society, where the logic of egalitarianism conflicts with the liberty of instincts." From this, he draws political conclusions:

> This is the dialectic at the heart of the conflict between liberal democracy with its emphasis on liberty and permissiveness and the scientific socialism of the Pentheus's of this world into [sic] feel that people should do what is good for them, even if they have to do so by force.
>
> (Milner 1975)

Second, the production obviously succeeded in getting the spectators involved – due to the spatial arrangements, the dance and the rhythm – not only in what is called audience participation but also and foremost in the sense of being aware that *tua res agitur*, that their own affairs were dealt with here, as clearly testified by Milner's review. However, the participation of spectators added another dimension:

> Our involvement is evidently central to this production's aims and achievements. It transforms the Little Theatre into a series of theatres in the round . . . It literally involves the audience in some of the action, enticing individuals into the dance. Actors mingle with us, speak from above, beside and behind us. Also, very importantly, by the choice of rhythms and (less happily) occasional words, the production discretely Jamaicanizes Wole Soyinka's version of *The Bacchae* of Euripides.
>
> (M. M. 1975)

The critic emphasizes that it was in particular "the rhythms of Dionysiac celebration" being "mainly Rastafarian or revival" that worked on the spectators and aroused a sense of communality:

> Overall the effect is to draw the Jamaican audience deeper into the heart of this universal myth and to suggest the dangerous incompleteness of those here who do not yet accept as part of themselves the energizing rhythms of most black Jamaican life.
>
> (M. M. 1975)

According to this review, because of the rhythms, the performance was able to restore a particular group of spectators to completeness and thus to strengthen the community of black Jamaican people who make up more than 90 percent of the population. This was also underlined and brought about by the chorus:

> The great glory of the production are the chorus and the resourcefulness with which they are deployed. They seem impressively free and impressively disciplined. They shift from solemn procession into frenzied orgy or reverent devotion or four-legged animalism with notable precision. They convey with equal force either ecstasy or calm . . . Perhaps most simply but with disturbing beauty, at the end, they are mourners, expertly directed to suggest a funeral cortege which is seen to move while virtually stationary on stage. A great deal of the play's emotional tone and its meaning is conveyed through them.
> (M. M. 1975)

As can be gathered from these reviews, Carol Dawes' production not only matched Soyinka's idea that the play should be staged as "a communal feast, a tumultuous celebration of life," but also, by doing so, strengthened the sense of a particular Jamaican communality.

After the failure of its London production, Soyinka became protective of the play, allowing only a few performances. It was first performed in Nigeria many years later, in 2008 by the National Troupe in Lagos. Its director, Ahmed Yerima, was a former student of Soyinka's. He commented as follows on his choice of the play: "We are concerned with realizing the aesthetic comprehensiveness of the play as well as dislocating it from the tight grip of western mythology and planting it in a soil that would give it a colour of its Africanness" (quoted by Nwachuku 2008), thus taking up once more the question of ownership. Accordingly, Yerima's production was set in Yorubaland and was "steeped deeply into the cultural aesthetics of the Yoruba" (Nwachuku 2008).

The "twinning" of Dionysus and Ogun was emphasized. It found expression in the god's appearance as well as in the mode and objects of worship:

> For instance, the bacchants, devotees of Dionysus, were costumed in adire, Yoruba traditional fabric and the thyrsus, the mystic staff borne by Dionysus, is similar to Opa Ogun held by the male devotees of the Yoruba deity, likewise is the ivy and the palm fronds.
> (Ayayi 2008)

Another critic describes them as "flaunting costumes that depict a life of the living, the dead and the unborn," which, at least, tells us that they referred to the unity of these three aspects so important in Yoruba

FIGURE 2.1 Dionysus (Albert Akaeze). Photo: National Association of Nigerian Theatre Arts Practitioners.

culture (Lasisi 2008). Although many productions of the National Troupe headed by Yerima were known for their serious musical performances, in the production of *The Bacchae* "too much music" was avoided (Yerima, quoted by Nwachuka 2008). However, some Yoruba cultural songs were introduced.

As far as can be judged from the reviews, the production was received as an African play. This understanding is not only grounded in its aesthetics. It also refers to its subject. For, in the view of many critics, the play deals with "the misuse and peril of power, especially in developing countries." This critic goes on to state that since the time when the play was written and "the crass opportunism of the military elite of that era" was obvious, "nearly 40 years after, little or nothing has changed. Nigeria, like most African countries, is still in the grip of dictatorship and maladministration, while crime, insecurity, nepotism and looting of the treasury remain a dominant feature" (Asoya 2008). Pentheus was thus no longer associated with the British colonizers but with "the visionless and purposeless political leaders, many of who occupy the political space not only in Nigeria but also in Africa and many other third world countries" (Nwachuku 2008). The communal rite that ended the performance could therefore be taken as a celebration of the hope for liberation from dictatorship and a utopian vision of new political communities in Africa.

Hereby, the question of ownership was settled. The rewriting of a Greek tragedy by an African playwright was recognized as an African play. As no one nowadays would call Racine's *Phèdre* an adaptation of Euripides' *Hippolytos* but a French tragedy, or Goethe's *Iphigenie at Tauris* an adaptation of Euripides' tragedy but a German play, so Soyinka's *The Bacchae of Euripides* is not to be regarded as an adaptation of Euripides' tragedy, but as a Nigerian play.[11]

Since Yerima's production did not refer to a Greek tragedy but to a Nigerian drama set in Yorubaland and openly criticizing the misuse of power and dictatorship, it comes as something of a surprise that, after a few performances at two different venues in Lagos, the play was "staged before Nigeria's President Umaru Yar' Adua and members of the Federal Executive Council . . . at the Sheraton Hotel and Towers, Abuja" (Anon. 2008). While reviews generally report an enthusiastic response from audiences of *The Bacchae*, no information could be found about the reception it was granted at this very special performance.

Notes

1. This "adapter's note" was prepared by Wole Soyinka both for the guidance of the director of his adaptation, Roland Joffe, and for the performance program. The last sentence was added after the production, as a result of the experience of it, when he prepared the publication of the play.
2. As Soyinka testifies, the performance in London was a failure because "the production was weak and amateurish" and could not cope with quite a number of technical difficulties, but most of all because "the European audience found itself estranged from the tragic statement." Here, an important aspect of the divergencies between the European and the African cast of mind came to the fore: "that on the one hand, which sees the cause of human anguish as viable only within strictly temporal capsules, and the other, whose tragic understanding transcends the causes of individual disjunction and recognizes them as reflections of a far greater disharmony in the communal psyche" (Soyinka 1976: 46).
3. See Hardwick (2004); also Gilbert and Tompkins (1996: esp. 38–42).

4. "The Fourth Stage" was first published in Jefferson (1969). It was reprinted in Soyinka (1976: 140–160; 1988: 21–34). Here, it will be quoted from Soyinka (1988).
5. For Poel's production, see Macintosh (2007) and in particular Sampatakakis (2005); who cites extensively the unpublished Murray–Poel correspondence which is part of the Gilbert Murray Papers, New Bodleian Library, Oxford, MSs 10, 14, 15.
6. See the introduction to the present volume.
7. Macintosh argues that Soyinka's insistence in his "Introduction" that the worship of Dionysus affords the "release [. . . of] the pent-up frustrated energy of all the downtrodden" and his inclusion of the slaves resonate with "Murray's consistent desire to emphasize that the wisdom of ordinary people lies at the heart of Dionysiac religion." In a footnote she quotes Murray: "This religion, very primitive and barbarous, but possessing a strong hold over the emotions of the common people"; and "No grudge hath of the great / No scorn of the mean estate . . . /The simple nameless heard of Humanity/Hath deeds and faith that are truth enough for me" (Murray 1902: 166; S. Macintosh 2007: 161).
8. The ritual of the slaying of the Old Year alludes to different contexts. On the one hand it refers to Yoruba rituals of carriers, kinds of scapegoats that take the burden of the old year away from the community. On the other hand, it might conjure up once more the Cambridge Ritualists with the idea of an *eniautos daimon* ritual, a year-god ritual, from which they tried to prove Greek tragedy originated.
9. When Pentheus answers Dionysus' question "And for this you raise the army of Thebes – Against women?" with "Those are not women. They are alien monsters/ who have invaded Thebes. I have a duty to preserve/The territorial integrity of Thebes" (283), he is associated with the federal government during the civil war.
10. In the context of this book my interpretation of Soyinka's adaptation focuses on the question of political liberation and the coming into being of a new political order, the celebration of a new community. Of course, many important aspects of the play are ignored here. For other interpretations highlighting other aspects and giving other judgments, see Baker-White (1993) and the further reading listed at the end of this chapter.
11. As the director confirms in a letter to me, he tried "to bring the play closer home": "Take the play from the Greeks, situate it within the Yoruba god, Ogun, and allow the other characters grow in mannerism, speech patterns and delivery within the Yoruba the reality of the everyday worldview so that they spoke to my audience directly. The ritual act in the play then became realistic and acceptable. And finally I enriched the play with the aesthetics through elements of performance by embellishing it with rich Yoruba costumes, music, dances, chants, and language, thus giving it a stamp of sociocultural ownership." Unfortunately, Wole Soyinka did not see the production, as I learned from the playwright himself.

References

Anon. 2008. "Soyinka's *Bacchae* of Euripides for Mr. President." *Vanguard*, 9 April.

Asoya, Sylvester. 2008. "*Bacchae* of Euripides, a satirical play by Wole Soyinka comes alive at the National Theatre." *A Warning Defied*, April 8.
Ayayi, Segun. 2008. "Soyinka's Bacchae opens theatre season in Lagos." *Daily Sun*, April 2.
Baker-White, Robert. 1993. "The Politics of Ritual in Wole Soyinka's *The Bacchae of Euripides*." In *Comparative Drama* 27. Edited by Clifford Davidson and John H. Stroupe, 377–397. Kalamazoo: Medieval Institute Publications, Western Michigan University.
Barber, John. 1972. "Vivid Political Slant on *The Bacchae*." *Daily Telegraph*, August 3.
Euripides. 1960. *The Bacchae*. Translated by William Arrowsmith. In *The Complete Greek Tragedies*, Vol. 3. Edited by David Grene and Richmond Lattimore, 189–261. Chicago: University of Chicago Press.
Gilbert, Helen and Joanne Tompkins. 1996. *Post-Colonial Drama, Theory, Practice, Politics*. New York: Routledge.
Goff, Barbara. 2005. "Dionysiac Triangle: The Politics of Culture in Wole Soyinka's *The Bacchae of Euripides*." In *The Soul of Tragedy: Essays on Athenian Drama*. Edited by Victoria Pedrick and Steven M. Oberhelman, 73–88. Chicago: University of Chicago Press.
Hardwick, Lorna. 2004. "Greek Drama and Anti-Colonialism: Decolonizing Classics." In *Dionysus in 69: Greek Tragedy at the Dawn of the Third Millennium*. Edited by Edith Hall, Fiona Macintosh, and Amanda Wrigley, 219–242. Oxford: Oxford University Press.
Hobson, Harold H. 1973. "Agony and Ecstasy." *Sunday Times*, August 5.
Hunt, Albert. 1980. "Amateurs in Horror." In *Critical Perspectives on Wole Soyinka*. Edited by James Gibbs, 113–115. London: Heinemann.
Jefferson, Douglas Williams. 1969. *The Morality of Art: Essays Presented to G. Wilson Knight by his Colleagues and Friends*. London: Routledge and Kegan Paul.
Lasisi, Akeene. 2008. "Soyinka is very protective of Bacchae – Yerima." *Punch*, March 30.
M. M. 1975. "Accept Dionysus." *Daily Gleaner*, March 26.
Macintosh, Fiona. 2007. "The Theatrical Legacy of Gilbert Murray's *Bacchae*." In *Gilbert Murray Reassessed: Hellenism, Theatre and International Politics*. Edited by Christopher Stray, 145–166. Oxford: Oxford University Press.
Milner, Harry. 1975. "Bacchic Diversions. School of Drama's production of The Bacchae of Euripides by Wole Soyinka." *Sunday Gleaner*, March 30.
Murray, Gilbert. 1902. "Introductory Essay: *The Bacchae* in Relation to Certain Currents of Thought in the Fifth Century in *Euripides translated into Rhyming Verse*." In *The Athenian Drama: A Series of Verse Translation from the Greek Dramatic Poets*. Edited by George Charles Warr, xix–lxviii. London: G. Allen.
Nouryeh, Andrea J. 2001. "Soyinka's Euripides: Postcolonial Resistance or Avant-Garde Adaptation?" *Research in African Literatures* 33 (4): 160–171.
Nwachuku, McPhilips. 2008. "National Troupe presents Soyinka's The Bacchae of Euripides as parable of power." *Vanguard*, March 29.
Sampatakakis, Georgios. 2005. *Bakkhai-Model: The Re-Usage of Euripides' Bakkhai in Text and Performance*. London: London University Press.

Soyinka, Wole. 1973. *The Bacchae of Euripides*. In Soyinka, Wole, *Collected Plays 1*, 233–307. Oxford: Oxford University Press.

Soyinka, Wole. 1976. *Myth, Literature and the African World*. Cambridge: Cambridge University Press.

Soyinka, Wole. 1988. *Art, Dialogue and Outrage: Essays on Literature and Culture*. Ibadan: New Horn Press.

Further Reading

Jeyifo, Biodun. 1999. *Wole Soyinka: Politics, Poetics and Postcolonialism*. Cambridge: Cambridge University Press.

Okpewho, Isidore. 1999. "Soyinka, Euripides, and the Anxiety of Empire." *Research in African Literature* 30 (4): 32–55.

Quayson, Ato. 2001. "The Space of Transformation: Theory, Myth, and Ritual in the Work of Wole Soyinka." In *Wole Soyinka, Freedom and Complexity*. Edited by Biodun Jeyifo, 201–236. Jackson: University Press of Mississippi.

Rhodes, Neil. 2007. "Tarzan of Athens, Dionysus in Africa: Wilson Knight and Wole Soyinka." In *Tragedy in Transition*. Edited by Sarah Annes Brown and Catherine Silverstone, 232–248. Oxford: Blackwell.

Senanu, K. E. 1980. "The Exigencies of Adaptation: The Case of Soyinka's *Bacchae*." In *Critical Perspectives on Wole Soyinka*. Edited by James Gibbs, 108–112. London: Heinemann.

Sotto, Wiweca. 1985. *The Rounded Rite: A Study of Wole Soyinka's Play The Bacchae of Euripides*. Lund: CWK Gleerup.

3

Sparagmos and *Omophagia*
Teat(r)o Oficina's *Bacantes* in São Paulo (1996)

"The production proved to be 'faithful' to the play's Dionysian spirit. At any time, it was ritual, festival, carnival and celebration of the tragic and sensuous joy, intensely integrating the audience" (Roston 2009).[1] With these words a critic summarized his experience of seeing *The Bacchae* staged by José Celso Martinez Corrêa (known as Zé Celso) and his Teat(r)o Oficina in São Paulo in 1996. The key words here are ritual, festival, and carnival. They refer to genres of cultural performance in which each participant fulfills particular functions without a clear separation between actors and spectators, all of whom "act" in one way or another. In line with this thinking, the critic emphasized that the performance "intensely integrated the audience." Almost all of the production's reviews highlighted this integration of the spectators. Not only the performers but the spectators, too, were said to have felt "joyful and complete devotion . . . to their songs" and their "convincing shamelessness" (Uzel 1997). Time and again, they seemingly entered "a state of being extraordinarily uncontrolled" (Santos 1996). Moreover, it seemed that participating in the performance marked an important social event which meant a lot to many spectators. The actress Leona Cavalli, who took part in the production, recalls on her website:

> After the premiere we performed the piece for six months. Each performance lasted for six hours, which means that it was actually a theatrical vigil involving the audience – so much so that they brought along drinks, snacks and clothes to change into (in case they got dirty or wet during the performance). People brought along flowers to throw to Dionysus or one of their other favorite gods.

Dionysus Resurrected: Performances of Euripides' The Bacchae in a Globalizing World, First Edition. Erika Fischer-Lichte.
© 2014 Erika Fischer-Lichte. Published 2014 by John Wiley & Sons, Ltd.

> People fought over how often they had participated in *The Bacchae* and many did not miss even a single performance. Birthdays would be celebrated during the performance on stage, love stories began and ended.
>
> (Cavalli 2012)

It follows from these memories that the performance marked a meaningful event in the lives of many spectators. The line usually drawn between theatre and ritual or festival and carnival was erased, as was that between theatre and life. What happened here seems to have come close to what Wole Soyinka had envisaged for his own production of the play: "a communal feast, a tumultuous celebration of life."

However, not all spectators reacted in the same, life-affirming way. One critic reported two opposing reactions. The common people in Ribeirão Preto's Greek arena, the spectators in Rio de Janeiro at the festival "Rio em Cena," who seemed to recognize themselves in the performance, and the audience at the first night in São Paulo responded with great enthusiasm. Others, however, vehemently objected to it. One critic alleged that it

> appears to them as a loose mixture of perfidious assaults on good taste, on intelligence, on any sense of shame or on the body of the spectators . . . In my view, the polarity (between complete distance or none whatsoever) is not to be viewed as a mere indicator of variations in the audience or of the heights and depths of a splendidly generous and creative spectacle. Rather, it is a sign of the radicalness with which this piece deals with the dilemma produced by its central question: the invasion of the Dionysian into the public order.
>
> (Wisnik n.d.)

The polarization caused by the performance was due to its political implications. Since it advocated "the invasion of the Dionysian into the public order," which was not only represented through the action on stage but also realized for all participants of the performance, it displayed a highly charged political dimension. It comes as no surprise, then, that it polarized the audience and became a "scandal, shocking and of great importance; it made people reflect and provoked extreme opinions; it brought legions of Pentheuses and Dionysuses into our present, going far beyond a merely theatrical production" (Cavalli 2012).

The history of the Teat(r)o Oficina speaks to this political dimension. Founded in 1958 by Zé Celso, it moved into its own building, a former factory in the immigrant neighborhood of Bexiga in São Paulo, in 1961. This burnt down in 1966, was rebuilt and extensively renovated in the 1980s, and finally completed in its current form in 1993. After the military coup of 1964, many artists and intellectuals found themselves oppressed and persecuted. The situation further deteriorated in 1969 when the regime issued its Institutional Act No. 5, which abolished freedom of expression in the arts and in artistic movements. In 1974 members of the Teat(r)o Oficina were arrested on charges of drug dealing. Zé Celso responded by spreading an SOS appeal to the public in Brazil and abroad, in which he asked for help and which led to his own arrest. After being tortured by the military police, he fled the country after his release, which had been brought about by the intervention of international artists, among them Jean-Paul Sartre. Zé Celso returned to Brazil in 1979. Two years later, despite the difficult political situation, he reopened the theatre under the name Teat(r)o Oficina Uzyna Uzona. As the name suggests, it saw itself as a workshop (*oficina*) and theatre as a form of work or labor "as any other" (Celso 1998: 149), its symbol being the anvil. The bracketing of the "r" allowed for the reading of the first term as "te ato," which means "I'm connecting you to someone" or "I'm tying you to someone." As such, the name itself reflected the theatre's objective. It implied that whatever audience participation was to happen was not the result of manipulation or a supposed act of liberation but a "seduction."

From 1982 onwards, i.e., one year after the reopening of the Teat(r)o Oficina, the military regime began to crumble, finally coming to an end in 1985. The theatre's fight against the military dictatorship now changed into a fight against a powerful capitalist – Silvio Santos, owner of a media empire. He tried to buy the theatre building in order to tear it down and erect a shopping mall in its place.[2] Although this never happened, he was still trying to do so at the time of *The Bacchae*. The potential double loss of its performance space and the unique opportunities afforded by its specific architecture remains a constant threat as well as a major source of inspiration for the company. Every production at least alludes to this ongoing battle.

In the 1980s the architect Lina Bo Bardi came up with a design concept for redoing the theatre. Apparently, the idea to rebuild it emerged around the same time as the first plans for staging *The Bacchae*. However, the process of rebuilding took longer than expected, so that the theatre could not reopen until 1993. Its first production was not *The Bacchae* but *Hamlet* – starring Marcelo Drummond, who would later play Dionysus in *The Bacchae*.

The new performance space, truly unique in its resemblance to the streets that host the carnival every year, ideally suited the mise en scène of *The Bacchae*. These so-called *sambódromos* are flanked by multistoried structures for the spectators. Below, on the streets, the parade of scantily clad sambistas passes through, drumming, singing, and dancing ecstatically. The performance space of the Oficina, which Zé Celso named *teatódromo* by analogy, is 45 meters long. Four-storied structures rise up on both sides, which can accommodate approximately 300 spectators either standing or sitting. The space is closed off from the outside by a red metallic door – frequently, the performance begins on the nearby street(s), making the passage from the street into the Oficina a part of the performance.

Approximately 20 meters inside, the wall to the left of the entrance is made of glass. The 10-meter high removable ceiling allows the actors and spectators to look up at the sky. The space thus opens itself up to the city as well as the sky. Tall trees stand in front of the glass wall and tall plants decorate the inside; thus, the space also opens itself to and includes nature. The walls are made of yellow brick. For the performance of *The Bacchae*, an underground opening was located halfway down the long passage. It was first covered by a wooden plank and later by an iron grate from which the flickering flames of a fire could be seen. The spot was mentioned and used variously as Semele's womb as well as Semele's tomb, Dionysus' prison, Pentheus' sepulcher and, lastly, a grill on which meat was roasted in a pan. On its right-hand side (as viewed from the entrance) was a cascading fountain, next to which the musicians stood and played.

The action of the tragedy was extended substantially. It included the birth of Zeus through Rhea, his love affair with Semele, Hera's jealousy, Semele's death, and Dionysus' birth, all enacted during the first hour of the performance after the procession of the actors into the performance space. At the end the action stretched to a meeting of the gods Zeus, Hera, Dionysus, and Apollo on a balcony – Mount Olympus – and to a festive common meal, for which the mortals, actors and spectators alike, assembled around the underground opening, where the "raw meat" was roasted in a pan.

The focus of the following analysis will be on the relationship between performers and spectators, the particular community brought forth by them, and the strategies and means by which the performers succeeded in "connecting" with, indeed "seducing," the spectators. I will explore the grounds for and the impact of such a "seduction" – during the performance itself as well as beyond.[3]

In my analysis I shall use as guiding concepts the three descriptions from the review quoted at the beginning of this chapter: carnival, festival, and ritual. These three concepts are interrelated insofar as carnival is a collective festivity that includes special rituals; generally speaking, rituals are performed as part of festivals which, because of their paradoxical nature (to be explained later) are ritualistic. They all have in common that they allow and partly even require their participants to enter a state of liminality and undergo transformations, so that they strengthen their sense of communality and affirm their particular community. However, each of them also displays another, unique feature.

Carnivals are based on the reversal of the social order; everything is turned upside down. Those in the lower ranks of society take over the positions of the upper class, if only in a mock ceremony. Moreover, the body plays a central role in carnival. As Mikhail Bakhtin has elaborated in his famous study, *Rabelais and His World* (2009), the carnivalesque body knows no boundaries. It exists only in contact with other bodies, highlighting its openings and all the actions they make possible – eating, drinking and excreting, copulating and giving birth.

In *The Bacchae* performances these two carnivalesque aspects stood out, albeit not always in the same way as in carnival. The performance opened like a Brazilian carnival. It began in the streets near the theatre as a procession of drummers, singers, and ecstatic dancers headed by Zé Celso, who would play the part of Tiresias. The procession made its way into the performance space, where the audience was already assembled. It included a curious vehicle, steered by the actor Marcelo Drummond, who would later appear as Dionysus (close to the end of the performance, Cadmus would use this vehicle for going into exile). As in a carnival, the parading actors danced in a choral formation, singing the words "the samba school will parade and people will sing." The allusion to the sambistas was obvious. However, while the sambistas are usually scantily clad, all the performers were dressed in hooded cloaks of different colors, the hoods drawn over their heads. Before the procession entered the theatre, a person dressed in a light-brown hooded cloak knelt on the floor and blew into a gigantic curved horn. Then the vehicle drove in, followed by all the others dancing and singing. At that point, the space was actually used as a sambódromo.

This setting established a carnivalesque atmosphere from the very start. The action of the play, i.e., the "intrusion of the Dionysian into the public order," turned this order upside down over the course of the performance. The ruler turned into the victim and the assaulted, persecuted, and imprisoned god and his followers into those trapping and killing him. The hunter became the hunted and vice versa.

The carnival atmosphere also turned the status of the spectators upside down, transforming them into performers. It engulfed all participants and allowed for ecstasy and all kinds of transgression. In particular, the twenty-five songs, always accompanied by dancing and structuring the performance, continually reinforced this atmosphere in which anything could happen. The spectators would frequently join in, either by simply clapping their hands and moving their bodies to the rhythms of the singers and dancers or by singing along or getting up and mingling with the dancers. As we have seen, the space not only allows the spectators to move closer to or further away from the actors over the course of the performance; it also facilitates, even encourages, the possibility of becoming part of the action and joining in – especially for the spectators at stage level. The carnival atmosphere was intensified by the almost – and later fully – naked singing and ecstatically dancing bacchants who radiated a high amount of energy that circulated in the space, turning the spectators into performers.

The other characteristic feature of carnival, the carnivalesque body, played a crucial role throughout the performance. The actors and spectators ate grapes and drank wine. The performers, either naked or dressed only in loose, flowing garments, repeatedly exposed their genitals. The bacchants, turning their back on Tiresias, leant down, lifted their robes, and mockingly confronted him with their bare bottoms. Zeus copulated with Semele by bringing a huge phallus, a stick of approximately two meters, close to her vagina. Clearly, body openings featured prominently.

By turning the given order upside down and exposing the carnivalesque body, the performance succeeded in transferring the spectators into a state of liminality and transformation.

The carnival atmosphere also created a festive mood among the spectators. Festivals are special events that transgress everyday life. Yet, since they take place at regular intervals, they also structure the daily routine. Usually, festivals are rooted in particular occasions of a religious, social, political, seasonal, or biographical nature. They constitute a genre of cultural performance characterized by the double dialectic of liminality and periodicity on the one hand, and compliance with rules and their transgression on the other. The first opposition refers to time. Since festivals recur regularly, they are embedded in the routine of everyday life; nonetheless, they constitute a time of their own and thus enable transgression, which disrupts the flow of regular time. In Zé Celso's view this particular quality of festive time is in fact the time of the performance. In an interview he states:

> I think that theatre is the eternal present. As now: we are here, but everything is charged with the past, everything is a series of future wishes. Everything is here; what exists is the here and now. While you concentrate on the here and now, you lead a dialogue with eternity. In this sense, you do something that becomes history and abstracts from the present. For history is here, it is in your body, in the body of the spectators, in the architecture of the space. We no longer have a linear concept of history. It is possible to deal with the present by proceeding from the past and the future, which is beyond time – it does not matter anymore.
>
> (Valente 2004)

The second opposition refers to the actions and behavior in the context of a festival. On the one hand, they are subject to strict rules; on the other, the essence of festive action and behavior can be defined as not only allowing for but also encouraging a transgression of certain rules, i.e., those that determine the behavior of everyday life. As the above-quoted reviews tell us, rules valid for everyday behavior were transgressed both by the performers and spectators. They testified to the performers' "shamelessness" and the spectators' "state of being extraordinarily uncontrolled." Each participant introduced new rules for themselves which they considered appropriate.

Certain dimensions concerning the festive effects on participants can be deduced from this concept of festival.[4] The first opposition highlights the liminal dimension: festival time is an in-between time, a time of passage, embedded in the everyday as well as in historical time. It requires that the participants detach themselves from their daily routines to which, hopefully transformed, they have to return after the end of the festival. As such, the liminal dimension is the *conditio sine qua non* of another dimension – the transformative one. What kinds of transformations are effected and how long they last depends on the nature of the festival and on the circumstances. In any case, it strengthens the sense of *communitas*.

The second opposition, on the one hand, entails a "conventional" dimension. It demands compliance with the rules valid for this particular kind of festival. On the other hand, a cathartic dimension is implied. When participants transgress the rules of everyday life by committing different kinds of excesses such as drinking too much and overeating, taking drugs, having sex in public, or enacting violence, a specific cathartic dimension is addressed. As we shall see, all these dimensions applied to the performance.

The festival reached its first peak with Song 10 (referring to the second chorus song in Euripides). Semele, who joined the chorus after her death, took a bottle of wine and drank from it. Subsequently, she approached the audience and poured wine into the mouths of willing spectators while the chorus of bacchants and satyrs, joined by some spectators, danced. At that point the festival literally turned into a bacchanal. Such moments recurred throughout the performance. After the performance came to an end, many spectators stayed behind and celebrated together with the performers. Not only did the performance take place as a festival; it also resulted in a communal feast.

Pentheus and his militia, all dressed in black and heavily armed, put an end to this first bacchanal. They cordoned off the space of revelry and, wielding their weapons menacingly, chased the bacchants away until they had fled through the red metallic door on to the street. The space hosting the tumultuous celebration of life was now to become one of repressive law and order.

Pentheus and his militia conjured up a wide range of associations. The bacchants addressed him as Pentheus Pentagonus. This and the flag resembling a dollar bill hanging from his palace – and later covering his coffin – connected him to the US military. On the other hand, the crushing of the festive spirit and the subsequent imprisonment, threats of torture, and killings by a military power and through sheer force alluded to the long-term military regime in Brazil. Another possibility was opened up when Pentheus appeared on the balcony facing the red metal door at the other end of the "teatódromo" before Song 10, in his hand a huge bag with "9 million $ $" written on it. Tiresias remarked: "Want to build a shopping mall?", clearly linking Pentheus – as well as the Cadmus family – to Silvio Santos.

The liberation brought about by Dionysus and celebrated by the bacchants and satyrs could thus be interpreted variously – liberation from the military dictatorship, the threat of US capitalism and military power and, one might hope, the threat of the Teat(r)o Oficina's closure through Silvio Santos. Ultimately, the whole performance could be regarded as a festival, celebrating liberation not only from political or economic oppression but also from restraints imposed on individuals by public order and other demands that repressed their need for transgression and excess. It celebrated a human state similar to that described by Nietzsche in *The Birth of Tragedy out of the Spirit of Music* when characterizing the tragic chorus:

> Not only is the bond between man and man sealed by the Dionysian magic: alienated, hostile or subjugated nature, too, celebrates her reconciliation with her lost son . . . Now, with the gospel of world harmony, each man feels not only united, reconciled, and at one with his neighbour, but one with him, as if the veil of Maya had been rent and now hung in rags before the mysterious primal Oneness. Singing and dancing, man expresses himself as a member of a higher community: he has forgotten how to walk and talk, and is about to fly dancing into the heavens. His gestures express enchantment.
>
> (Nietzsche 1995: 17–18)

In fact, the performance centered on the chorus, just as Nietzsche described the coming into existence of Greek tragedy out of the chorus of satyrs. It was a choric performance, not merely representing but bringing forth a festive community that extended to the spectators and actively incorporated them.

The performance came into being out of the dancing and singing chorus. It seemed as if everyone, at one point or another, would join the community – even Pentheus, who became one with it by being dismembered and then eaten.

As the fate of Pentheus indicates, the chorus acted not only as a festive community but also as a ritual community. As such, it drew heavily on the practices of the Afro-Brazilian religious cult *candomblé*. Zé Celso emphasized the relationship of his theatre to the *candomblé* by calling its space a *terreiro*, a term used to designate the temple and ritual space in *candomblé*. Marcelo Drummond compared the Dionysian cult to *candomblé*, strongly relating the working practices of the Teat(r)o Oficina to the latter:

> What makes the aesthetic of the Teat(r)o Oficina so special is the ritual. The Dionysian cult is a ritualistic religion of trance and incorporation. Here, in Brazil, *candomblé* . . . exists. This, too, is a religion of incorporation. It is extremely important for our aesthetics and our way of doing theatre. We work a lot with energy . . . We work with the shamanistic elements in us. Quite often, we get into great difficulties during rehearsals because of it, since we need to transpose ourselves into this kind of a trance, without which we are unable to work. This is why we dance and sing in a circle until we move into another state of consciousness, until we become mad. We cannot work in our everyday state of consciousness. We dance, talk, sing until we turn into Indios, for the Indio says everything at the same time.
>
> (Drummond 2008: 241)

FIGURE 3.1 Chorus of the bacchae. Photo: Associação Teat(r)o Oficina Uzyna Uzona.

In *candomblé* the participants achieve ecstasy by way of singing, drumming, and dancing in order to become permeable, so that an *orixá* (a god) can enter them. The universe is conceived of as an energetic merging of the material and the immaterial. The relationship between these two levels is defined and stimulated by a never-ending movement of giving (sacrificing) and receiving (incorporating). This is the state which the performers of the Teat(r)o Oficina aim to enter in order to allow other beings to pass through, enter, and leave their bodies.

To achieve this end, music played an important role, for the music served as the basis for the dancing through its rhythm, which worked on the bodies of the performers and the spectators. Music invades the body through the ear and the skin, resonates inside the body and often triggers physiological and affective reactions. The listeners shudder, get goose bumps, their pulse accelerates, they breathe faster and heavier, become euphoric and are set in motion. Sometimes only parts of the body move, other times it is the whole body. In the performance it always set the whole chorus in motion. How this happened depended on the music played. Zé Celso took great care to choose music from the most diverse Brazilian traditions, ranging from *candomblé* to opera, so that various rhythmic schemes were realized, which determined the relationship between actors and spectators. Rhythm as an organizing principle stands in contrast to temporal units of beat and meter, for it is repetition and deviation. In rhythm, the foreseeable and the unforeseeable interact. Most importantly, it is a principle based on the human body. The heartbeat, blood circulation, and respiration each follow their own rhythm, as do the movements we carry out when walking, dancing, swimming, writing, etc. The same goes for the sounds we make when speaking, singing, laughing, or crying. Even the inner movements of our bodies down to each cell, which we are incapable of perceiving, are also organized rhythmically. The human body is indeed rhythmically tuned.

We have a particular capacity for perceiving rhythms and tuning our bodies into them. When the temporality of a performance is organized and structured through rhythm, as was the case in *The Bacchae*, different "rhythmic systems" clash – the rhythm of the performers collides with the various rhythms of each individual spectator. If the spectators prove responsive to the rhythms set by the performers they tune in: their own rhythmic system changes and adapts to that of the performer. A rhythmic community comes into being, as was here the case. Through rhythmic singing and dancing, accompanied and supported by instrumental music including drums, flute, cymbal, piano, etc., the chorus radiated a vast amount of energy, drawing in the spectators. Joining in the dance, they tuned in with their own rhythm, thus incorporating themselves into the choric community.

In *The Bacchae* the chorus repeatedly danced in a circle (*roda*), worshipping not only Dionysus but also Xango, the Yoruba god of thunder and lightning and one of the *orixás* of the *candomblé*. Ritual and theatre merged in the singing, drumming, and dancing of the chorus that transposed them into a trance or at least a trance-like state. The scenes represented the worship of a god in trance while the performers at the same time actually entered this state. The distinction between theatre and ritual was blurred. Moreover, the ritual practices used here were not borrowed from distant foreign cultures but were familiar to all those assembled in the theatre. Thus it was entirely possible that spectators who joined the singing and dancing chorus might also have entered a state of trance.

Embedded in this overall ritualistic structure as established by the chorus, three different kinds of rituals were performed in the course of the performance – birth rituals, rituals of dismemberment (*sparagmos*), and those of incorporation (*omophagia*). The whole chorus took part in all of these rituals. Mainly, the rituals were performed as an enactment of the chorus' songs and the messengers' reports.

The two birth rituals constituted the *entrada*, the "entrance" or *parodos*, which was followed by the prologue enacting the arrival of Dionysus in

Thebes, i.e., the proper beginning of Euripides' tragedy. The *entrada*, which spanned the first chorus songs of the tragedy narrating the prehistory of Dionysus' conception and birth, was extended back to Zeus' birth. The *entrada* also included the story of Hera's jealousy. When Hera cursed Tiresias and robbed him of his eyesight because he had sided with Semele and Zeus thereupon conferred on him the gift of prophecy ("But you'll know it all"), the gauze veil which had been hanging from the ceiling in front of the multistoried structures, thus obscuring the spectators' view, fell down. Following this scene, the spectators had a clear sight of the action on stage.

The two birth rituals – Rhea giving birth to Zeus and Semele to Dionysus – strikingly differed from each other, not only because the spectators had a veiled view of Zeus' birth and an unobstructed one of Dionysus'. Hidden underneath a white cloth behind Rhea, who was dressed in a flowing white garment, the naked Zeus was born by crawling out through her splayed legs. The Afro-Brazilian actress playing Rhea (and who later took on the part of Agave) used the tune of *candomblé* songs in her solos. She appeared as the Great Mother from whom all life sprung. Zeus' birth was ritualistic only in the sense that it reenacted a myth and that the chorus' and Rhea's singing created a ritualistic setting. The overall impression of the scene was humorous.

Dionysus was born twice. When Semele died after being touched by Zeus, he was "born" by ascending from the opening in the floor – Semele's womb – and crawling through Zeus' splayed legs. There he lay down on the floor in a fetal position. The ritual creation of his fetus had already taken place immediately after Zeus had begot him: around Semele's wreath of ivy, with which she had earlier crowned Zeus' huge phallus when he approached her, Tiresias wrapped golden ribbons – the umbilical cord. Now Zeus picked up the wreath with the ribbons.

Tiresias also acted as a kind of midwife at Dionysus' second birth. It was performed as an obvious allusion to the birth ritual in Schechner's *Dionysus in 69*. The still-naked Zeus squatted down. Behind him, first hidden under a huge white cloth, the naked satyrs and bacchants lay side by side. Tiresias stood next to Zeus. When Zeus rose to his feet, standing with his legs splayed, Tiresias began moving his body as if in labor, after which Dionysus emerged crawling through Zeus' legs out of the now-visible pile of bodies, followed one by one by the others. Having been born they formed a line by standing behind each other. They surrounded the opening, now Semele's tomb, dancing and singing, quoting the words from Dionysus in *Dionysus in 69* after his birth: "I am a god. I have come here to perform my rites and to be born." Whereas in the production of the Performance Group the birth ritual, replicating the adoption ritual of the Asmat tribe, was essential, because it worked as a bond between the members of the group and because the subsequent circle dance around the spot of Dionysus' birth was the first event that encouraged audience participation, here the inclusion of this scene was done tongue-in-cheek. It served as a quotation easily incorporated into the overall ritualistic setting and as a mock-performance of a ritual. This aspect of mockery was emphasized when all those just "born" posed naked as if for a group photo standing in two rows, the front row squatting, while those at the back casually had their arms around each other's shoulders. Zeus stood in the middle. During the *entrada* some of the spectators joined in and became very involved by singing along, clapping their hands to the rhythm of the songs or by moving their bodies rhythmically without, however, interfering in the main action.

This involvement increased during the first rituals of dismemberment. It could be said that there were three of these: two scenes and the overall dismemberment of the text. The latter provided the basis for the performance. It was dismembered in such a way that its fragments could be connected to the other elements brought in by the artists and spectators. Such a dismemberment of the text allowed for an element of unpredictability to enter the performance. The text did not serve as an incontestable authority controlling the artists and spectators. On the contrary, its dismemberment was the precondition for the coming into being of the performance out of the unforeseeable encounter between the performers and spectators.

The first ritual of dismemberment in the performance took place as an enactment of the herdsman's report on what happened in the Cithaeron mountains. After he had uttered the words, "and they out of vengeance attacked our cattle," the dismemberment of an ox was enacted. The chorus sang "Eh ox, eh ox," holding up a toy head of an ox impaled on a stick. When the women tore it apart, red ribbons flowed out of it. One member of the chorus donned an ox suit and mask and danced wildly. The bacchants chose a willing volunteer from among the spectators. They – the group included Dionysus – undressed, caressed, and kissed him while the herdsman recounted "that they have eaten up his flesh." (The Portuguese word for eating, *comer*, also means to make love, rendering the "eating up" of the ox rather ambiguous.) Some spectators usually joined in.

One night, at a performance in Rio de Janeiro, the famous Brazilian musician and composer Caetano Veloso, a good friend of Zé Celso's, was in the audience. The bacchants chose him as the ox, to be dismembered and eaten. The audience responded with frenetic applause. Everybody wanted to participate. Subsequently, the pop singer and composer Adriana Calcanhotto, also a good friend of Zé Celso's and of Veloso's, wrote the song "Vamos comer Caetano Veloso," which translates as "Let's eat up/make love to Caetano Veloso"; the lyrics continue:

"Undressed by the bacchants/During a performance/We feast on ourselves and each other/Order and orgy/In a super-bacchanal/Flesh and carnival" (quoted in Horan 2012). On another night the musician Chico César was chosen. The spectators spontaneously began singing the song *Mama Africa*, which was his greatest hit at the time (Cavalli 2012). The dismemberment of the "ox" was one of the climaxes of audience participation on many nights. It did not induce a sense of horror but of communal festivity and celebration.

The scene's popularity and success was most likely also due to the fact that it openly alluded to a famous Amazonian festival celebrated by the Indios – the Boi Bumbá (*boi* meaning ox) or Festa do Boi. There are two Bois (Caprichoso and Garantido) – as there were two in *The Bacchae*: the one in the costume of an ox and the other one chosen each night. After the dismemberment, both were led to the fountain of Dirce by Dionysus and stood under the cascade. In the Boi Bumbá, the teams consisting of two oxes each play the same story in a competition:

> The play tells the story of Pai Francisco, who worked on a farm, and Mâe Catirina, his pregnant wife, who longed to eat beef tongue. Pai Francisco kills an ox to satisfy his wife's craving. Unfortunately, this ox is the farm owner's favorite. A priest and a doctor fail to revive the Boi, for whose death Pai Francisco would be sent to jail. The story has a happy end thanks to the ritual performed by a pajé (pa-zhe, shaman). Pai Francisco is forgiven and the whole ordeal ends in a major party that celebrates the Boi's life.
> (http://www.boibumba.com/brief_en.htm, accessed June 18, 2013)

This party always also includes the spectators. After the three-hour show of each Boi, the city provides food and drinks for everybody. Thus, it ends with a common meal.

It can be assumed that many spectators, if not all of them, would have been familiar with the Boi Bumbá. It follows, then, that the ritual dismemberment performed as the enactment of the herdsman's report "seduced" the spectators to join in because of this knowledge.

The final ritual of dismemberment showed Pentheus being hunted down and killed by the bacchants. When they perceived Pentheus sitting high up on a tree trunk, they addressed each other as well as the audience: "Attack him with applause!" They applauded and the audience joined in. When the trunk came down, Dionysus caressed Pentheus, the bacchae undressed and kissed him and each other. While Dionysus, now in the costume of a bull with horns, cracked his whip to the rhythm of the drums, the bacchants formed a pile of bodies kissing each other. Again in an allusion to *Dionysus in 69*, Pentheus was chased through the "death channel" formed by the women. While Pentheus lay motionless on the ground, the women mimed his dismemberment. Tiresias brought a bowl of grapes, put it on Pentheus' belly and fed him these grapes, thus preparing him for his impending transformation into Apollo, who appeared at the end in a golden cloak on the balcony among Zeus, Hera, and Dionysus. Then a red cloth was spread over Pentheus' body and a wreath of ivy placed on top. Agave took a piece of raw meat handed to her by Tiresias, which she addressed as the head of the young lion she had hunted down. She speared it with her thyrsus, covered it with the hairpiece first worn by Dionysus and later by Pentheus, and invited everyone to feast on the meat: "Let us eat. In this banquet all are invited to participate."

In contrast to the dismemberment of the ox, spectators did not participate in Pentheus' dismemberment. They refrained from joining the bacchants beyond applauding them. This scene did appear to horrify the spectators as they turned into involuntary witnesses. Having joined in the applause marking the beginning of the hunt, they had somehow taken part in and sanctioned it. Despite Dionysus' frightening appearance, the first moments of caressing, kissing, and undressing seemed to suggest a certain analogy to the Boi Bumbá scene. This changed when Agave stepped forward, establishing an atmosphere of horror from one moment to the next. It continued until the beginning of the official funeral ceremony, which opened with the words "I leave your pain in my heart," sung by Tiresias. In the ceremony the black cloth brought in by Cadmus, in which bones were wrapped, was covered with the flag resembling a large dollar bill from the palace and taken to the opening. All on stage stood motionless, holding a hand before their mouths.

While the dismemberment of the ox was performed as a joyous, highly erotic encounter in which performers and spectators alike participated with great enthusiasm, Pentheus' dismemberment through his own mother and her sisters was portrayed as a terrifying and shocking event. The spectators looked deeply horrified – they fell silent, became almost motionless, and were clearly highly involved emotionally.

However, the *sparagmos* was followed every time by a common meal. The first had already taken place after Dionysus' final birth, when Zeus had cut off some golden ribbons from around Dionysus' legs, the last remains of the umbilical cord. A bowl filled with grapes was brought in. While they were distributed among the bacchants, satyrs, and spectators, Zeus said, "Drink the blood, eat this raw flesh," thus marking the event as a communion rite, in which everyone present participated. His words echoed the words of consecration that traditionally accompany the Catholic Eucharist.

The first dismemberment, that of the ox, was performed as a banquet. As implied by the play on the Portuguese word *comer*, beyond the obvious eroticism the ludic, joyful, and erotic caress and kissing scene hinted at both – the dismemberment and the common meal. It was not performed literally, as was the case with the communion rite in the *entrada*, as well as in the communion rite at the end.

Here, Dionysus put the piece of raw meat that had been impaled on Agave's thyrsus and represented Pentheus' head into a pan, put it on the flames flickering from Semele's tomb, and beat it as if it were a steak. Cadmus returned from exile distributing grapes among the spectators. A wooden tub with grapes was brought in. The barefoot Dionysus climbed inside it and stomped on the fruit. Later, others took his place. While the chorus sang the words from Aristophanes' *The Frogs*, "Breke Breke Coax Coax," mockingly in honor of Dionysus, wine circulated and was poured into the flames of Semele's tomb, making it blaze. While the spectators got up and applauded, a man, dressed in a similar way to Dionysus, tore morsels from the now-roasted meat in the pan and distributed them to those around him – bacchants and satyrs as well as spectators. The *sparagmos* was completed with a common meal. The sacrificial meal celebrated the establishment of a new utopian order which excluded no one. It included the gods and the mortals, the bacchants, the satyrs, and all the members of the Cadmus family, as well as the spectators – the "beloved friends and detested enemies," as Dionysus put it.

As Dionysus' words indicate, this sacrificial meal did not hark back to a mythical, archaic, or ancient past. Rather, it was rooted in a specifically Brazilian tradition – that of Brazilian *modernismo* as strongly influenced, if not invented, by the brothers de Andrade, in particular by Oswald de Andrade's *Manifesto Antropófago*. Published in 1928, Dionysus' words clearly alluded to it, especially to Andrade's phrase "absorption of the holy enemy" (Andrade 1990: 51). In the *Manifesto* modernism is understood not as an imitation of Western thought and practices, nor as a recourse to precolonial tradition, but as something completely new that emerges from the fusion of one's own and other cultures. It dismisses all dichotomies underlying the formation of Brazilian culture since the beginning of colonization – e.g., civilization–barbarism, modern–primitive, original–derivative. They all collapse when viewed from the perspective of anthropophagy, meaning cannibalism. Andrade chooses as the founding myth for the "Ur-Brazilian" cultural practice of *antropofagia* the sacrificial meal at which the Portuguese bishop Sardinha was killed and eaten by indigenous people in 1544. Andrade imagines this sacrificial meal as a barbaric, joyful festival of dance and music. He embraces the conviction of indigenous tribes such as the Wari that through the consumption of body parts one takes possession of the person's qualities. He shares the belief that Brazilians should continue to incorporate the best of other cultures, appropriating them so that they become part of themselves through the shared process of transformation. Andrade emphasizes the importance of being insatiable and of transgressing all boundaries in order to aid the mixing of cultures, styles, etc. This form of cannibalism thus implies a constant transformation with no particular goal, but which goes on forever.

After the military coup, the idea of cultural cannibalism – *antropofagia* – experienced a revival in the founding of the *tropicália* movement. Among its founding members were Zé Celso and Caetano Veloso, who turned *antropofagia* into a bulwark against the military dictatorship. With his production of Oswald de Andrade's play *O Rei da Vela* (The King of the Candle) in 1967, Zé Celso for the first time realized his new theatrical aesthetics of *antropofagia*. Keeping this in mind, *The Bacchae*, in particular the sacrificial meal at its end, could be understood as a reflection on the Oficina's own aesthetics and on the notion of *brasilidade*, Brazilian identity.

As regards aesthetics, it was obvious that the old dichotomies and oppositions could not sustain themselves. Be it cultural differences or those between sexes, genres of cultural performance and styles, they all lost their significance and were incorporated. Here, the question of ownership that haunted Soyinka's version of the tragedy and its London production did not even arise. In the third song of the *entrada* the chorus sang: "Dionysus arrives from the mountains of Phrygia to the wide roads of Greece, of Brazil." He belongs to Brazil as much as he belongs to Greece. The performance was theatre, ritual, festival, and carnival. It was called "Opera Elektrokandomblaika carnaval" – "electrocandombleique de carnival opera" and "Tragicomédia Orgya." It incorporated the most diverse musical and poetic styles. It seems that there was nothing it could not incorporate. However, in stark contrast to Roland Joffe's strikingly incoherent plundering of different cultures, here all elements underwent transformation. It was only through the process of being incorporated that this could happen, thus contributing to the transformation of the performance itself. The need to control the spectators by manipulating or supposedly "liberating" them was thus eliminated. Everything the spectators contributed became a part of the performance. Yet this had nothing to do with postmodernism. Rather, it followed Andrade's *Manifesto* that demanded "a permanent transformation of taboos into totems" (Andrade 1990: 50). Two important consequences of this statement are significant in this context. The first is a political one, insofar as the "absorption of the holy enemy," of anyone or anything representing opposition, e.g., a foreign culture or a particular morality, etc., undermines or even invalidates given laws, rules, or hierarchies. The second refers to creativity, for incorporation is not a process of judgment or mindless appropriation but one of productive use. *The Bacchae* presented such a "cannibalistic" aesthetics and reflected on it.

Since, by doing so, the production emphasized the rituals of dismemberment and the common meal that were performed together, the resulting community was affirmed and at the same time extended to everyone present. If we agree that this sort of transformation lies at the heart of Brazilian cultural identity – *brasilidade* – then we have to acknowledge that *The Bacchae* reflected on this notion, too, defining it as an ever-changing – a Dionysian – identity. Since a community of performers and spectators as negotiated and brought forth in the course of a performance can never be regarded as fixed but must be seen as undergoing permanent transformation, this could theoretically also be extended to the whole nation, to be constantly renegotiated, transforming existing taboos into new totems.

The production deeply resonated with audiences wherever it was shown in Brazil. It was always sold out during its six-month run in São Paulo. People stormed the two or three performances in other places, such as in Rio de Janeiro and Bahia. The performance allowed them to experience themselves as ever-changing – as truly Brazilian.

Notes

1. All reviews originally written in Portuguese were translated by Senia Hasicevic.
2. Today, the struggle revolves around the question of whether the shopping mall will be erected adjacent to or at a short distance from the theatre and, if adjacent, what architectural style should be used.
3. I shall refer closely here to a video recording of the production as well as to the script and a number of reviews.
4. For this concept of festival, see Köpping (2002); in particular "The Festive: Structure and Contingency," 121–138.

References

Andrade, Oswald de. 1990. "Manifesto Antropófago." In *A utopia antropofágica*, 47–52. São Paulo: Globo.
Bakhtin, Mikhail. 2009. *Rabelais and His World*. Bloomington: Indiana University Press.
Cavalli, Leona. 2012. Leona Cavalli website. At http://www.leonacavalli.com.br/index.php?option=com/content&task=view&id=26&/tern/id=26. Accessed June 11, 2013.
Celso Martinez Corrêa, Zé (José). 1998. *Primeiro Ato: Cadernos, Entrevistas (1958–1974)*. São Paulo: Edeteria 34.
Drummond, Marcelo. 2008. "Interview with Mirjan Nikola Rehmet." In *Mirjam Nikola Rehmet, Poesie des Verrats: Erotik in der Aufführungspraxis des Teatro Oficina*, 240–244. Trier: Wissenschaftlicher.
Horan, Eduardo. 2012. "Uma questão de gusto" [A question of taste]. At http://www.adrianacalcanhotto.com/sec_textos.php?page=3&type=1&id=215. Accessed June 11, 2013.
Köpping, Klaus-Peter. 2002. *Shattering Frames: Transgressions and Transformations in Anthropological Discourse and Practice*. Berlin: Dietrich Reimer.
Nietzsche, Friedrich. 1995. *The Birth of Tragedy out of the Spirit of Music*. Translated by Shaun Whiteside. Edited by Michael Tanner. London: Penguin.
Roston, André Esposito. 2009. "Assista ao Bacanal." Data da Mensagen: March 23, 12:01am. http://www.setedoses.com/2009/03/23/assista-ao-bacanal/. Website no longer available.

Santos, Mario Vitor. 1996. *Folha de São Paulo*, September 24.
Uzel, Marcus. 1997. *Correio da Bahia* 3.
Valente, Augusto. 2004. Interview with the stage director José Celso Martinez Corrêa as part of the Ruhrfestspiele in Recklinghausen. April. www.dw-world.de. Accessed February 25, 2012.
Wisnik, José Miguel. n.d. *Folha de São Paulo*.

Further Reading

Candomblé

Bastide, Roger. 2001. *Le candomblé de Bahia*. Paris: Plon.
Capone, Stefania. 2010. *Searching for Africa in Brazil: Power and Tradition in Candomblé*. Durham, NC: Duke University Press.
Voeks, Robert A. 1997. *Sacred Leaves of Candomblé: African Magic, Medicine, and Religion in Brazil*. Austin: University of Texas Press.

Anthropophagy

Forsyth, Donald W. 1983. "The Beginning of Brazilian Anthropology: Jesuits and Tupinamba Cannibalism." *Journal of Anthropological Research* 39: 147–178.
Helena, Lucia. 1982. *Uma literature antropofagia*. Rio de Janeiro: Livraria Editora Cátedra/Instituto Nacional de Livro.
Jackson, David K. 1994. "Three Glad Races: Primitivism and Ethnicity in Brazilian Modernist literature." *Modernism/Modernity* 1: 89–112.
Ziebell, Zinka. 1999. *Numa terra de canibais*. Porto Alegre: EDV FAGS.

BLACKWELL BRISTOL LECTURES ON GREECE, ROME AND THE CLASSICAL TRADITION

Part II
Renegotiating Cultural Identities

In many respects, Dionysus is related to issues of identity – the identity of individuals as well as of communities. He has the power to change his identity, adopting human form and oscillating between male and female, or likening his appearance to that of animals such as a bull, lion, or snake. He has his epiphany at the moment of crisis of the community, enabling him to reverse the debilitating disintegration that threatens it and to reconfirm the group's common identity. Yet he never takes a clear stance. He blurs the line between god and man, man and beast, male and female, between the dissolution and the affirmation of a common identity. At stake is always the transformation of identity.

The same holds true for Dionysus' role in the mystery cults. He invites his followers to pass from life to death, keeping them on the threshold

---

Dionysus Resurrected: Performances of Euripides' The Bacchae in a Globalizing World, First Edition. Erika Fischer-Lichte.
© 2014 Erika Fischer-Lichte. Published 2014 by John Wiley & Sons, Ltd.

between the two states (Seaford 2006: 45–75). He is the god of liminality – destabilizing a given identity, status, or order and opening up the possibility for transformation by retaining an individual or a community in a prolonged state of being in-between. Frequently, it remains uncertain whether the transformation can be completed successfully.

This function of destabilization, of transferring individuals and communities into a liminal state, played a key role in the performances dealt with in the second part of this book. They subverted a given cultural identity held by the spectators in Germany, Greece, and Poland and lured them to the threshold, where they remained. The cultural identity they had hitherto believed in was not simply disrupted but shattered, perhaps even dismembered. The restoration to "wholeness," i.e., the adoption of a new cultural identity valid for the whole group – in the German case, for instance, the educated middle class – was beyond reach. The passage could not be completed. The spectators remained in a liminal state.

In these cases, the performances did not reflect Dionysus' role in mystery cults and rituals as the restorer of order and wholeness, but his characterization in *The Bacchae*. Just as Pentheus' dismembered body remains at the end, never to be restored to wholeness and life, the prevalent collective identity was dismembered in each of the cases presented in this part of the book, without any possibility of restoration. Yet this brings to light an important difference between rituals and theatre performances. While the first brings about a new identity, status, or order, no such thing happened or was even hinted at in any of the three performances under discussion. It was up to the spectators and to society to find a solution to the problem or to at least reflect on and discuss what kind of a cultural identity might be possible in a time of globalization.

Reference

Seaford, Richard. 2006. *Dionysus*. New York: Routledge.

4

On the Strangeness and Inaccessibility of the Past

The Antiquity Project at the Schaubühne Berlin (1974)

The opening images already show ... that Grüber "makes" theatre by "destroying" several predominant expectations we have of theatre ... Here, nothing is "narrated" or whittled down to its essence or restricted to some "realistic" minutiae of representation; no "Spielfreude" [joy of performing] is going to arise here ... Instead we stare into dreamlike images, which never tell a story but simply unfold, which are entirely unrealistic but still deal with reality, in which one is at once actor and spectator.

(Baumgart 1974)

What we have is a monstrosity, entirely unmoving, merely astonishing. An autistic performance, totally sunk into itself, into the beauty of suffering, of blood, of ecstasies, into the cult of refinement; elitist artistry and the appeal of the morbid as an end in itself: the new decadence – nowhere as accomplished as at the socialist Schaubühne.

(Hensel 1974)

The endeavour uses quotes from the aesthetics of the early happenings, the works of Beuys, it spells out inventions on stage which had defined the last documenta in Kassel. The ensemble has set itself the challenge to explore new, radical forms of performance ... Any discussion on theatre in the next months will include talk of these two evenings. Perhaps they mark a turn onto

---

Dionysus Resurrected: Performances of Euripides' The Bacchae in a Globalizing World, First Edition. Erika Fischer-Lichte.
© 2014 Erika Fischer-Lichte. Published 2014 by John Wiley & Sons, Ltd.

the wrong path, because the social value of the achieved results is questionable.

(Iden 1974)

The critic Günther Rühle summarizes the irritated responses of most of the spectators of the Antiquity Project of the Berlin Schaubühne with the words: "Why? Why? This was the most commonly heard word that evening; it was difficult for the spectator to read the production he was faced with" (Rühle 1974).

The Antiquity Project consisted of two evening performances, the first presenting *Exercises for Actors* by Peter Stein, while the second was a production of *The Bacchae* by Klaus Michael Grüber. As can be gathered from the reviews excerpted above, the surprise, even shock, of many critics and other spectators was especially due to the expectations raised by the image of the Schaubühne as a "socialist theatre" that prioritized the "social value" and social relevance of the "achieved results" of its artistic work.

The Schaubühne Berlin was widely recognized as a political theatre. It was founded in 1970 by a group of theatre practitioners that included Peter Stein, who in 1968 directed Peter Weiss' *Vietnam-Discourse* at the Munich Kammerspiele. On the first night, after the applause had died down, Stein and his actors descended from the stage into the auditorium and lounge and asked for donations for the Vietcong. This provoked an enormous scandal and Stein had to leave the Kammerspiele.

The Schaubühne was organized as a collective in which all members received the same salary. It was founded at a time when the Social Democratic Party had for the first time in the history of the Federal Republic of Germany become the ruling party, with Willy Brandt as Chancellor. This more or less marked the end of the so-called APO (extra-parliamentary opposition), even though the Baader-Meinhof gang and the Red Army Faction continued to exist. The Schaubühne explicitly responded to the student rebellion and to the change in West Germany's society and politics. Its early productions included Brecht/Gorky's *The Mother* (1970), Enzensberger's *The Havana Inquiry* (1971), Vishnevsky's *An Optimistic Tragedy*, and Marieluise Fleisser's *Purgatory in Ingolstadt* (1973).

In 1973 the Schaubühne embarked on the Antikenprojekt (Antiquity Project). The year before, the leaders of the Baader-Meinhof gang had been arrested. On September 5 of that year, Palestinian terrorists shot eleven Israeli athletes and a German policeman at the Olympic Games in Munich. Five terrorists were killed during the release operation. The Antiquity Project opened in February 1974. Three months later, Chancellor Willy Brandt resigned because an East German spy had infiltrated his office. Helmut Schmidt took over. A few months later, in November, members of the Red Army Faction shot Günter von Drenkmann, the president of West Berlin's

Superior Court of Justice. Those hoping to find a direct response in the Antiquity Project to the ongoing social and political situation were deeply disappointed. However, as we shall see, the Antiquity Project and, in particular, Grüber's production of *The Bacchae*, did adopt a clear stance. Here, the aesthetic turned into the political.

It is said that the idea of staging *The Bacchae* at the Schaubühne had been around from the theatre's very inception but that the project was postponed because it seemed too challenging. After a series of more or less successful productions the Schaubühne finally decided to begin the project. Schaubühne members not only traveled to Greece but also extensively studied literature on ancient Greek theatre, mythology, and rituals. As a result of this research they came to the conclusion that *The Bacchae* could not be presented to an audience without an introduction. The first night, with the staging of *Exercises for Actors*, was meant as such an introduction.

At the beginning of the 1970s *The Bacchae* did not have an extensive performance record on German-speaking stages. Although there was a steady tradition of putting Greek tragedies on stage, beginning at the latest with Goethe's productions of Euripides' *Ion* (1802) and Sophocles' *Antigone* (1809), *The Bacchae* was not among them. In 1973, however, there had been two productions of the tragedy, one by Hansgünther Heyme in Cologne and another by Luca Ronconi in Vienna. Both productions tried to explain the tragedy and make it more accessible. While Heyme did so by staging it together with Aristophanes' *The Frogs*, presenting Dionysus in *The Bacchae* as a comic figure and in *The Frogs* as an out-and-out clown, Ronconi staged *The Bacchae* as "theatre within theatre," setting it at the time of the Renaissance and the rediscovery of antiquity.

The Schaubühne took a very different approach. By drawing on a wealth of literature about the origin of Greek tragedy from rituals and on the ritualistic structure of *The Bacchae* – including works by Burkert, Kott, and Murray – the directors, actors, and stage designers set out to test the idea of such an origin through theatrical means before embarking on the enterprise to stage *The Bacchae*. It was decided not to stage the play at the small theatre building of the Schaubühne at Hallesches Ufer, but instead create a set for the performances inside a huge exhibition hall at the Berlin fairgrounds, the Philips Pavilion.

The stage for *Exercises for Actors* was designed by Karl-Ernst Herrmann.[1] The floor of the hall, sloping slightly on three sides, was covered in soil. Wherever the soil piled up it was overlaid by wooden planks – the seats for the spectators. Flowing white sheets of cloth hung on the walls. This created a unique space, which barely separated the actors from the spectators. Before entering the space the spectators could watch the actors from behind a glass pane, not putting on their makeup but wiping it off. The performance lasted for three hours. In the hall a huge clock, reminiscent of a railway station, hung from the ceiling. Every five minutes the voice of Bruno Ganz (who played the role of Pentheus on the second night) announced the time over a loudspeaker. The actors, dressed in white blouses and wide dark trousers, entered the hall one by one; they spread out in the space, adopting a relaxed posture with their heads slightly bowed. At eight o'clock there sounded the signal to begin.

The *Exercises* consisted of six parts: "Beginnings," "The Hunt," and "The Sacrifice" were followed by an intermission, which featured a satyr play. After the intermission an initiation rite of sorts was performed, and the evening concluded with Prometheus' response to the second stasimon of the chorus from the Aeschylean *Prometheus Bound* (436–506). The titles of the three parts before the intermission as well as the initiation rite after it recalled Burkert's book *Homo Necans*, which had been published the year before the Schaubühne began their preparations for the Antiquity Project. In it, the Swiss philologist and anthropologist connects the sacrifice with the hunt and the meal on which the hunters feast after a successful hunting expedition. Burkert had identified three parts of the sacrifice: the beginnings (which consisted of cleansing rites, putting on new clothes, self-decoration, often sexual abstinence, forming a procession, and all the procedures right up to the killing of the sacrificial animal); the killing of the animal and its dismemberment (*sparagmos*); the burning of the bones on the altar and the shared meal of meat (*omophagia*). The titles used by the Schaubühne – "Beginnings," "The Hunt," "The Sacrifice" – drew heavily on this theory. Later in the book, Burkert delved further into Greek initiation rites, to which that part of the *Exercises* also alluded. In adopting these very specific headings, *Exercises for Actors* directly referred to the most up-to-date theory on Greek sacrificial rituals. As can be gathered from the eighty pages of program notes regarding the "initiation," van Gennep's *The Rites of Passage* (1960) and George Thomson's *Aeschylus and Athens* (1941) were also taken into account. In his book, Thomson argued that the origins of Greek theatre could be found in particular initiation rites.

At eight o'clock, when the beginning was signaled, the actors started to move around. They walked deliberately, breathing slowly, moving their limbs and reaching out with their hands. Certain movements or patterns were repeated: the breathing led to sounds, which turned into screaming (for a specific description, see Jäger 1974). The exercises seemed to emphasize the differences between the actors. While one actor walked in an elegant and refined manner, another was more clumsy, and so on.

"Beginnings" was an ambiguous piece. On an obvious level, it simply marked the beginning of the performance. However, as the beginning of an "antiquity project" it also implied much more. It could be interpreted as the beginning of theatre itself, in that the human body has always been the primary material of theatre. Wherever theatre exists, human bodies are involved. A performance is created out of the particular possibilities offered by the body. It therefore seems to follow that the beginning of the Antiquity Project was a meditation on the birth of theatre.

The second part, "The Hunt," began with the separation of the three protagonists from the community of actors, which was reminiscent of the separation of the actor from the chorus in Greek theatre and of the further development of theatre: Aeschylus is said to have introduced the second actor and Sophocles the third (Aristotle, *Poetics* 4. 1449^a). As such, ancient Greek theatre never featured more than three actors. In Berlin the three actors took over the parts of the hunters and the victim. The hunters (Otto Sander and Peter Fitz) were dressed in long, pale rubber coats, which made a creaking sound with every movement, and wore large dark hats and sunglasses. They looked as if they had stepped out of a spaghetti western. The victim (Heinrich Giskes) looked half-human, half-beast – a mythical figure. He had a huge beetle's shell buckled to his torso, covering his chest and belly. The hunt was thus rooted in archaic as well as modern culture. The hunted figure, genuinely exhausted, finally fell into a mud hole. Tracking down the victim not only entailed allusions to Burkert's theory of sacrifice and of the function of the hunt, but it also turned out to be one of the main subjects of theatre (and later film) from the age of the Greeks until the present day. In the third part, "The Sacrifice," the actors brought in a sculpture made from animal skulls and bones. They wound woolen threads around it, recalling Burkert's description of how the horns of the sacrificial animal were wrapped in bandages. The actors danced around the sculpture; they explored different ways of creating a collective body from their individual bodies, e.g., by experimenting with complicated rhythms. While Burkert, as explained in the introduction to this book, grants the sacrifice the power to strengthen or renew the communal bond between the different members of a society, it clearly did not serve this function here. Rather, the focus in "The Sacrifice" was on bringing forth a collective body through rhythm. Generally speaking, Burkert's descriptions were used or at least alluded to without, however, referring to his or any other explanation.

The second and third parts were as ambiguous as "Beginnings." Perhaps they referred to Burkert's ideas on how hunting and sacrifice were related to each other. They may also be seen as a tentative statement concerning the origin of Greek theatre or as a precursor to the second night, the performance of *The Bacchae*, in particular the tracking down and dismemberment of Pentheus.

During the intermission the spectators were sent out into the snow-covered winter garden where a satyr with a huge phallus jumped around among several fires. Meanwhile, a dividing wall was set up inside the hall.

After the intermission the actors and spectators were grouped according to sex – an initiation rite of sorts. Three actors from each group were undressed, beaten, buried, excavated, smeared with slime, and their faces painted to resemble masks. Actions were performed – such as the unearthing of bodies covered with slime – to be picked up again in *The Bacchae*. They had to relearn how to perceive and how to move. Finally, they were reincorporated into the community. This part could easily be associated not only with Burkert but also with Thomson's theory on the origin of theatre.

It seems, then, that *Exercises for Actors* did indeed reflect on the beginnings of theatre – suggesting different kinds of rituals, e.g., of sacrifice or initiation, as possible origins – and on the human body, which constitutes the main material and fundamental condition of theatre. *Exercises* did not, however, attempt to provide evidence to support particular statements. Instead it opened up different possibilities by putting emphasis on the performing human body moving through space and uttering sounds, e.g., while enacting ritual patterns such as those in "The Hunt," "The Sacrifice," and the initiation rites.

Language was not used until the final part. Previously, the actors had only employed voice to produce different kinds of sounds and to scream. Now the spectators of different sexes were reunited. They were pushed through a narrow opening into another part of the hall where Prometheus (Eberhard Feik) was bound to one of the walls. Two actors were in the process of covering him in plaster. As Prometheus began stammering the first words of the evening, delivering the monologue cited above, his body steadily disappeared underneath layers of plaster. When he spoke his last sentence, "All arts that mortals have come from Prometheus" (*Prometheus Bound*, 505), only his mouth was visible and the words were reduced to stammers once again. This part was no less ambiguous than the previous ones, yet it did introduce a material which, in European theatre, proved to be as fundamental as the human body (language), and the exercises turned out to be exercises in language: the actor tried out different kinds of vocal delivery (melodrama, ridicule, exaggeration, and so on). Nonetheless, language was shown not as supplemental to but opposing the body insofar as the more language developed, the more the body vanished. However, once the body was "gone," language also ceased to exist and deteriorated into the stammers from which it sprang, highlighting the complicated relationship between body and language in theatre. Language emerged out of a "bound" body which was incapable of moving; it separated itself from the body (just as the texts of Greek plays handed down to us are detached, as disembodied language, from the original performance from which they derive). But without a body, language in theatre seems to degenerate. In the theatre, language only makes sense as embodied language. Disconnected from the body, language is unable to constitute theatre. By reflecting on the origins of theatre, on its possible roots in different kinds of rituals as well as on its main materials, primarily bodies and language, the piece actually ended up reflecting on the particular relationship between body and language in the theatre (and perhaps even between performance and text).

On the other hand, the words spoken prefigured the next evening:

> . . . but listen to the tale
> Of human sufferings, and how at first
> Senseless as beasts I gave men sense, possessed them
> Of mind . . .
> In the beginning, seeing they saw amiss,
> And hearing heard not, but, like phantoms huddled
> In dreams, the perplexed story of their days
> Confounded; knowing neither timber-work
> Nor brick-built dwellings basking in the light,
> But dug for themselves holes, wherein like ants,
> That hardly may contend against a breath,
> They dwelt in burrows of their unsunned caves.
> Neither of winter's cold had they fixed sign,
> Nor of the spring when she comes decked with flowers,
> Nor yet of summer's heat with melting fruits
> Sure token: but utterly without knowledge
> Moiled, until I the rising of the stars
> Showed them, and when they set, though much obscure.
> Moreover, number, the most excellent
> Of all inventions, I for them devised,
> And gave them writing that retaineth all,
> The serviceable mother of the Muse.
>
> (v. 444–66)

In the minutes of the preparations of the project (excerpts of which were included in the program notes), Prometheus' perspective on his own achievements is harshly criticized as "the 'scornful review', the break with the past and the final stipulation of one's own beginning" (program notes of Antikenprojekt 1974). Such a "rational" and "enlightened" view is also characteristic of Pentheus. Prometheus' words can thus be understood as a suitable introduction to the performance on the following night. In retrospect, they can also be regarded as a description of the spectators' state during the performance of *The Bacchae*, as the reviews quoted above suggest. For the spectators, "seeing . . . saw amiss/And hearing heard not, but, like phantoms huddled/In dreams." Peter Stein's statements in *Exercises for Actors* on the origins of theatre or on the relationship between body and language were not explicit. He opened up different perspectives on these issues without favoring any particular solution. Moreover, by instructing the actors to perform strange actions such as those in the second, third, and fifth parts, and by exposing the alien nature of these actions, he intimated that whatever the origins of Greek theatre may be, they are inaccessible and, in the end, incomprehensible.

While contemporary classicists and anthropologists tried to explain the origins of Greek theatre by referring to pieces of evidence from different contexts and putting them together as in a puzzle in order to tell a consistent story and explain "the birth of theatre," *Exercises for Actors* denied such a possibility. It made reference to the very same evidence but demonstrated that the attempt to assemble it into a coherent picture was misguided. The pieces of evidence remained fragments removed from their contexts, transformed in particular ways without claiming to restore them to a complete body of knowledge. The performance negated the contention that we possessed this knowledge about ancient Greek theatre and its origins. What we had at our disposal were mere bits and pieces that did not speak as *pars pro toto* but, transformed by the lens through which we looked at them, it was left up to us to put them back together in which ever way we saw fit in order to make sense of them – by no means leading to the original, authentic, or "true" one.

This posed a challenge to the German audience at the beginning of the 1970s, composed mostly of the educated middle class. The majority of these spectators would have grown up studying ancient Greece and would have felt confident in their knowledge of it as a part of their intellectual history and property. Moreover, as will be explained later, the German educated middle class (*Bildungsbürgertum*), until the late nineteenth century lacking any kind of national identity, developed a tendency to identify strongly with ancient Greek culture. The writings of Johann Joachim Winckelmann played a significant role in shaping this self-image, in particular his essay *Thoughts About the Imitation of Greek Works in Painting and Sculpture* (1755), in which he hails Greek culture as the epitome of all culture. The *Bildungsbürgertum* proved eager to mold their own self-understanding and cultural identity on this model as they understood it – often wildly divergent and yet consistent in their belief that what they had in mind was the "true" antiquity. *Exercises for Actors* questioned this conviction, undermining the foundation upon which the cultural identity of the educated middle class had been built.

Even in this respect, the first night proved a meaningful introduction to Grüber's production of *The Bacchae*. The director not only broke with all the conventions of staging classical dramas prevalent from the 1950s onwards, but he also defied those norms newly established after the late 1960s by the so-called Regietheater – directors' theatre – that was accused of demolishing the classics (*Klassikerzertrümmerung*). As suggested by the critical responses cited at the beginning of this chapter, Grüber went so far as to refuse to present any actions and objects on stage which the spectators would be able to "read" (Rühle 1974), decipher, or make sense of while watching. Instead he confronted them with dreamlike images which "never tell a story but simply unfold" (Baumgart 1974).

In my analysis of the performance I shall proceed from these enigmatic images in order to answer the question of how they affected the spectators with regard to their understanding of ancient Greek culture and their own cultural identity rooted in it.

Gilles Aillaud and Eduardo Arroyo were the artists who redesigned the exhibition hall for the performance of *The Bacchae*, which lasted four hours. A huge white-planked area marked the stage. It was flanked on two sides by the spectators, seated at right-angles to each other. The back wall had four openings. On the left, a road-sweeping machine was parked and manned by workers in yellow plastic suits, their faces covered by fencing masks of sorts; in the middle were two openings – one, a hatch, was closed, and the other, a door, stood open to reveal a man dressed in a tuxedo, drinking a glass of champagne and watching the arena. Later on, he would reappear in a white summer suit. On the right, two horses were positioned behind a glass pane. A ventilator hung from the ceiling and neon lights lit the hall brightly. The space had a cold, sterile atmosphere, keeping the spectators at a distance and alienating them.

Excerpts from Stravinsky's *Apollon Musagète* then filled the space. One of the masked workers in yellow pushed a stretcher onto the stage through the open middle door. On it lay Dionysus (Michael König) holding a woman's shoe of a dark color in his hand. He was naked except for a G-string, which made his penis appear artificial. All male figures in the performance were dressed this way, reminding one of ancient Greek statues. A dark stripe, reminiscent of Zeus' lightning, went along the right side of Dionysus' body down to his toes. When the stretcher came to a halt, light from a dark lampshade, which was lowered from the ceiling, illuminated the god. Dionysus began the prologue stammering, searching for the word "I." He giggled, babbled incomprehensibly, caressed the shoe, and then began to speak. While delivering the line "on my lightning-married mother's grave" (v. 7) he flung away the shoe as if in a fit of madness and, almost instantly and accompanied by wild, imbecilic gestures directed at his attendant, demanded it back. Clutching the shoe with both hands he continued his monologue, partly in German, partly in ancient Greek. The act of speaking the words "Like it or not, this city must learn its lesson" seemed to trigger convulsive spasms in his body that made the stretcher topple, depositing Dionysus on the floor. At the line "Therefore I shall prove to him and/every man in Thebes that I am a god" (v. 47/48), Dionysus stood up, collected the different parts of the stretcher and put it back together. He got back on it, ending his prologue by repeating the first line "I, Dionysus, the son of Zeus" and caressing the shoe.

What are we to make of such an image? Was this a hospital? A madhouse? Was the man on the stretcher a shoe fetishist, fantasizing about being Dionysus? And why was he brought onto the stage to the sound of *Apollon Musagète*? Each of the elements evoked different associations, but they did not complement each other in ways that allowed for a coherent attribution of meaning. The image could be experienced but not interpreted. It remained an enigma.

After Dionysus' final words, the right wall opened to reveal a group of women stepping in from the Berlin night, all similarly yet highly individualistically dressed in black cloaks or capes over white blouses, skirts, or dresses. They remained standing there for a moment before walking onto the stage. Behind them, the wall closed again. The sounds of cymbals and bells were heard. Slowly, bringing to mind a dreamlike state, they moved barefoot through the space, forming a circle around the stretcher. Then they separated in different directions. One of the women – the chorus leader – sat down on the floor in front of the stretcher, slowly speaking the lines of the first chorus song. The others inspected the room, poked at the ventilator and the walls that surrounded the stage, turned off the neon lights, and began to tear out the planks from the floor. This last act brought to light a mass of wool, and they began to weave a woolen net from the stretcher all across the space, thus recalling parts of the "Sacrifice" from the preceding night. One of the women went to a huge pipe at the wall and turned a wheel. Grain poured onto the floor. She took a pestle and began to pound the grain. Others threw clumps of soil, lettuce, and grapes from underneath the planks. A bust of Dionysus was lifted from the bed of salad, cleaned, and put on the back of the stretcher, which Dionysus had vacated in the meantime. Salad, grapes, wool, and grain were arranged on the stretcher around the bust, thus turning it into an altar with offerings to the god. A fire was started in an earthen pit. Finally, from the steaming mud, the women unearthed the elderly Cadmus (Peter Fitz) and Tiresias (Otto Sander), completely covered in slime. The scene was strongly reminiscent of the "initiation" scene and the mud hole into which the hunted mythical animal had stumbled the preceding night. Moreover, what at first glance appeared to be slime later on turned out to be the remains of plaster, another allusion to the *Exercises*. The two men evoked plaster casts of Greek statues – a plaster antiquity. This association was strengthened by Tiresias. On a bench at the wall before the left opening, he struck a "classical" pose, lying down with one leg stretched out, the other bent at the knee, one forearm resting on the bench, the other raised, bent at the elbow. He remained in this pose for quite a while – until joining Cadmus for another pose for the journey to the Cithaeron mountains.

While the chorus leader finished the song to the sound of soft percussion, the other women assembled around the stretcher as if it were an altar and they were performing a rite of sacrifice and worship to the god.

The appearance of the bacchants in this sterile cold space happened like the intrusion of something long forgotten and repressed. They unearthed elements of nature such as soil, mud, and fire, dug out products of a cultivated nature such as grain, grapes, salad, and wool as well as "elements" from the past – a bronze bust of the god Dionysus and figures from a plaster antiquity. The women performed all their activities with great precision and thoroughness as if following a strict pattern. It was the intrusion of a world of mystery, unknown to the spectators and allowing only for fragmentary recognition even while casting a spell on them.

Even Pentheus' (Bruno Ganz) entrance was enigmatic. Stark naked, his left arm was covered in a layer of plaster – corresponding to and clashing with the black line on the right side of Dionysus' body. He entered the stage from the same opening as Dionysus and his stretcher. His entrance was accompanied by the low sounds of a different music. He crossed the stage, passing the stretcher, and then stopped. His first words were not from the play but passages from Wittgenstein's diaries, more precisely, the entries for May 31, 1915 and July 8, 1916:

> One cannot achieve any more by using names in describing the world than by means of the general description of the world!!!
> Could one then manage without names? Surely not.
> Names are necessary for an assertion that this thing possesses that property and so on.
> They link the propositional form with quite definite objects.
> And if the general description of the world is like a stencil of the world, the names pin it to the world so that the world is wholly covered by it.
> (Wittgenstein 1961: 53e)
> I can make myself independent of fate.
> There are two godheads: the world and my independent I.
> I am either happy or unhappy, that is all. It can be said: good or evil do not exist.
> A man who is happy must have no fear. Not even in face of death.
> Only a man who lives not in time but in the present is happy.
> Für das Leben in der Gegenwart gibt es keinen Tod. For life in the present there is no death.
> Death is not even in life. It is not a fact of the world.
> If by eternity is understood not infinite temporal duration but nontemporality, then it can be said that a man lives eternally if he lives in the present.
> (Wittgenstein 1961: 74e–75e)

How did Wittgenstein's deliberations on names, death, and eternity relate to Pentheus? Why was he introduced in this way? Some of the sentences reflect Pentheus' attitude toward the world, e.g., "I can make myself independent of fate" or "There are two godheads: the world and my independent I." At the same time, Wittgenstein's words link Pentheus to our world without actually transferring him into it. Other images related to him, however, were not as ambiguous. When Pentheus gave the order to demolish Tiresias' place, the road-sweeping machine drove onto the stage and swept away the "filth" created by the bacchants. The yellow figures replaced the boards and turned the neon lights back on. Since the women lay immobile on the ground, the road-sweeping machine had to circumvent them. After that, the bacchants slowly began to move again. They tried to combine the words "Pentheus" and "hubris" into one and completed verbal exercises with Greek terms such as *orgiazein*, "to perform a sacred act."

The image of the road-sweeping machine cleaning the stage and the act of switching the neon lights back on could undeniably be taken as an interpretation of Pentheus as a man of law, order, and reason. On the other hand, the bacchants interpreted it as an act of hubris. Here a hermeneutic approach seemed possible, something that turned out to be the exception rather than the rule in this production.

As the performance continued, the audience was presented with many other striking and enigmatic images which, superimposed on each other,

FIGURE 4.1 Pentheus (Bruno Ganz) with bacchae. Photo: Helga Kneidl.

intersected with and cut through the linear succession of the dialogues and the choral passages.

Before the first encounter between Dionysus and Pentheus, the latter demarcated a space at the wall and on the floor with adhesive tape, as if marking his territory. The music of *Apollon Musagète* softly swelled up. Pentheus stepped into his "territory" and contemplated the long shadow cast by his body. Dionysus appeared, unnoticed by Pentheus, who slowly squatted down so that his shadow diminished. Then he knelt, leant forward, and placed his head on his knees, making the shadow vanish. Dionysus approached very slowly, stepped behind him and cast a long shadow over him. Pentheus, noticing it, got to his feet and turned around to confront Dionysus, who gave him a long intimate kiss, seized his arm and caressed it. Pentheus put this arm on Dionysus' buttock and gently caressed it, then sought out Dionysus' penis and continued the caress there. It was a very intimate moment, both figures almost melting into one and recalling Girard's idea that Dionysus and Pentheus represent each other's "monstrous doubles" (Girard 1977: 160). All of a sudden, Pentheus slapped Dionysus hard in the face, stepped back and hurried away, creating a lengthy distance between them. Dionysus stretched out his arms on both sides, casting a huge shadow, then squatted down and put on the floor the woman's shoe which he had held the whole time.

Dionysus in 69 and the Teat(r)o Oficina's *Bacantes* both featured homoerotic encounters between Dionysus and Pentheus. In these two productions the scene took place after the reversal of roles between the seemingly effeminate god and the emphatically masculine ruler. In *Dionysus in 69* this was the dressing scene, while in the Brazilian *Bacchae* it followed it. In this production it happened at their very first encounter. After dressing up, the focus was on Pentheus' transformation into a bacchant. It took place on an empty stage, deserted by all except Dionysus and Pentheus. The chorus members had disappeared into the audience or behind a side wall, with only their heads visible at the top. From there they could also watch the scene unfolding on stage as spectators. Dionysus was seated in the lit hatch when Pentheus came in through the door. He wore a long black dress partly covered by a short light fur, imitating and reversing the clothes of the bacchants. After Dionysus had helped him with his makeup, Pentheus made some tentative dance steps, striking the pose of a maenad found on Greek vases – a pose which one of the bacchants had struck during the last chorus song. (In the program notes there is a picture of the so-called Pronomos Krater, displaying a Dionysian thiasus, performing these movements.) Dionysus threw the woman's shoe to the ground. Pentheus slipped on the shoe and with another tentative dance step approached the place where the horses stood. Dionysus, who up to then had also acted as a kind of spectator to Pentheus' transformation, helped him mount one of the horses.

And while the bacchants took turns speaking the lines of the chorus song "Run to the mountains, fleet hounds of madness!/Run, run to the revels of Cadmus' daughters!" (v. 978–1021), Dionysus led the horse with Pentheus on its back in a circle around the horses' area that was lit by a warm light. This continued until the bacchants had ended their song. For a substantial period of time the spectators saw nothing but this image on stage – except for the two or three heads peeking over the wall. It was this image that became deeply imprinted on the audience's perception and memory.

Both images – the homoerotic encounter and Pentheus' ride to the Cithaeron mountains – evoked a wealth of associations, memories, and emotions in the spectators. However, they denied a hermeneutic approach to the performance with reference to the dramatic text of the tragedy. They were able to bewitch and fascinate the spectators but did not contribute to a clear understanding or fixed reading of what was going on. Rather, they once more raised the question dominating the production: "Why?"

The same applied to the two messenger reports. The herdsman (Heinrich Giskes) was enshrouded with a mythical air. Fur sprouted from the skin on his right shoulder. His feet were also furry and prominently hooved. Was he one of the satyrs whose chorus, according to Nietzsche, can be regarded as the origin of tragic theatre? He was accompanied by two leashed dogs, one black, one white – the colors of the bacchants. While speaking, he occasionally fed raw meat to the dogs. When he quoted Agave's call "Hounds who run with me, men are hunting us down! Follow, follow me!" (v. 731/32), Pentheus went down on his knees and, resembling a four-legged animal, approached the black dog, which instantly barked at him. Pentheus crouched beside the messenger and snapped at the piece of flesh which the herdsman held in his hand. Like a dog, he tore it with his teeth, hurling it around so that it slapped his cheeks, before the black dog snapped it away from him and devoured it. At the end of his report, the herdsman ate a piece of the raw meat himself before feeding the rest to one of the dogs.

Was Pentheus enacting what the messenger told him about the actions of the bacchants? Was he embodying the hounds that tore apart his cousin Actaeon? Or was he himself anticipating what would later happen to him? This scene could also hint at the unavoidable kinship between a man of law and order and the beast in all of us, in that there always lurks the danger that a rational human being degenerates into an animal. As can be seen from these suggestions, they are associations triggered by the scene rather than a scholarly interpretation.

The second messenger's (Günter Hacker) report was even more puzzling. He entered through the middle opening, where he remained standing until he left the stage in the same way as he had arrived, long after he had finished his report. He was accompanied by all the laughing bacchants, so that Agave spoke her address to the city (v. 1202–14) on an empty stage before her encounter with Cadmus.

During the messenger's report the man from the beginning had taken up position in the horses' area. Now dressed in a trench coat and black trousers, wearing a dark hat and sunglasses, he was reminiscent of the two hunters from the previous night. The bacchants were spread out all over the space, most of them standing, one sitting on the floor, another leaning against the wall. They were positioned to create the impression of a picture painted according to the principle of central perspective. They formed two uneven diagonal lines that ran from the front of the stage to the middle opening, thus fixing the center of attention on the messenger. The messenger reported the events in the Cithaeron mountains, which culminated in Pentheus' dismemberment, all the while remaining almost motionless as brownish-yellow slime dripped from his naked body, a likely reference to the initiation scene from the *Exercises*. He spoke at an excruciatingly slow pace and in a slightly singsong tone of voice. He did not once change his position – only his face was grimacing and one could see how his chest rose and fell with every breath. When he repeated Dionysus' words "Women, I bring you the man who has mocked/at you and me and at our holy mysteries./Take vengeance upon him" (v. 1079–81), he drew out the vowels to an extent that was almost unbearable and physically painful for the listeners. It took him more than half an hour to deliver his report, which was underlined and punctuated by a very low music playing on an organ or harmonium. After having told the story of the killing he erupted in long screams, "alalah, alalah . . . ," punctuated by the organ that was now clearly audible. Up to this point there was no movement in the space, except for that of the ceiling fan and of the horse's head and tail. Now the bacchants slowly began to move, performing stylized dance steps as Pentheus had done before his departure, e.g., with one leg raised and the head thrown back. They continued to dance and laugh until Agave emerged from the left opening (where the road-sweeping machine stood parked), wrapped in bloody bandages and holding up a very realistic head in her right hand.

The scene was composed as in a painting. The spectators were confronted with it for a very long time. On the other hand, the report was delivered as a kind of aria in a melodrama, accompanied by music, even though it was not always audible. While the vocal delivery in some instances recalled Prometheus' way of speaking in the *Exercises*, the composition as a whole, i.e., the clash of the visual and aural components, reminded one of a seventeenth-century opera performance in the allusion to its staging conventions: the virtuoso at the center, displaying his wondrous skills of vocal delivery, framed by the chorus, watching and admiring his art along with the other spectators. In the same way or perhaps even more so than the image of the ride to the Cithaeron mountains, this extensive, tortuous yet fascinating scene not only imprinted itself on the spectators' perception and memory but also made them aware of the act of watching as witnessing.

The performance ended as it began – as an enigma. This time, however, Dionysus did not reappear on stage. Cadmus and Agave, still holding Pentheus' head, sat on two chairs before a silver tray, on which the "poor boy's body" (v. 1298), ripped to pieces, lay piled up: stand-up collar, white gloves, white sleeves, white handkerchief, and a pair of gray patent leather shoes with shoe trees – all items of clothing that the man in the tuxedo, the contemporary spectator of the scene, had worn in the beginning. Agave was still in her bloody bandages and Cadmus was naked, his body partly covered in plaster. One of the yellow figures took Pentheus' head from Agave and replaced it with the stand-up collar from the tray. Gradually, the light dimmed. The lamp which had been lowered from the ceiling over Dionysus on the stretcher in the first scene was once again brought down, now shedding light on Agave and Cadmus for the recognition scene. While delivering the lines from "I feel as though – /my mind were somehow – changing" (v. 1270) through to "Dionysus has destroyed us all" (v. 1290), Agave, motionless, stared at the stand-up collar in her hand. After the recognition she slowly raised her legs, rolled sideways off the chair, and crawled to the left opening from which she had appeared. For a long time, only her sighs, sobs, and screams could be heard, resembling those of a wild beast in deepest agony. When Agave finally reappeared at the left opening, she was clothed in a white dress with a beige cloak or blanket draped over it. Cadmus approached her, covered himself with a blanket and both returned to the chairs. The light in all the openings went out. While Agave spoke the lines, alternating between German and Greek and beginning with the sentence "O Father, now you can see/how everything has changed," which she repeated as her final words, Cadmus took a glove from the tray and began to sew. After Agave's last words, string music swelled up. When it died down, both sat silently in the cone of light shining down from the lamp, sewing together the pieces from the tray without ever coming to an end.

This finale did not answer any of the previous questions posed by the performance but only raised new ones. Why was Pentheus' head replaced by a stand-up collar? And why were the pieces of Pentheus' dismembered body represented by the pieces of the suit worn by the man in the tuxedo drinking a glass of champagne and watching the stage as well as parts of the auditorium – the same person who, dressed differently from but still to be identified as the spectators' contemporary, was also present at the messenger's report on Pentheus' death? Why did Dionysus not reappear in the end, explaining once more the reasons for what had happened? Why did Agave alternate between German and ancient Greek at that moment?

These and related questions can hardly be answered by referring to the tragedy's text. I have provided an abundance of examples of scenes from the performance in order to substantiate my argument that as a whole it is to be regarded as a chain of such enigmatic images. In order to deal with them in a productive way, I will group the questions they raised into three sets of problems concerning

1. the relationship between text and performance;
2. the concept of theatre underlying the production;
3. the relationship of theatre to the past.

The keyword to all of them is *sparagmos*: something seemingly whole is torn apart and the question is how the scattered pieces can be restored to the former – or a new – wholeness.

The first question had already been raised by the last part of the *Exercises for Actors* by exploring the relationship between language and body, text and performance. The same could of course be said of any production of the so-called Regietheater, and of Schechner's *Dionysus in 69*. In the latter, the dismemberment of the text was performed as a process of rewriting it by using biographical material from the performers' lives and justifying the procedure by citing oral traditions. Soyinka rewrote the text by including actual elements from oral traditions. This was not Grüber's concern. Although he also abridged the text, using not only Wolfgang Schadewaldt's translation but also seven others and incorporating excerpts from the original Greek text and from other texts such as Wittgenstein's diaries, the production did not focus on or try to justify the rewriting of the text. Rather, a wholly new kind of relationship between the textual excerpts and the spoken words, the bodies, actions, objects, and images on stage was established, one which did not allow for a linear or mutual explanation, interpretation, or clarification. The *sparagmos* of the text did not result in the restoration of the old or a new wholeness or in a common meal that would bind together all those participating in a community. Rather, the production revolved around fragments, each of which enabled the spectators to complete the picture in their own imagination while denying the possibility of uniting the individual pieces in one meaningful whole.

In this manner the production realized a completely new concept of theatre – a theatre of images – radical at the time of the production. From the end of World War II until the beginning of the 1960s, the dominant understanding of the function of theatre was that it had to stage the classics in order to convey the timeless ideas, ethical norms and values to audiences hungry for such intellectual nourishment after the shattering effects of the Third Reich. This implied a certain hierarchy: since the poet built these values into the text, it was of prime importance to the performance; without a text there would be no performance. It was the task of the performance to convey the meanings of the text and be as "true" to it as possible. It was the text which first and foremost constituted theatre.

In the 1960s this idea was challenged by a new generation of stage directors including Peter Zadek, Hansgünther Heyme, Claus Peymann, Peter Stein, and Klaus Michael Grüber. They not only developed new forms of political theatre in the broad sense of the word but also brought about a new retheatricalization in their work by advocating and applying a deliberate return to the "proper" means of theatre, such as the human body and its performative as well as expressive potential. Theatre, they believed, needed to evolve from a "hermeneutic" interpretive institution conveying timeless values formulated in the classics into an unmistakably performative art and interventionist "political" institution. The primacy of the text was refuted. The classical texts were now read with regard to their potential topicality or their particular historicity. Peter Stein's production of Goethe's *Tasso* (Bremen 1969), for instance, equated Tasso's dilemma with Goethe's and thereby with that of an artist in a bourgeois society. The spectators, in turn, were faced with the challenge of developing a new attitude toward theatre performances. Instead of slapping a particular reading on the play, they were required to "read" a performance as a commentary on the text, i.e., as an explanation for a particular historical moment or development which continued to have an impact on them. In this sense, spectatorship still entailed deciphering a "message" conveyed by the performance.

Grüber's theatre of images did away with this claim once and for all. Here, the so-called director's theatre turned into a spectator's theatre. The enigmatic images liberated the spectators from the demand to decipher any message at all. The images were self-referential in a very peculiar manner. From the point of view of the spectator, they were arranged in a completely haphazard and unpredictable manner, neither relating to the text nor to the preceding or following images. The sudden, seemingly unmotivated appearance of an image drew the attention of the spectators toward it alone; they directed their attention toward the particular bodies, movements, objects, and sounds before them. Through the very nature of these images the spectators' perception adopted a certain quality. The images excluded the possibility of other ulterior meanings, purposes, or contexts. Perception was performed as a contemplation of the image for its own sake. In this contemplative mode of perception, free of any intention, the perceived image presented itself to the spectator in a way that seemed to reveal its innermost mystery – it had nothing to do with the text and was different for each and every spectator.

Paradoxically, however, the same images achieved quite the opposite after a while. They triggered, almost explosively so, the most diverse memories, fantasies, and associations in the spectators and aroused various physiological, emotional, energetic, and motoric responses. Neither the text nor the dramatic characters could be credited with the outcome of this process; rather, it was the encounter of the individual spectators with their own imagination. Of course, in retrospect, each of the images could have been interpreted differently. The first image, for instance, could be read and explained in terms of Foucault's impressive studies on *The Birth of the Clinic* (1963), *Mental Illness and Psychology* (1954), and *Madness and Civilization* (1961). In order to deal with Pentheus' first appearance one could delve into Wittgenstein's *Philosophical Investigations* (1953) and discuss the relationship between theatre and theory – both terms rooted in the Greek word θεά (thea) meaning "show." How does theatre reflect on itself by theatrical means? Does it need "names" or even concepts?

Each image, particularly in retrospect, seemed to invite the spectator to engage in such kinds of investigations and inquiries. Each was able to set in motion an endless process of interpretation without allowing for an unambiguous, consistent reading that could be logically related to that of other images. Of course, such a thought process could have been set in motion while the performance was going on, especially due to the long duration of some of these images. However, serious reflection could only begin afterwards. This mode of perception greatly contributed to the individualization of the spectators. However, it did not isolate them from each other. Rather, they all shared certain experiences triggered by the images – experiences that bore the potential to transform.

The experiences were caused by the particular attitude toward the past which the images revealed, thus developing an idea Stein introduced in *Exercises for Actors*. Both parts of the Antiquity Project, and in particular *The Bacchae*, could be experienced as a meditation on the fundamental strangeness and inaccessibility of the distant past – be it archaic or classical Greek culture. Grüber's production demonstrated in an impressive way that the theatrical elements meant to represent the past were primarily related to our own world and told us more about ourselves and our present than about the past world. On the contemporary stage, a revival of the ancient Greek world will always be impossible, because resurrecting the past is not within our power. What remains are only fragments – play texts torn out of their original contexts – which cannot convey their original meaning. They are distant and alien, and therefore it is not possible to stage them as if they were contemporary plays.

This insight, which was deepened by the enigmatic images, was conveyed with a particular intensity in the final image. Instead of having Cadmus put the fragments and pieces of Pentheus' dismembered body back together, Grüber created the image of a never-ending process of sewing together the bits and pieces of the contemporary spectator's clothes. I read this image as a commentary on the process of staging Greek texts. In this process, the textual "body" had to be dismembered. It was accessible not as a whole but only as individual components. It would be a delusion to think that the performance could ever render the text on stage. The performance could be no more than an endless sewing together of the pieces of a contemporary spectator's clothes. Even sacrificing the text-body would not redeem us or admit us into the paradise of an unmediated understanding of ancient Greek tragedy. By performing a sacrificial ritual on the text, the production of a Greek tragedy at best would allow us to reflect on our fundamental distance from it and perhaps insert some fragments of it into our present theatre and contemporary culture. It cannot accomplish a return to the origins – whatever they might have been. Those are gone and lost forever.

The idea of the cultural identity of the German educated middle class as based on an identification with Greek culture hence was not simply undermined – as in *Exercises for Actors* – but shattered in its very assumptions. *The Bacchae* performed a *sparagmos* of the cultural identity of the educated middle class to which the majority of the spectators belonged.

Around 1800, the school reform initiated in Prussia by Wilhelm von Humboldt declared the gymnasium the only branch of school with the exclusive right to prepare its pupils for university study. This followed a grammar school system privileging the study of Greek and Latin. It was not until 1900 that other schools that did not teach Greek or even Latin were accorded the same right. However, the identification of the educated middle class with Greek culture was by then firmly established. It was manifest not only in the growing number of productions of Greek tragedies since the famous and popular production of *Antigone* in Potsdam (1841), for which Felix Mendelssohn had composed the music for the chorus songs and the epirrhematic passages (for more on this production, see Fischer-Lichte 2010: 329–338). It also found expression in the great public interest aroused by the excavations in Olympia. Ernst Curtius systematically began unearthing Olympia in 1875, thus bringing it to the awareness of a broader public. Between 1875 and 1881 the government of the newly established German nation-state contributed to the popularization of Olympia by publishing annual reports on the progress of the excavations, highlighting the various findings by Curtius and his team. This meant that Curtius' own reports were eagerly awaited when they finally appeared between 1890 and 1897.

Moreover, it was quite common to compare the political situation of the German states with that of the Greek states. Goethe, for instance, in his speech "Zu brüderlichem Andenken Wielands" (1813), argued: "The constitution of the Reich, composed of so many small states, therein resembled the Greek one" (Goethe 1893: 311). Thus, Weimar was either called "German" or "Ilm-Athen" ("Athens-upon-Ilm"). In the Prussia of Friedrich Wilhelm IV, who had commissioned the Potsdam *Antigone* at the beginning of his reign, Berlin was frequently labeled "Spree-Athen" ("Athens-upon-Spree"), while the people of Munich, too, liked to refer to their city as "Isar-Athen" ("Athens-upon-Isar"). The different German states rivaled each other in naming their own capitals "Athens."

By the end of the nineteenth century there were two competing images of Greek culture. The first was introduced by Winckelmann in the essay cited above. It propagated "noble simplicity" and "quiet greatness" as the main characteristics of Greek culture. This image, more or less unquestioned until the 1870s, remained dominant until the late 1950s, and even partly survived into the early 1970s. The other was created by Nietzsche in his *Birth of Tragedy*, which put forward the thesis that Greek tragedy had grown out of competing Apollonian and Dionysian forces, despite the clear bias toward the latter. While most classicists fought this image – with the exception of the Cambridge Ritualists, who developed it further – theatre practitioners took to it. Max Reinhardt's productions of *King Oedipus* (1910) and the *Oresteia* (1911) in the Circus Schumann popularized the Nietzschean version. By touring all over Europe with *Oedipus*, this notion was spread far beyond Germany. However, the majority of the educated middle class in Germany was rather hesitant to subscribe to it. They preferred the Winckelmannian image for their own self-understanding. One might assume that the Nazis were partial to the Nietzschean image. However, they – and Hitler in particular – also hailed Winckelmann's version. Nazi Germany promoted itself as the legitimate heir to and true successor of ancient Greece. For the Olympic Games in Berlin in 1936, Curtius' findings were used for the design of the Reichssportfeld, the site of the Olympic Games. It was decided to replicate the topography of ancient Olympia in many respects, thus reviving ancient Olympia in Berlin. The effect was further enhanced by the newly invented ritual of igniting the Olympic flame in the holy precinct of Olympia and carrying it in a relay race from there to Berlin, thus creating a living bond between ancient Olympia and modern Berlin. On the second day of the Games, Aeschylus' *Oresteia* was shown at the Schauspielhaus am Gendarmenmarkt (Fischer-Lichte 2008). Even during the theatre season of 1940/41, in the second year of the war, fifteen new productions of *Antigone* were staged, two at prominent places, namely the Schauspielhaus am Gendarmenmarkt in Berlin and the Burgtheater in Vienna (Fischer-Lichte 2010). It seems that the Nazis thought it useful to confirm the educated middle class's cultural identity as based on Winckelmann's ideas of ancient Greek culture in order to further their own ends.

Although after the war classicists and stage directors both alleged that Greek tragedy and Greek culture had been suppressed, even destroyed, by the Nazis, their own claim of "returning" to the eternal values embodied in ancient Greek culture was nothing but an encouragement to confirm the self-understanding of the educated middle class – to which they themselves belonged – that had not been seriously challenged, let alone fractured, by the Nazis. It is no exaggeration that from around 1800 onwards until the Antiquity Project, the identification of the educated middle class with Greek culture constituted an uninterrupted and stable tradition.

Against this backdrop, the enormous importance and lasting impact of the Antiquity Project, in particular Grüber's *The Bacchae*, becomes obvious. The productions denied the very possibility of referring to what for almost two hundred years had been conceived as a stable foundation on which to build one's cultural identity – the unhindered access to and familiarity with ancient Greek culture. What was believed to be unshakeable knowledge of ancient Greek culture was exposed as nothing but images composed of elements from modern times based on our own imagination of ancient Greece and on desires generated by our contemporary world. A return to the paradise of a stable and shared cultural identity seemed impossible. Like the angel with the fiery sword, Grüber's *The Bacchae* had chased the spectators away and denied them any means to re-enter it.

The cultural identity of the educated middle class was dismembered, never again to be restored to wholeness. Any attempt to mend it – to sew the pieces back together – would only create a patchwork consisting of fragments from our own contemporary world.

This was a political statement. It denied any possibility of "owning" ancient Greek culture. *The Bacchae* prevented spectators from falling back on a convenient but fictitious cultural identity. Instead, the production challenged its audiences to reflect on the issue of identity, both cultural and individual, and on its foundations. As Kott has demonstrated, *The Bacchae* is also to be understood as a tragedy dealing with identity and the end of the polis. Thus, it was no coincidence that the exposure of a self-delusional common cultural identity was accomplished by a production of *The Bacchae*. Grüber's production, it turned out, marked a turning point in the cultural history of Germany.

Note

1. I base my analysis of the two productions of the Antiquity Project on my own memories of seeing them both, plus video recordings, reviews, and program notes. I also build on my earlier work in Fischer-Lichte (2004: esp. 332–334) and Fischer-Lichte (2005: 229–239).

References

Aeschylus. 1975. *Prometheus Bound*. Translated by James Scully and C. John Herington. Oxford: Oxford University Press.

Aristotle. 2002. *Poetics*. Translated by Seth Benardete and Michael Davis. South Bend: St. Augustine's Press.

Baumgart, Reinhard. 1974. "An den Grenzen des Theaters: Das Antikenprojekt der Schaubühne." *Süddeutsche Zeitung* 49, February 16/17, Feuilleton Beilage.

Fischer-Lichte, Erika. 2004. "Thinking about the Origins of Theatre." In *Dionysus since 1969: Greek Tragedy at the Dawn of the Third Millennium*. Edited by Edith Hall, Fiona Macintosh and Amanda Wrigley, 329–360. Oxford: Oxford University Press.

Fischer-Lichte, Erika. 2005. *Theatre, Sacrifice, Ritual: Exploring Forms of Political Theatre*. New York: Routledge.

Fischer-Lichte, Erika. 2008. "Resurrecting Ancient Greece in Nazi Germany – the *Oresteia* as part of the Olympic Games in 1936." In *Performance, Iconography, Reception: Studies in Honor of Oliver Taplin*. Edited by Martin Revermann and Peter Wilson, 481–498. Oxford: Oxford University Press.

Fischer-Lichte, Erika. 2010. "Politicizing Antigone." In *Interrogating Antigone in Postmodern Philosophy and Criticism*. Edited by S. E. Wilmer and Audrone Žukauskaité, 329–352. Oxford: Oxford University Press.

Foucault, Michel. 1965. French 1961. *Madness and Civilization: A History of Insanity in the Age of Reason*. London: Tavistock.

Foucault, Michel. 1976. French 1954, re-ed. 1995. *Mental Illness and Psychology*. Translated by A. M. Sheridan-Smith. New York: Harper and Row.

Foucault, Michel. 1994. French 1963. *The Birth of the Clinic: An Archeology of Medical Perception*. New York: Vintage.

Girard, René. 1977. French 1972. *Violence and the Sacred*. Translated by Patrick Gregory. Baltimore: Johns Hopkins University Press.

Goethe, Johann Wolfgang. 1893. "Zu brüderlichem Andenken Wielands" (1813). In *Goethes Werke. Weimarer Ausgabe, Part I, Vol. 36: Tag- und Jahres-Hefte als Ergänzung meiner sonstigen Bekenntnisse, II. Part*. Weimar: Böhlau.

Hensel, Georg. 1974. "Im Anfang war das Fleisch." *Weltwoche*, February 13.

Iden, Peter. 1974. "Mit den Griechen an die Grenzen: 'Die Bakchen' des Euripides als zweiter Abend des 'Antiken-Projektes' der Berliner Schaubühne." *Frankfurter Rundschau*, February 11.

Jäger, Gerd. 1974. "'. . . wie alles sich für mich verändert hat'. Das Antikenprojekt der Berliner Schaubühne und die 'Bakchen' des Euripides, von Grüber in Berlin, von Ronconi in Wien inszeniert." *Theater heute*, March: 12–21.

Program Notes *Antikenprojekt*. 1974. Schaubühne am Halleschen Ufer. Leaflet.

Rühle, Günther. 1974. "Keine Liebe in Theben: 'Antikenprojekt 2. Teil'/'Die Bakchen' des Euripides in der Berliner Schaubühne." *Frankfurter Allgemeine*, February 11.

Thomson, George. 1941. *Aeschylus and Athens: A Study in the Social Origins of Drama*. London: Lawrence and Wishart.

van Gennep, Arnold. 1960. *The Rites of Passage*. London: Routledge and Kegan Paul.

Wittgenstein, Ludwig. 1961. *Notebooks 1914–1916*. Chicago: University of Chicago Press.

Wittgenstein, Ludwig. 2001. German 1953. *Philosophical Investigations*. Oxford: Blackwell.

Further Reading

Remshardt, Ralf E. 2004. *Staging the Savage God: The Grotesque in Performance*. Carbondale: Southern Illinois University Press.

5

Performing or Contaminating Greekness?
Theodoros Terzopoulos' *The Bacchae* in Delphi (1986)

In 1985 Melina Mercouri, Greek Minister for Culture, launched the Greek Drama International Meetings in Delphi in order to give the ongoing discussion on ancient Greek drama in the age of globalization an official forum. From the very beginning, performances from non-Western countries were invited – for instance, at the first meeting, Suzuki Tadashi's *Trojan Women* and at the second meeting Luo Jinlin's *Oedipus the King*, as well as an *Antigone* by the Indian director Kavalan Narayana Panikkar. The internationally experienced Theodoros Terzopoulos was appointed artistic director. After a four-year stint at the Berliner Ensemble (1972–1976), he had staged his first productions at the State Theatre of Northern Greece in Thessaloniki, among them Brecht's *The Rise and Fall of the City of Mahagonny* (1977) and Lorca's *Yerma* (1981). At the second meeting in Delphi in 1986 he contributed to the debate by presenting his production of *The Bacchae*, the result of a nine-month rehearsal period with his newly founded Attis Theatre.

The response of most critics was overwhelmingly negative. They based their disapproval and, in a few cases, vehement rejection of the production on several, partly interrelated, arguments. The first was the objection that it was not even a real staging of Euripides' *The Bacchae*:

> Where were *The Bacchae* in his [Terzopoulos'] production? In this performance Euripides' tragedy worked neither as language nor as intellect nor as

---

Dionysus Resurrected: Performances of Euripides' The Bacchae in a Globalizing World, First Edition. Erika Fischer-Lichte.
© 2014 Erika Fischer-Lichte. Published 2014 by John Wiley & Sons, Ltd.

praxis – not even as sound. Not even as a pretext was it justified. It would have been better if it would not have been used at all. (Polenakis 1986)[1]

The second argument lamented the "misreading" of the text: "*The Bacchae* is no ritual. It is a work that deals with the subject of rituals. And this work we have not seen" (Lignadis 1986). As this review continued, a third argument emerged: the production was not Greek at all: "The overwhelming visual stimuli reduced the function of the ancient and modern Greek language and completely eliminated the myth, ethos, and spirit of this deeply moving Euripidean tragedy." The fourth argument condemned the contamination of Greek tragedy through foreign influences:

> The spectators felt that they were confronted more with a Japanese spectacle than with a seemingly Greek ritual . . . I am afraid that Mr. Suzuki will have a strong influence on the easily impressionable Greek stage directors and that in the near future, we shall see more Japanizing performances.
> (Lignadis 1986)

A similar charge was made in another review by an actress who had performed in many Greek tragedies since the foundation of the Epidaurus Festival in 1956. She alleged that such "disastrous experimental tendencies go together with the newest fashion trend of bringing together European and Asian culture" (Synodinou 1986). This argument was picked up by another critic, who emphatically stressed the uniqueness of Greek tragedy that, according to him, was far removed from Asian theatre:

> This tragic pattern [i.e., conflict between instinct and logic] was interpreted by the director as a ritual, as an enactment through ritualistic elements. On stage, however, the ritual refutes itself, it becomes a spectacle, and is not an end in itself. Folk-rites lend ritualistic elements to the form and to the theatrical expression; tragedy, however, is not a ritual in itself. Otherwise the myth is cancelled: this is so to say one of the major differences between Greek tragedy and Eastern theatre.
> (Heimares 1986; quoted from Sampatakakis 2005: 203.)

Just as the stranger Dionysus had come from Asia to Thebes in order to destroy it, according to these and many other Greek critics, Terzopoulos' *The Bacchae* had arrived in Delphi in order to destroy the Greekness of the tragedy by contaminating it with elements from Asian cultures. In their extreme hostility toward his production, these critics proved quite akin to Pentheus, who met the stranger – his cousin – with such strong resistance.

The same and the following year Terzopoulos' production toured extensively in Germany, Austria, Spain, the United States, and Australia. Since the production won nothing but the highest praise and acclaim abroad, its negative and almost offensive reception at its premiere in Delphi begs for an explanation which seems unrelated to its artistic achievements. Rather, we have to investigate the implications of the concept of Greekness and to confront it with the main elements of the new kind of theatre created in Terzopoulos' production.

Before the war of independence in 1821 – after nearly four hundred years of Ottoman rule – Greek intellectuals, partly educated in Western European countries, had established and widely disseminated "archaiolatreia, the worship of antiquity, and the progonoplexia, ancestor obsession or 'ancestoritis' . . . that has been such a striking feature of the cultural and educational life of post-independence Greece" (Clogg 2003: 20). Here, for the first time, an unbroken continuity stretching from the fifth century BC to modern times was proclaimed, totally disregarding the cultural impact of the Christian Byzantine and Ottoman rule. Greek intellectuals of the late eighteenth and nineteenth centuries, as well as Greek people of the twentieth century, saw themselves – and partly still do – as the lineal descendants of the citizens of ancient Athens and other ancient Greek cities. This "direct line" between ancient and modern Greece was the basis on which Greek national identity was/is built. In our context, only two factors meant to guarantee this identity will be considered: ancient monuments and the performance of ancient Greek plays. Both were seen as constituting a cultural "heritage" of the highest order. Their reappropriation seemed a fundamental prerequisite for letting "the new State appear as the natural heir and the descendant of ancient Greece" (Roilu 1999: 195).

Hamilakis and Yalouri explained the function of ancient monuments as follows:

> Ancient monuments . . . provide the most powerful currency of [a] specific form of symbolical capital due to their materiality, visibility (especially in case of prominent architectural monuments), authenticity, age and sense of time-lessness, . . . continuity and eternity. They [are] instruments in constructing a topos that [is] at the same time within history and outside it. A topos structured by a specific temporality: a monumental time distinct from the "social" experiential time of everyday life.
>
> (Hamilakis and Yalouri 1999: 125)

On the one hand, monuments sacralize the past; on the other, they constitute a material continuity. In order to emphasize this continuity, the excavation and preservation of monuments takes on a crucial role. They serve as acts of witnessing to the greatness of the past and also as extant bonds to it, testifying to the continuity between past and present and guaranteeing an unchanged cultural identity. In monuments, "identity is immediately recognized by others." The exclusive interest of Greek archaeology in classical antiquity thus "had a recognizable political content, juxtaposing a constructed orientalism with Greek culture" (Kotsakis 2003: 64). The rigid and uncompromising delimitation of Greek from "oriental" or "Asian" cultures that haunted Greek archaeology also resonates in the reviews quoted above.

The heritage value of monuments is complemented by that of ancient Greek plays, the performances of which again and again turned into battlegrounds for the exclusive and legitimate "ownership" of ancient Greek culture. At the beginning of the twentieth century it was also to a large extent a battle over language. The question was whether the official language of the new Greek state should be an artificial language – *katharevousa* – which aimed to purify the modern language and thereby bring it closer to ancient Greek, or the modern language – *demotiki*. The debate was finally resolved in 1976 after the military dictatorship had come to an end and *demotiki* was recognized as the official Greek language.

Three performances of Greek tragedies that used *demotiki* took place in Athens at the beginning of the twentieth century: *Alcestis* with music by Gluck (November 1901), *Antigone* with Mendelssohn's music (1903), and the *Oresteia* (1903), which used instructions formulated by Paul Schlenther for the production at the Burgtheater in Vienna in 1900. The music, stage design, and costumes followed the Viennese model. The philologist Georgios Sotiriadis translated the text into *demotiki* not from the ancient Greek original but from the German. All three productions adhered to the principles of historicism, aiming to "revive" the past as it has been in order to provide the people of modern Greece with a model with which to identify. While *Alcestis* and *Antigone* were more or less favorably received – nobody taking offense at the use of *demotiki* – the *Oresteia*, for that very reason, "provoked violent public demonstrations of university students and enraged citizens who feared for the integrity of Greece's classical heritage. Three citizens died in the confrontation of the mob with the police in this flare-up of fanaticism over the fate of classical heritage" (Kitromilides 2003: 49). As can be gathered from the first review of Terzopoulos' production quoted above, the language issue continued to be of prime importance with regard to cultural identity, even if in a different sense.

At the theatre festivals of Epidaurus and Delphi, these two decisive identity-building factors – monuments and ancient plays – came together. The monuments served to sacralize the past. It comes as no surprise, then, that in the 1930s the ancient theatre of Epidaurus, erected in the fourth century BC as part of the Asclepius sanctuary, was identified as an "adequate site for a revival of ancient drama" (Bastias 1936: 4), even though no performances of plays were documented at this site in ancient times. When the Epidaurus Festival was founded in 1956 it was intended only for the staging of ancient plays for which, the statement said, the theatre had originally been built – constituting the invention of a tradition. The Greek

National Theatre, founded in 1930, was awarded the privilege of staging Greek plays there. It was granted the power to decide on the "correct" and therefore dominant understanding of Greek plays. The artistic director of the National Theatre declared that

> all Greek plays . . . remain an artistic inheritance for every Greek, which we must make productive. The Epidaurus Festival is an effort in progress. Its achievements reflect on modern Greece, and its failures are failures in our artistic advancement.
> (*Ta Nea*, June 21, 1962, quoted after Sampatakakis 2005: 152)

The General Secretary of the Greek Organization for Tourism went even further:

> I have the opinion that nothing should change in the artistic form of the Epidaurus Festival, but it should remain an institution as it is today: motherland of classical drama.
> (*Ta Nea*, June 21, 1962, quoted after Sampatakakis 2005: 152)

These statements depict the Epidaurus Festival as the epitome of Greek culture as it was ideologized: unchanged since antiquity, self-contained, sealed off from any outside influence. Such a notion of culture has since been challenged by academia (e.g., cultural studies) and the arts and long rendered obsolete.

The Bacchae was staged twice in this "sacred" space. In 1962 a production by Alexis Minotis declared itself the tragedy's "world premiere" and starred Katina Paxinou as Agave. It was staged again in 1977 by Karolos Koun. It is worth noting that the first of these productions took place before the end of the military dictatorship (1967–1974) and the second after. Both productions will be examined briefly with regard to the concept of Greekness underlying them in order to better understand why Terzopoulos' production caused such a scandal.[2]

When we proceed from the assumption that "the prevailing Modern Greek tradition of staging Greek drama . . . demanded high stylization, screams and yells" (Sampatakakis 2005: 153), it is evident that Minotis (1898 or 1899–1990) deviated from this tradition insofar as he favored a psychological acting style. This provoked a mixed response among the critics and, as it seems, the audience. One critic wrote: "the audience was not entirely satisfied by the performance of the two protagonists. Not that they didn't cry or screech . . . but they didn't feel the part burning in their inner being and tearing their heart apart" (Babis D. Klaras, quoted after Sampatakakis 2005: 153). Another states just the opposite about Paxinou's acting: "Katina Paxinou in Agave's part is overwhelming; she forces the spectator to participate in her horrifying lament by expressing all of its human truth, overpowered nonetheless by her fortune" (K. B. Paraskos in *Kathimerini*, June 19, 1962, quoted after Sampatakakis 2005: 156)

Overall, the production was not well received. The stage design, costumes, and music, as well as the choreography of the chorus, seemed neither to have worked together nor with the acting style. However, nothing in the reviews hints at a fundamental rejection of this kind of theatre. The production seems to have been regarded as more of an accident, without at all questioning the traditional concept of Greekness. The critics did not even blame Minotis for the failure, but found fault with the play itself: *The Bacchae* "is not of course one of Euripides' best plays" (Babis D. Klaras, quoted after Sampatakakis 2005: 153); "rightly buried in the haze of the centuries, it is the worst of his tragedies" which adds "absolutely nothing to the unblemished magnitude of his renowned masterpieces." This latter critic even went so far as to claim that "theatre had nothing to benefit from the revival of *The Bacchae*" (KOK 1962; quoted after Sampatakakis 2005: 153). Were these critics insinuating that the play itself was rather un-Greek?

While Minotis' production does not appear to have contributed anything to the concept of Greekness, i.e., demanding or bringing about any changes to it, this definitely was not the case with Koun's production. After 1975 the National Theatre lost its privilege and Koun's Theatro Technis (Art Theatre) was allowed to perform at Epidaurus. By then Koun (1908–1987) was already a living legend. "For Greeks, Koun is the director who globalized Modern Greece and transformed any Greek drama production into a pan-Hellenic assembly" (Sampatakakis 2005: 171). His productions of Aristophanes' comedies, particularly *The Birds*, earned him international acclaim. It was "revived" several times even after his death.

Koun's production of *The Bacchae* transformed the concept of Greekness. On the one hand, it reintroduced elements that had faded into oblivion during the years of the dictatorship. On the other hand, it incorporated new ones, thus far neglected if not completely overlooked because they were not regarded as authentically ancient. All of them were related to Dionysus.

Mimis Kougioumtzis, who played Dionysus in Koun's production, was a fiercely masculine god who acted as the liberator of the people of Thebes, oppressed by the dictator Pentheus. He appeared as the god of the people, a democratic god. In this manner the idea of democracy, lost during the years of dictatorship, was reinscribed into society via the concept of Greekness. This concept, elaborated by philologists, historians, and archaeologists, at that time still disregarded Christian Byzantine traditions even though most ordinary Greek people understood themselves as Christians. Koun's production seemed to identify Dionysus with Christ – in accordance with Jan Kott's earlier analysis. Kott interpreted Dionysus' reappearance from Pentheus' prison in analogy to Christ's resurrection from the grave. On Koun's stage this was performed as "the elevation of Dionysus in white amidst special effects of smoke, multi-coloured lights, and fear-provoking music" (Sampatakakis 2005: 177). Critics discussed this scene in a similar manner: "The conception of Dionysus went directly to pre-Raphaelistic Art, and to the paintings of Mantegna and El Greco with the arrest of Jesus Christ" (Kostas Yorgousopoulos, in *To Vima*, August 28, 1977, quoted after Sampatakakis 2005: 177).

Koun also drew on folk traditions in which Dionysian and Christian elements seem to have merged. In order to present trance as a religious practice once more, he used elements from the *anastenaria* ritual, performed every May 21 in northeastern Thrace in honor of St. Konstantinos. "The sacred thiasos walks barefoot to the mountains where it prepares itself for fire-walking. After descending the 'cleansed' actors dance on burning coal with the icon of the Saint in hands without getting hurt" – which echoes the lines in *The Bacchae*, "Flames flickered in their curls and did not burn them" (v. 757/55) – "probably due to the anaesthetization of the feet from walking barefoot on rocks" (Sampatakakis 2006: 100).

Some of the actors' movements alluded to this ritual, which is said to have its roots in the Dionysian mysteries.[3] (Terzopoulos would incorporate this ritual into his production in an even more pronounced way.)

Thus, the concept of Greekness was considerably expanded to include not just the elite but also the common people. As would happen in Zé Celso's production of *The Bacchae* twenty years later when the spectators experienced themselves as truly Brazilian – in their case this meant ever-changing – the audiences of Koun's production were able to experience themselves as truly Greek.

> An audience of 28,000 people attended the performance during the weekend shouting at the end Koun . . . Koun . . . Koun . . . This is indicative of Koun's idolization into a cultural icon who expressed with his Art the lower-class Greek's hopes for social equality after – and before – the restoration of Democracy.
>
> (Sampatakakis 2005: 179)

With this production, Koun revived the Dionysian spirit that the military dictators had oppressed for such a long time. In this sense, he topicalized the tragedy through particular aesthetic means.

> Karolos Koun treats every ancient drama as if it was modern, and in that sense he manages to cover the chronological gap between text and audience. With any new re-performance he offers us theatre, living and, to a possible extent, modern, not merely restorative theatre.
> (E. Alexandros, in *Politika Themata*, August 20–26, 1977, quoted after
> Sampatakakis 2005: 180)

While Koun's production of *The Bacchae* in a "sacred" place – the theatre of Epidaurus – fundamentally redefined the concept of Greekness and was celebrated for this by critics and audiences alike, Terzopoulos' production of the tragedy in a similar space, the stadium at Delphi, was passionately rejected and accused of robbing the site of its power to sacralize the past. It was denounced as blasphemy desecrating the heritage value of the monument as well as the tragedy. What exactly was it about this production's aesthetic that appeared to redefine the concept of Greekness in a way that critics and audiences experienced it as an insulting attack and threat to their cultural identity?

In order to answer this question, my analysis of the performance will refer to the four objections raised by the critics of Terzopoulos' production: (1) "the function of the ancient as well as the new Greek language was reduced"; (2) it was a "Japanese spectacle" instead of a Greek one; (3) it was the performance of a ritual rather than a tragedy; and (4) the production had nothing to do with the text of the tragedy.[4]

(1) In Yorgos Patsas' stage design in Delphi, a round platform was fastened to the ground by centrifugally attached pieces of rags that produced an effect of lightness and circular motion through the gentle movements of the stage. It was reminiscent of the orchestra but was used as a ritualistic space. It was covered with light, partly reddish sand. At the beginning of the performance, six figures were squatting on the ground near the edge of the circle, their upper bodies naked and painted white. Loincloths were wrapped around their hips in thick layers. These six actors played all the parts, including that of the chorus.

When the figures stood, one could see that the face, chest, and armpits of one of them were covered in red dust. Another figure squatted in front of a large crystal globe, while a third wore a fur thrown over his back. Two others clung to sticks as thick as an arm. A woman with long black curls squatted behind a drum, her mouth gaping open. She was breathing in and out loudly – as were the others. Her upper body was erect. She alternated lifting each arm to her shoulders, forming a right angle with her upper and lower arm as well as with her lower arm and palm. The loud rhythmic breathing was occasionally punctuated by a drumbeat.

From the very beginning of the performance, then, it was established that its focus was on the bodies of the actors, not the ancient or new Greek language. The latter was not reduced by the visual stimuli. Focusing on the bodies changed the language both in terms of its status and in the way that the words were uttered. The most important artistic device was the performers' particular use of their bodies and voices. Their movements were not meant to express an individual emotion or psychic state of a character. Instead, firstly, they were rooted in the specific space, i.e., the circle, delineating clear boundaries, preventing transgression. Secondly, they had to define the relationship between the figures within the circle. Thirdly, and most importantly, the actions on stage were performed in order to generate energy and let it circulate in the whole space so that it would be transferred to the spectators and become contagious – "infecting" them so that they might be able to tap into it themselves.

These three functions were not paired with three different kinds of movement. Rather, every movement sequence had to serve all three purposes simultaneously. The actors leaned forward; they squatted in the sand and crawled across it, crouching. During the "earthquake" they all prostrated themselves on the ground, shaking their entire bodies, limbs trembling. Tiresias (Sophia Mikhopoulou) moved around in a squatting position, holding a huge crystal globe over his head. Cadmus (Thodoros Polyzonis) kept dragging himself across the ground, seemingly unable to lift up his body. Dionysus (Akis Sakellariou) used a much greater variety of movements, all meant to conjure up energy and circulate it in the space. Initially, he stood motionless. Then he started moving one arm, flinging it back and up. One leg was stretched out to the front. Then he began to move like a dancer. At his first words he squatted down with one leg stretched out in front of him, his body leaning back; he ran his hand through the sand and let the reddish dust trickle onto his face.

When Dionysus and Pentheus (Dimitris Siakaras) faced each other for the "agon" they never stood or moved with their bodies upright, although their feet remained on the ground. Their legs were mostly bent at the knees and their upper bodies leant forward sharply. The feet were firmly planted on the ground, leaving footprints, as if the performers wanted to draw energy from the earth and to channel it into their bodies. There were only a few instances of the bodies straightening: as Dionysus placed the veil with the wig over Pentheus' head (to dress him up for his journey into the Cithaeron mountains) and as Pentheus pulled it over his temples. The most impressive and deeply moving moment of this kind was when Agave (Sophia Mikhopoulou), holding Pentheus' head/mask over her head, which was inclined back, stepped forward with carefully measured steps to announce her triumph.

These movements also defined the relationship between the figures. As Dionysus and Pentheus faced one other, they defined their relationship as antagonistic and yet as equally matched, denied, however, by Dionysus' words. When Pentheus straightened and stepped up to Dionysus, the latter held the veil with the blonde wig over Pentheus' head, who seized it and pulled it on. They drew nearer to each other, Dionysus reaching under Pentheus' arm as if wanting to hug him. Instead, however, Dionysus took hold of the stick which Pentheus had been clutching from the very beginning. They seemed almost to melt into each other. Here, it was the dressing scene that showed both as each other's "monstrous double" (Girard).

When Agave stepped forward, arms still stretched upwards and holding the mask with the bloody veil in her hands, her position marked her as someone apart from and superior to the others.

FIGURE 5.1 Agave (Sophia Mikhopoulou) with Pentheus' head. Photo: Johanna Weber/Theodorus Terzopoulos and the Attis Theatre.

When Cadmus challenged her to look at the head, she pulled the mask over her face as if looking at the world through Pentheus' eyes. When she realized what had really happened her mouth opened wide and her tongue rolled out again and again, without uttering a sound. She flung her head back and rolled up her eyeballs. Then she sank to her knees and threw herself to the ground. The mask pulled over her head, she let out heart-rending sounds of lament that resembled the cries of a wild animal. She separated herself from the others, shut herself off from the community, and buried herself in the earth along with her sorrow.

The movements which the actors carried out were very unusual. They were hardly ever flowing or even graceful in a way that would lead energy back into the body or diffuse it in space. Instead, they were extremely powerful and controlled, with a high degree of dynamism, which continually brought the limbs together in angled positions. They often began and ended abruptly. These movements forged and forced energy out of the body like an eruption, so that the other actors and the audience were struck by it.

A key factor here was that the movements followed certain rhythms, as did the breathing, the speaking, the sounds, and the music (excerpts from the

Mystery by Yannis Christou and from Australian aboriginal music). However, the rhythms were rarely fully synchronized. The rhythm of the movements and that of the speech often conflicted. Nonetheless, they followed the same principle insofar as they both emerged from the body, their flow repeatedly interrupted, setting free a tremendous energy that circulated in the space. As elaborated in the previous chapter, the human body is rhythmically tuned. We are therefore able to perceive rhythm as an external as well as internal principle. However, rhythm as an energetic principle can have an impact only when it is sensed physically, such as with our own bodily rhythms, so that we begin to tune into it.

In Terzopoulos' *The Bacchae* the human body not only featured prominently but also constituted the *conditio sine qua non* for the performance to come into being. The bodies on stage drew attention to themselves as this condition because of how they were used by the performers. This body usage was the result of a particular training method – Terzopoulos' biodynamics – as well as of the inclusion of elements from Greek popular and religious culture. Elements from the *anastenaria* ritual or of the dance of Pontos were incorporated into the training as well as the performance. The dance of Pontos, for example, served as a model for the chorus: hands trembling in a mimesis of flying, feet marching steadily on the ground.

> Three different, concurrent movements were explored as the dance of the chorus: the head is quickly shivering left and right, the hands are up with the palms tremblingly loosely open, while the feet are either fixed to the ground in the kabuki semi-squatting position or with the knees shaking uncontrollably.
> (Sampatakakis 2006: 95–96)

By including such elements, Terzopoulos provided further evidence for the claim that his approach to body usage was akin to that practiced in ancient Greece. In a talk about *The Bacchae* he stated:

> I began to search into the mysteries, the Greek theatrical events, to explore the popular festivals, to search for all information about Dionysus. I found one vital information in a book which was found in Leipzig, an edition of the seventeenth century. I read there that in Attica, where there is the hospital of Asclepius, the patients had to follow a certain ritual. When the sun was setting, they had to walk naked in a circle on wet sand, on wet earth, one around the other. In the second hour, they had to quicken their steps, in the third more. In the fourth, they had to bend their knees just as in Kabuki. In the fifth, they had to bend the elbows, and little by little advancing and quickening this motion, with the extremities bent, the physical pains started to go away, and the clots to break up. One had pain in the heart, another in the stomach, and suddenly it was gone. Little by little these people, for eight hours, did this same thing and they began to have so much energy. This is like what happens in Kabuki. The

Kabuki actor can walk with bent knees for ten hours, and plays with the same secret. And from this, gradually, the pains began to break up and go away.
(McDonald 1992: 164)

This statement is highly relevant to our question. For, on the one hand, it insists on the Greekness of these movements, performed in this very way and for similar reasons at the sanctuary of Asclepius at Epidaurus in ancient Greece. Centering on the body and developing its full potential appears as a traditional Greek idea and practice. This notion of the central and constitutive role of the body in Greek culture must therefore be incorporated into the concept of Greekness.

Moreover, the body is considered equally important as words when it comes to individual and collective memory. Terzopoulos proceeds from the assumption that

the real source of our energy and knowledge comes from the interior of the body, from memories which have been printed inside us from long ago. There exists an inner energy which carries images and repressed memories of other lives and of other eras. Namely, there exists all the knowledge of the world inside our very bodies, and there is no need for us to refer to a hundred books in order to extract this.
(McDonald 1992: 163)

A concept of Greekness excluding the body and its inherent potential seems unacceptable.

On the other hand, the human body is addressed as an anthropological given. As Marcel Mauss has explained in his pioneering study "Techniques of the Body" (1973 [orig. 1934/5]), every human being is able to stand, sit, walk, run, swim, dive, etc., because the anatomy of the human body allows for all these different kinds of movements. However, members of different cultures perform them each in their own way. As he demonstrates with regard to swimming, techniques can also correlate with new ideas about a more efficient use of the body which might lead to different usages within the same culture. The kinds of body techniques that will be acquired depend on the processes of learning involved. Even within one culture they are not fixed once and for all. Mauss also compares the way in which American and French women walk and reports that, probably due to the popularity of American movies in France in the 1930s, many French women changed their gait through imitation – whether this happened intentionally or involuntarily cannot be said with certainty.

Mauss' insights suggest that the body's potential, determined anatomically, will be developed and exploited in every culture, albeit differently. Of course, a similar technique could be developed in two cultures located far away from each other. Movements used in an ancient Greek healing ritual could just as well be performed in Japanese Kabuki theatre, enabling us to consider them Japanese. Human anatomy makes such movements possible, even if not all cultures will make the same use of them.

(2) This leads us to the second argument, that *The Bacchae* was a "Japanese" spectacle. In Terzopoulos' production the performers did in fact use elements from the Japanese performing arts. As Sampatakakis has shown, Dionysus in the opening scene danced the *bugaku* military dance of *bu-no-mai*. When Dionysus and Pentheus met, "Dionysus is schematically paired off with Pentheus who dances the antistrophic dance. As in ancient *bugaku*, the dancers follow each other in pairs" (Sampatakakis 2005: 198). Pentheus' dance can thus be regarded as the "answer dance" – the *kotae ma*. It is revealing that it was Dionysus, the new god from Asia, who introduced movement patterns from the Japanese performing arts and, moreover, made even Pentheus employ them. Sophia Mikhopoulou's use of her body in the recognition scene, flinging back her head and rolling her eyeballs up to signal epilepsy, are also to be found in other cultures, such as "in Japanese shamanistic rituals, the Anastenaria dance, and in the *kaiko* dance of New Guinea, and often represented as *rasa* in *kathakali*" (Sampatakakis 2005: 200).

This particular use of the body – described as genuinely Greek and, at the same time, also Japanese or generally "other" – challenged the idea of the fundamental uniqueness as well as difference of Greek culture from any other culture – in particular from Asian cultures. It presupposed a basic kinship of Greek culture with others insofar as the human body is regarded as "the existential ground of culture and self," as the anthropologist Thomas Csordas put it (Csordas 1994). In this respect, all cultures resemble each other. Moreover, from this it follows that no culture can be conceptualized as monadic. They all have elements in common and are in principle able to incorporate new elements from each other. Cultures in a globalizing world in particular constantly engage in exchanges of all sorts. The idea of a monadic, unchanging culture that maintains some kind of a fundamental difference from all others has long become obsolete. This insight was embodied in Terzopoulos' production, and it made sense that it was presented at the second Greek Drama International Meeting that aimed to relocate Greek drama in a globalized world. However, as can be guessed from the reviews cited above, the majority of the critics and the audience saw these meetings as an opportunity to demonstrate to the world their "Greekness" and thus ownership and superior understanding of ancient Greek drama, which led to more accomplished theatre productions. It is therefore no surprise that this staging of *The Bacchae* infuriated them.

(3) Long passages of the reviews are devoted to explaining that ancient Greek theatre should neither be regarded nor enacted as a ritual, implying that the critics felt that Terzopoulos' *The Bacchae* had done just that. It is

difficult to assess on what grounds they reached this conclusion. Not only Gilbert Murray but also the classicists and anthropologists of the 1960s and 1970s described in great detail the ritualistic structure and elements of *The Bacchae* without identifying the tragedy itself as a ritual. Terzopoulos' production made use of ritualistic elements such as the circle – as Zé Celso would do ten years later with the *roda*, the circle dance of the *candomblé* – or the ecstatic body movements performed by Agave or the chorus. Using "ritualistic" elements, however, is not the same as enacting a ritual. Is it possible that the critics who saw the performance as the enactment of a ritual were seduced into doing so by the "strange" appearance of the actors and their unusual movements?[5]

It seems that they mistook the loincloths, the movements and the "strange" music for elements of a ritual that might be an acceptable practice among "savages" but not among Greeks. As such, they were unable to recognize the particular understanding of the body underlying and informing this production – an understanding to which critics outside of Greece responded with enthusiasm.

Another reason might be found in the particular state into which the performance transferred the spectators, including the critics, right from the beginning. It was induced by the unique atmosphere of the performance, which could be characterized as a mood that may occur when waking up at the crack of dawn, the first rays of light and noise from the outside world merging with the last terrible images of a nightmare and creating an irrefutable feeling of impending disaster. This atmosphere was not due to any single element, such as the drumbeats, the twilight, the music, or the appearance or movements of the actors. Rather, it was their sum total and their particular interplay that allowed this atmosphere to emerge.

It is difficult to observe atmospheres because they don't confront us directly and instead unfold somewhere between the stage and the auditorium. They also might emanate from objects on stage. Nevertheless, spectators also play a part in their creation through their mood and the degree of their responsiveness. They perceive atmosphere by becoming immersed in it and sensing it with their entire body. The atmosphere generated at the beginning of the performance, which spread through the space and pulled the spectators in, transposed them into a threshold state, a state of "in-betweenness." This was true for the whole performance, even though the atmosphere changed.

This state of "in-betweenness" was probably intensified by a destabilization of the spectators' perception: the perceivable elements of the performance were selected in such a way that they challenged the perception of the spectator to oscillate constantly between the very special phenomenality of the elements and the meanings one might attribute to them – between their materiality and semioticity. This applied to the appearance of the actors and to their actions, to the objects they used, and to the light and the music.

From the outset the fact that the actors were merely wearing loincloths directed the spectators' attention to their phenomenal bodies regardless of what role they were playing or what figure they were supposed to represent. The spectators' attention was drawn to the different faces, hairstyles, and physical features. This tendency was enhanced by the unusual movements described above. Spectators seemed spellbound by the way in which Sophia Mikhopoulou moved around the circle in a squatting position, her feet bouncing, without asking themselves what this could mean with regard to the figure of Tiresias, whom she played. Some spectators might have felt challenged to ask this question and, unable to answer it, would have felt confused. The same happened when Akis Sakellariou – Dionysus – stepped over those squatting on the ground with his legs spread apart after the announcement of his imprisonment, or when the messenger delivered his report about the activities of the Theban women in the Cithaeron mountains, his hands stiff, breathing heavily, convulsive spasms shaking his entire body. At moments such as these, which occurred on numerous occasions over the course of the performance, the phenomenal body in its specific, peculiar being completely absorbed the attention of the spectators before they were able to perceive it as a semiotic body – as a sign for the dramatic figure or his/her actions or words. This was particularly true of the loud breathing. It defied all interpretation and was experienced by the audience exclusively as an accumulation and emission of energy. The spectators responded to this release of energy by focusing their attention on the phenomenal corporeality and the emerging effect it had on them. The question of the possible meaning of the actions came up only later. What was perceived as a performer's intense presence during these moments, setting free a stream of energy, was perceived as a dramatic character – as Dionysus, Pentheus, or Agave – the next.

Similar experiences were enabled by the objects on stage. The crystal globe, which the actress held in her hand, leant on, or did a head stand in front of, at first glance was perceived as a round, glassy object that took on different shades and colors depending on the light. Only later did the question arise whether it alluded to our planet, to the significantly smaller crystal balls used by fortunetellers or perhaps to something else altogether. Because of its particular materiality, the crystal globe first and foremost referred back to itself; its self-referentiality was so strong that any attempt to interpret it as something else became secondary.

If the actor playing Dionysus had held a stick in his hand when he revealed his identity it would have undoubtedly been taken for a thyrsus. However, Pentheus and one of the messengers held sticks. Since it was far from clear to the audience at the beginning of the performance who was playing what role, the spectators' attention was drawn to the objects in their specific phenomenality. This triggered a range of associations which, in the case of the stick, included the thyrsus, a walking stick, and a weapon. After the stick was used as a kind of lance by Pentheus, its phenomenal being receded into the background and its semiotic character came to the fore. Now it was perceived as a weapon with which Pentheus wanted to fight the Stranger; later on, when Dionysus and Pentheus held the stick and seemed to melt into one another, it became a thyrsus. At the same time, the whole process appeared as a sign for Pentheus' transformation.

In all of these cases, as in several others, the spectators became aware of their own perception as it oscillated between the specific phenomenality of bodies and objects and the possibilities to interpret them as signs. Secondly, the performers and the objects proved to be extremely ambiguous – what might appear to be something at one moment became something completely different the next. The spectators had constantly to change the meanings they attributed to actions and things, making it difficult for them to see consistency in what they perceived.

At the moment of the switch between phenomenality and semioticity, a break occurred. The former order of perception was disrupted and a new one established. To perceive the performers in their bodily being-in-the-world established a specific order of perception; to perceive their bodies as a sign for a dramatic figure established another. The same applied to the perception of the objects.

What exactly happened during the transition when the old order was disturbed but the new one was not yet established? Perception was destabilized. A state of instability emerged. It transposed the perceivers between the two orders. They found themselves on a threshold, which is to be characterized as the passage from one order to another. As their perception constantly switched during the performance and the spectators were forced between the two orders of perception, the difference between the two orders receded more and more into the background, and the attention of the spectator focused instead on the transitions and disturbances, the state of instability and the production of a new stability. The more frequently the switches occurred, the more frequently the perceivers wandered between these two worlds and orders of perception. At the same time they became gradually more aware that they were not in control of the transitions. They could repeatedly try to focus their perception but, after a few failures, it was clear that these switches occurred without intent. They simply happened or befell them. The spectators entered a state between two orders without wanting to or being able to prevent it. At this moment, they experienced their own perception as an emergent phenomenon, i.e., happening beyond their will and control, albeit still consciously. This experience might have evoked a deep sense of disturbance and destabilization, enhancing the state of in-betweenness.

We can label this a state of liminality. Victor Turner even identified this state as typical of rituals, marking their second or threshold/transformation phase as described by van Gennep. Since spectators entered such a state of liminality during the performance of *The Bacchae*, undergoing physiological, affective, energetic, and motor changes that led to transformations, the conclusion was drawn by the critics that they were witnessing a ritual – one typical of some "savage tribe" unknown and incomprehensible to them.

This argument overlooks the fact that a liminal experience is not just ritualistic in nature but also aesthetic. In this respect, theatre and ritual overlap: both are capable of transferring the participants into a liminal state. However, there is a crucial difference between liminality as a ritualistic or as an aesthetic experience. The transformation brought about by a ritual is irreversible – e.g., the transformation of a boy into a warrior cannot be undone – and requires the acceptance of the whole group, community, or society. However, the physiological, affective, energetic, and motor changes which the spectators undergo during a theatre performance are only temporary and therefore reversible. They also do not require the acceptance of others.

Terzopoulos' production of *The Bacchae* used artistic means and strategies to enable the spectator to undergo liminal experiences. Potential transformations induced by them were essentially reversible, even if they had a long-lasting impact on some members of the audience. This production insisted not only on the possibility but on the necessity that a spectator's aesthetic experience is liminal without being ritualistic.

It seems that the destabilization that went with this kind of aesthetic experience was perceived as a threat. A performance of a Greek tragedy done by a Greek director was expected to stabilize the spectators by confirming the predominant concept of Greekness. Terzopoulos' production, in contrast, seemed to encourage a destabilization of their own cultural identity.

(4) The way in which the production dealt with the text further enhanced this feeling of destabilization. Instead of serving as a controlling authority, the text was subordinated to the body. It was not only cut substantially, but what was left of it was not "shown" on stage. Neither the space nor the appearance of the performers, e.g., their actions and movements, illustrated the text. Speech alternated with intervals during which no words were spoken at all – even if other sounds were always heard, if only as breathing. Moreover, the words were not spoken so much as hurled out of the body like an eruption. This impression was not just created by the energetic and dynamic movements preceding and accompanying them but was mostly due to the specific way of breathing. Here, breath, which first wrung itself loudly out of the body, turned into a stream of air and energy, lifting the words from the depth of the body and hurling them out. They did not point back to a text but to the body that expelled them.

It can be assumed that this created the impression among some critics that the text was nothing but a "pre-text" and that the production could have done without it. This is clearly a delusion. The particular ecstasy that the production aimed at and achieved is closely related to the subject matter of the tragedy. It also deals with the crisis in the community, i.e., in the polis of Thebes. The production referred to it by dealing with the crisis caused by clinging to a concept of Greekness that had long become obsolete. By incorporating the constitutive function of the body into this concept, the performance not only expanded it but also broke it open. The much-hailed Greekness, instead of being immune to the influence of other cultures, turned out to be similar and permeable to them. By performing the tragedy that deals with the devastation of Thebes as a consequence of the refusal of its ruler to accept the Stranger, the new god from Asia, in the polis, a new concept of Greekness was outlined that welcomed the inclusion of "Strangers," i.e., elements from other cultures, because all cultures spring from a common source, the human body.

Notes

1. Greek reviews are translated by Anastasia Siouzouli unless otherwise indicated.
2. My analysis is indebted to Sampatakakis (2005), which discusses both productions at great length.
3. Greek anthropologists of the 1930s, drawing heavily on the Cambridge Ritualists, declared this ritual a remnant of the Dionysian cult – therefore not Christian but ancient Greek in origin.
4. The analysis is based primarily on my observations of a guest performance in Berlin in 1987, on a video recording, and on a number of reviews of the Greek premiere and guest performances in Spain, Germany, the United States, and Australia.
5. Max Reinhardt's production of *King Oedipus* in 1910 featured some torchbearers in loincloths, which made the critics rage. They fiercely objected to the "naked torchbearers who shot through the orchestra bearing their torches and ran up the steps of the palace and down again like madmen" (Jacobsohn 1910: 1177). After Reinhardt's production premiered in London, a similar discussion erupted there. Gilbert Murray, who had translated *King Oedipus*, referred to the above scene in order to challenge the claim that the production was not Greek: "Professor Reinhardt was frankly pre-Hellenic (as is the Oedipus story itself), partly Cretan and Mycenaean, partly Oriental, partly – to my great admiration – merely savage. The half-naked torchbearers with loincloths and long black hair made my heart leap with joy. There was real early Greece about them, not the Greece of the schoolroom or the conventional art studio" (cited in Styan 1982: 85). It seems that the figures in Terzopoulos' production – loincloths slung around their hips – had a similar effect on the Greek critics as Reinhardt's had on the German critics before World War I. The complaints were the same in both cases: the performers were "savages," not Greeks.

References

Bastias K. 1936. "Week of Ancient Drama." In program of the performance of Sophocles' *Electra*.

Clogg, Richard. 2003. "The Classics and the Movement of Independence." In *The Impact of Classical Greece on European and National Identities*. Edited by Margriet Haagsma, Pim den Boer and Eric M. Moormann, 20–45. Amsterdam: J. C. Gieben.

Csordas, Thomas J. 1994. "Introduction: The Body as Representation and Being in the World." In *Embodiment and Experience: The Existential Ground of Culture and Self*. Edited by Thomas J. Csordas. Cambridge: Cambridge University Press.

Hamilakis, Y. and E. Yalouri. 1999. "Sacralizing the Past." *Archaeological Dialogues* 6 (2): 113–160.

Heimares, H. 1986. "I athootita kai to peirama." *Proti*, June 25.

Jacobsohn, Siegfried. 1910. No title. *Die Schaubühne*, November 17, 1176–1178.

Kitromilides, Paschalis M. 2003. "From Subservience to Ambivalence." In *The Impact of Classical Greece on European and National Identities*. Edited by Margriet Haagsma, Pim den Boer and Eric M. Moormann, 47–54. Amsterdam: J. C. Gieben.

KOK. 1962. No title. *Akropolis*, June 12.

Kotsakis, Kostas. 2003. "Ideological Aspects of Contemporary Archaeology in Greece." In *The Impact of Classical Greece on European and National Identities*. Edited by Margriet Haagsma, Pim den Boer and Eric M. Moormann, 55–70. Amsterdam: J. C. Gieben.

Lignadis, Tasos. 1986. "Theatrical Encounter in Delphi." *Ekathimerini*, June 22.

McDonald, Marianne. 1992. "Theodoros Terzopoulos' Talk." In *Ancient Sun, Modern Light: Greek Drama on the Modern Stage*, 159–169. New York: Columbia University Press.

Mauss, Marcel. 1973. French 1934/35. "Techniques of the Body." *Economy and Society* 2 (1): 70–88. DOI 10.1080/03085147300000003.

Polenakis, Leandros. 1986. "Bacchae without Euripides." *Avgi*, June 21.

Roilu, Joanna. 1999. "Performances of Ancient Greek Tragedy on the Greek Stage of the Twentieth Century." In *(Dis)Placing Classical Greek Theatre*. Edited by Savas Patsalides and Elizabeth Sakellaridou, 191–201. Thessaloniki: University Studies Press.

Sampatakakis, Georgios. 2005. *Bakkhaimodel: The Re-usage of Euripides' Bakkhai in Text and Performance*. London: London University Press.

Sampatakakis, Georgios. 2006. "Dionysus Restitutus – The Bacchae of Terzopoulos." In *Journey with Dionysus: The Theatre of Theodoros Terzopoulos*. Edited by Frank M. Raddatz, 90–102. Berlin: Theater der Zeit.

Styan, J. 1982. *Max Reinhardt*. Cambridge: Cambridge University Press.

Synodinou, Anna. 1986. "The Victim-Bacchae. An experiment of Mr. Terzopoulos." *Politika Themata*, July 18–24.

Further Reading

Fischer-Lichte, Erika. 2008. *The Transformative Power of Performance: A New Aesthetics*. New York: Routledge. For aesthetic experience as liminal experience, see pp. 174–180 and 190–200.

Hamilakis, Yannis. 2007. *The Nation and Its Ruins: Antiquity, Archaeology, and National Imagination in Greece*. Oxford: Oxford University Press. The relevance of ancient monuments for the notion of Greekness.

Ortolani, Benito. 1995. *The Japanese Theatre: From Shamanistic Ritual to Contemporary Pluralism*. Princeton: Princeton University Press. For the ancient Japanese *bugaku* dance, see pp. 39–53.

Sansom, Jane A. 2002. "Appropriating Social Energy: The Generation, Accumulation and Conversion of Capital in the Performance of Anastenária." *Journal of Modern Greek Studies* 19: 143–168. The anastenária ritual.

Terzopoulos, Theodoros. 2000. *Theodoros Terzopoulos and the Attis Theatre: History, Methodology, and Comments*. Athens: Agra. Terzopoulos' biodynamics.

6

In Search of New Identities
Krzysztof Warlikowski's *The Bacchae* in Warsaw (2001)

In Krzysztof Warlikowski's *The Bacchae* (Teatr Rozmaitości, Warsaw 2001), a creature resembling a mutilated animal or possibly a human being without a head comes out of the darkness in the opening scene. It is a Dionysian goat which transforms into a human being or, rather, out of which a human being grows like a rampant weed in order to finally turn into an evil god. The birth of this being is also the birth of theatre. Dionysus, in Warlikowski's production, is a vessel for words. The sounds he makes in the beginning are unintelligible, childlike, animalistic; his sounds, words and sentences can be deciphered only with difficulty. The goat, man and god, recognizes the words and the words recognize him. They grow, swell and nest in him, shake his torso, take possession of his body . . . Andrzej Chyra plays Dionysus and we witness his theatre god learning how to speak, learning to be himself. At the same time, he scripts the alphabet of the stage world, teaching the spectators how to listen. Warlikowski's god, made of vowels and consonants, patches up the idea of man in order to tear it apart in the final scene. If I had to choose a single image to symbolize what has happened to Polish theatre since 1997, it would be this very scene.

(Drewniak 2006: 102)

Dionysus Resurrected: Performances of Euripides' The Bacchae in a Globalizing World, First Edition. Erika Fischer-Lichte.
© 2014 Erika Fischer-Lichte. Published 2014 by John Wiley & Sons, Ltd.

The above quote identifies the year 1997 as a turning point in the history of Polish theatre, which was embodied by Warlikowski's *The Bacchae* in 2001. Tomasz Plata, the editor of the first book on Polish theatre between 1990 and 2005, holds a similar view. He lists three facts from the year 1997 to support his argument: Jerzy Grzegorzewski became artistic director of the Teatr Narodowy in Warsaw; the performer Paweł Althamer began his international career with his action/performance at the documenta X in Kassel; and Krzysztof Warlikowski (born 1962) staged Sophocles' *Electra* at the Teatr Dramatyczny in Warsaw. According to Plata, these three very different events marked the beginning of a new search for how to re-anchor the Polish performing arts in society.

In order fully to understand it, this search has to be seen in the context of recent Polish history, especially the fall of the Iron Curtain and the end of communist rule in 1989. How did the collapse of communism affect Polish theatre and what was significant about these effects?

Finding answers to these questions requires us first to look back at the era preceding 1989. In 1981 martial law was introduced, which brought severe censorship to the theatre, where opposition to the regime had been articulated openly. Consequently, actors boycotted state television, which served as the main tool for government propaganda. The artistic directors of the two most important theatres were removed – Adam Hanuszkiewicz from the Teatr Narodowy and Gustaw Holoubek from the Teatr Dramatyczny (the latter institution undoubtedly having been the most acclaimed in town in the 1970s). The ensembles were dissolved. To avoid instrumentalization by politics, theatre shifted to other places. Many performances were staged in churches, which at that time were the only spaces exempt from censorship. On stage, the theatre artists were forced to hone the art of political allusion. Post-1989, they were weary of any kind of political commitment, as evidenced by a review in the journal *Polityka*, in which Jacek Sieradzki recalled: "After the collapse of communism, our theatre was released from its many social commitments and was finally able to deal with what is actually important, namely the human soul" (Plata 2006: 220).

Plata emphasized that political and social engagement had been the highest duty of Polish theatre for decades. He distinguished between two models for this form of engagement, defining the first as a theatre of allusion. It opened up possibilities for addressing political issues even in times of censorship. As a classic example he mentioned Kazimierz Dejmek's production of Adam Mickiewicz' *Dziady* at the Teatr Narodowy in Warsaw in 1965. Mickiewicz wrote the play between 1823 and 1832, finishing it after the November Uprising of 1830. In four parts it deals with the political situation after the three divisions of Poland of 1772, 1793, and 1795 (the latter lasting until 1918). The third part, which he wrote last, is devoted to the national catastrophe, the November Uprising, brutally put down by the

Russian military. This part included the scene entitled "Vision of the Priest Piotr" which, among others, could be read as a response to "Great Improvisation," in which the poet Konrad raged against God's cruelty for forgetting about Poland and the Poles. This third part introduced the image of Poland as the crucified Christ and articulated the mystical promise of Poland's redemption, which is at the heart of Polish messianism. The *Dziady*, thus, can be regarded as the national drama, embodying what was later called the Romantic paradigm.

Dejmek did not openly topicalize the play but put it together in such a way that a particular reading was encouraged. Konrad, the protagonist played by Gustaw Holoubek as a rebellious intellectual, could be regarded as a symbolic figure personifying Poland and inaugurating a period of political disobedience. In the final scene he appeared before the audience silent and in chains, captive but not broken. The production (as one among other reasons) caused a political uproar. After the first performances the production was cancelled by order of the authorities. The student protests which followed were used by one of the communist factions to maneuver the struggle for power within the party in its own favor. This model over and over again provoked the direct intervention of the authorities.

The other model proved to be more resistant to such interventions. The works of Jerzy Jarocki, Andrzej Wajda, and Konrad Swinarski serve as examples here. In their productions they dealt with the vulnerability of man to the wheels of history, whereby history was conceived as utterly absurd. As Plata explained, Swinarski in his adaptations of the Romantic classics (plays by Mickiewicz, Juliusz Słowacki, and Zygmunt Krasiński), Jarocki in his productions of plays by Stanisław I. Witkiewicz (Witkacy), Witold Gombrowicz, and Sławomir Mrożek, and Wajda in his theatre as well as in his movies (*Kanal*, *Ashes and Diamonds*, *Legionnaires*), showed a common collective reality as concurrent with the tragic myth. They presented the fate of the individual as inextricably bound to the overarching and precarious historical process.

After 1989 grand narratives lost their place in Polish theatre, which instead set out to explore various smaller, individual narratives. It is not surprising, then, that the writer whose plays were performed most often immediately after 1989 was Chekhov. Tellingly, the above quotation by Sieradzki is from his review of Jarocki's production of *Platonov* at the Teatr Polski in Wrocław (1993). According to Plata, there were only a handful of artistically interesting Chekhov productions, among them Jarocki's and the two productions of *Uncle Vania* by Grzegorzewski in Warsaw and Rudolf Zioło in Cracow. Plata considered the majority of Chekhov productions between 1989 and 1997 as examples of an escapist tendency in Polish theatre and declared them to be an expression of the widespread conviction that theatre should not deal with the "here and today" but with what is "always and everywhere." However, it is difficult to assess whether they still contributed to a "private" discourse while neglecting social and "public" affairs. "When the old dissolves and the new has not yet taken a clear shape, when there are no plays addressing the present situation directly – then one has to play Chekhov. He knew everything about people living in times of change," as one critic wrote in defense of the current Chekhov mania (Wanat 1997: 127).

Even if there was a certain concern that relating to politics would inevitably result in the ideologization of theatre, this did not mean that the "small narratives" about the private lives of people were necessarily apolitical. In his early productions, beginning with *The Marquise of O* – after the novella by Heinrich von Kleist (Stary Teatr in Cracow 1993), for example, Warlikowski dealt with sexual and moral diversity, while Piotr Cieplak, in his production of *The History of the Glorious Resurrection of Christ* (Teatr Współczesny in Wrocław 1993), presented religious experience as something dissociated from the institution of the church and something deeply personal. Here, the private became the public and the personal turned political.

Keeping this in mind, the question arises as to what exactly happened in 1997 that justified the claim of a turning point marking a new relationship between theatre and society. In order to clarify it, let us return to the three events Plata lists in order to substantiate the claim.

When Grzegorzewski (1939–2005) took over the directorship of the Teatr Narodowy, he continued to stage the canon of classical Polish plays on which the Polish cultural and national identity had been based for such a long time, i.e., the Romantic poets, as well as plays by Witold Gombrowicz and Stanisław Wyspiański, whose *Acropolis* had become world-famous in Jerzy Grotowski's version (1962). Grzegorzewski, however, was not interested in continuing this tradition. Rather, by using theatrical means, he tested its validity and value for contemporary Poland. In his production of *Dziady*, which is exemplary even though the play had already been staged in 1995, he fragmented the play and put the scenes together in an unfamiliar order. Moreover, he implemented a new reading, radically questioning the meaning and significance of the play for his contemporaries. "Does *Dziady* continue to be an important part of our collective memory? The production liberated the play from its ideological residues . . . Ultimately, it focused on the existential problem of the dramatic figures with respect to the disintegration of their shared myths" (Plata 2006: 228). Grzegorzewski used the canon to question the shared myths and the national identity based on them, as well as the way they were put on the stage until that day, thus creating possibilities for its renegotiation.

While Grzegorzewski questioned the traditional, common self-understanding, the two other examples cited by Plata dealt with more recent social and political developments. The action and performance artist Althamer (born 1967) began his career as a sculptor, initially creating nude sculptures out of natural materials (e.g., hair, tissue, wax), utilizing instruments and spaces meant to shut off the perception from the outer world, such as capsules, spacesuits, and darkrooms. As a performer, he dealt with social issues. At documenta X in 1997 he broke down the barrier between art and social life by walking through the streets of Kassel dressed in a spacesuit, observing the everyday life of the people in the streets from an "extraterrestrial" perspective. The same year, Althamer engaged the residents of Bródno, a suburb of Warsaw, in a number of activities which resulted in an exhibition at the gallery A.R. in Warsaw and, later on, in the spectacular piece *Bródno 2000*, in which he persuaded some hundred families living in the same high-rise apartment building to switch the lights in their homes either on or off at a given time, making the inscription "2000" appear on the façade of the building. In addition, he organized a music festival in front of the building, bringing over three thousand residents of this "problematic" neighborhood together for this event. Later he handed over the exhibition spaces in which he showed his work to people largely voiceless or even excluded from society, for example to prisoners in Münster, Germany in 2002, to immigrants in Frankfurt am Main in 2003, and to children in Warsaw in 2003. In Vienna he invited homeless people to live in the gallery where he was exhibiting for the duration of the project (for more on his work, see Szablowski 2006).

As can be gathered from this short list of Althamer's actions/performances since 1997, that year he began embarking on projects that transferred the marginalized from the periphery to the center. In this way the spaces in which the privileged, adored artists and their works were admired by an audience, i.e. the public, were relinquished to the marginalized, thus enabling them to become the center of public attention themselves. These artistic actions were clearly deeply political. They might not have dealt with the question of national identity, but they certainly negotiated a common self-understanding. At the heart of Althamer's project lies the issue of the distribution of attention and of possibilities of participation in society – a question theorized by the French philosopher Jacques Rancière (2004) at around the same time. This issue is not restricted to Poland but addresses all contemporary democratic societies. Tackling these issues would open up new perspectives in any of these societies.

Althamer's actions can be seen within the context of the works of certain stage directors working in Germany and Austria at the beginning of the new millennium. Volker Lösch composed the chorus in his Dresden production of the *Oresteia* (2003) with thirty-three unemployed male and female citizens of the town. They spoke for the millions of voiceless unemployed people by discussing their problems and raising their concerns. At the Vienna Festival of 2003, Peter Sellars cast sixteen young male asylum seekers as the mute chorus of the refugees in his production of *Children of Heracles* (after Euripides), which took place inside the historic Reichsratssaal of the Viennese Parliament. The actors discussed the fate of the refugees in Euripides' words. They stood either at the lectern or were positioned on the government's benches. The young men of the chorus, meanwhile, sat on the floor right in the center of this historic place, dressed in their own everyday clothes. The audience was seated on the semicircular benches usually reserved for the members of parliament. Every performance was preceded by a public debate on asylum, in which the refugees could tell their stories before the audience as well as the invited guests from the government and human rights organizations. While in these two cases putting the marginalized on stage not only made them visible but also entailed the risk of exposing them to the gaze of the spectators and exoticizing them, Althamer managed to circumvent this risk through the space distribution, which did not allow for such an exposure.

Taking into account the respective local conditions, be it Warsaw, Frankfurt, or New York, Althamer opened up new possibilities for marginalized groups, empowering them to seize public spaces and gain agency and visibility. In New York, for example, he used the budget provided by the Wrong Gallery for hiring unemployed Polish immigrants first to demolish and then completely renovate the gallery space. His works thus always brought into sharp focus the question of participatory democracies and the criteria for inclusion and exclusion operative within them – a question not only crucial in Poland but in all democracies. Althamer thereby broke open the traditional Polish self-understanding that was hitherto centered on their own particular conditions. Instead, he reached out to connect these conditions with those in other European and Western countries, thus opening up Polish culture to them.

The third example from Plata's list is Krzysztof Warlikowski's abovementioned production of *Electra*. It was his first production of a Greek tragedy, followed one year later by *The Phoenicians* (Municipal Theatre, Beer Sheva, Israel, 1998) before staging *The Bacchae* in 2001. In contrast to other European countries such as England, France, Germany, Italy, or Greece, "in Polish theatre there is no tradition of staging ancient plays" (Niziołek 2001). There had been a few isolated productions, e.g., *The Bacchae* directed by Wacław Radulski at the Teatr Wielki in Lwów in 1933, mentioned in the preface to this book. *Antigone* was staged several times, for example by Helmut Kajzar (Teatr Polski we Wrocławiu 1971), Adam Hanuszkiewicz (Teatr Mały 1973), Andrzej Wajda (Stary Teatr 1984), and Jerzy Grzegorzewski (Teatr im. Stefana Jaracza 1972); Ludwik Ren directed *King Oedipus* (Teatr Dramatyczny 1961) and Zygmunt Hübner the *Oresteia* (Stary Teatr 1982). Konrad Swinarski staged two operas that used adaptations of Greek tragedies as libretti: Igor Stravinsky's *King Oedipus* (Teatr Wielki 1965) and Hans Werner Henze's *The Bassarides*. There were two other productions of *The Bacchae*, the first directed by Eugeniusz Aniszenko in Gniezno in 1979, the second, more than fifteen years later, by Paweł Łysak in Częstochowa in 1995. As stressed in a Warsaw newspaper review, the production in Gniezno was the first performance of the tragedy in Poland since 1933 (*Życie Warszawy*, no. 13, May 17, 1979). It was performed on a bare stage with palace architecture in the background. The only review I found provided two readings of the "austere and static performance." One related the opposition between reason and "the magic of religion and its church appealing to the feelings and emotions of the masses" to the political struggle between the "Shah and Khomeini" far away in Iran. The other emphasized the "universal truth . . . of Euripides' text in a highly readable and expressive manner conveyed to us by the actors" (Blażewicz 1979).

The second production was staged after the collapse of communism. The town in which it took place, Częstochowa, houses the Black Madonna, the national saint and treasure. The actor who played Dionysus, Omar Sangare, was also "of black skin" (Drewniak 1995). According to Drewniak, in the performance "Dionysus and Christ are one, although Euripides' Thebes is not the same as Jerusalem – Jesus/Zagreus arrives today . . . " "Arriving today," he could not take the same appearance as two thousand years ago. It made sense that

> Sangare does not only play the messiah of a new, orgiastic religion; he also appears as a kind of sex idol. His androgyny . . . , enhanced by the exoticism of his dress (a simple bronze-colored tunic) and appearance, is seductive. He announces the possibility of breaking all taboos.

However, the point made by the performance was another one. It turned out that with

> the death of the king, the sacrificial goat, order is restored. Old Cadmus is not chased away but . . . returns to the throne. End of crisis. Order is reestablished, the bacchants leave the messiah. *Ite missa est*. Sangare remains alone and at a loss on the empty stage; folding his hands and arms in a Christ-like gesture, as if to demonstrate that he has an innocent heart, it is as if he was saying: "I did not want this!"
>
> (Drewniak 1995)

According to Drewniak, the reborn Christ/Dionysus was able to overcome the crisis in the community caused by an authoritarian regime only by sacrificing the one who embodied it, even while regretting having to take such brutal measures. If Drewniak was right, the liberation of Thebes from the dictator Pentheus was to be translated as the liberation of Poland from communism brought about by the reborn Christ (the Black Madonna or even Pope John Paul II). After analysis of Warlikowski's *The Bacchae* we shall return to this performance.

None of the productions mentioned above were part of a particular tradition of staging Greek tragedies. When Warlikowski staged Sophocles' *Electra* in 1997 there was no need to refer to or even struggle against an established tradition. He was free to use Greek tragedy in order to rethink and redefine the relationship not only between theatre and society in Poland, but also between Polish and Western European theatre.

With this production, Warlikowski explicitly referred to the war in Yugoslavia, which then no longer interested either the critics or the audiences in Poland. In the reviews it is referred to as "the war we can always see on TV" (cited in Mogilnicka 2010: 77). The female chorus resembled the village women in the documentary photograph in the program notes. It showed the funeral of an immigrant from Offenbach who was killed by Serbians. Underneath it says: "As a dead man he came back to his house in Kosovo where, according to Islamic ritual, the women wept over him for hours" (cited in Mogilnicka 2010: 78). The women in the photograph wore white headscarves and were clothed in simple black dresses with long sleeves, as were the members of the female chorus. The chorus sang partly in ancient Greek, which seemed to have alienated the audience, and moved according to a ceremonial choreography, linked by some critics to a sacrificial ritual.

Warlikowski was accused not only of quoting from his so-called masters, for example Peter Stein's *Oresteia* (Schaubuehne am Halleschen Ufer, Berlin, 1980) in the case of the male chorus dressed in suits and hats in the prologue. The production was also repeatedly denounced as generally resembling German theatre too much with its excessive use of blood, cruelty, and cold distance (Gruszczyński 1997; Węgrzyniak 1997; Drewniak 2007). Moreover, the reviews were patronizing in their mockery of the allusions to the war in Yugoslavia. Only one critic remarked: "If a contemporary director or spectator does not connect the tragedy on the Atrides to the generally known outbursts of hatred, the play will always be a failure . . . Without thinking of Yugoslavia and other situations in which hatred is sown today, *Electra* will remain a bloody fairytale" (Dziewulska 1997). Later another critic not only defended the production but also declared it to be a very special event, stating that with this production Polish theatre had entered a dialogue with Western theatre (Nowak 2005).

Grzegorzewski's directorship at the Teatr Narodowy, Althamer's actions and performances since documenta X, and Warlikowski's *Electra* did in fact mark a turning point. They all redefined the relationship between the performing arts and society. While Grzegorzewski did so by testing the traditional canon and questioning its relevance after the fall of communism,

Althamer and Warlikowski dared to embark on a completely new beginning. Instead of focusing exclusively on the Polish scene, they followed paths that connected Polish art and theatre with that of Western European countries. In their artistic work, both opened up the possibility for a dialogue with other European cultures, emphasizing what Polish culture shared with them instead of highlighting its "otherness."

However, critics felt that with *Electra* Warlikowski had gone "too far." His topicalization of the tragedy in the eyes of the Polish audience was marked by two "mistakes." The first was the choice of the issue. While all over Europe the Yugoslavian war was the topic of heated debates, it did not arouse much interest, let alone passion, in Polish society, whatever the reasons for this may have been. The second was the absence of subtlety in addressing this topic, doing away with trusted hidden allusions that could be interpreted in various ways. However, at least the two critics cited above noted that staging a Greek tragedy in order to establish a particular relationship between theatre and society not only entailed a radical redefinition of this relationship but also a new self-understanding of Polish theatre and society. Staging a Greek tragedy meant opening up Polish theatre to Western cultures where Greek tragedies were a shared and widespread reference point.

When Warlikowski staged another Greek tragedy in Poland four years later, he avoided the two "mistakes" of *Electra*. *The Bacchae* did not address one particular political or social issue which was to be read by all spectators in the same way. It also avoided any kind of "foreign folklore" as the costumes of the female chorus there might have been described. Rather, it used images, objects, sounds, and music known to the spectators from their everyday lives and the omnipresent Catholic Church. Furthermore, even if some objects were used only once for a particular purpose, they were as ambiguous as the images. They allowed for a number of different associations, memories, meanings, or even "readings," as can be gathered from the reviews. While the critic quoted at the beginning of this chapter, for instance, interpreted the first scene as a symbol for the most recent developments in Polish theatre and thus as a self-reflection of theatre (Drewniak), another, referring to the theory of the psychoanalyst Melanie Klein, deemed it the "clinical picture of a disordered, unbalanced childhood" (Niziołek 2008: 87), citing as evidence for this interpretation the "dropped toy, buried in the sand" beneath Dionysus.

My analysis of the performance[1] will focus on two questions. Firstly, how did it redefine the relationship between theatre and society? Secondly, what kind of a search for a new common self-understanding was undertaken and what were its criteria?

The stage space (designed by Małgorzata Szczęśniak, who also designed the costumes) was shared by the actors and some spectators. Stage-left, there was a row of chairs for spectators, the first three remaining empty. The stage and the auditorium were close to each other, with no clear demarcation between them. Some actors entered the stage from the auditorium. The spatial arrangement emphasized that what was going to happen over the next few hours was going to happen to everyone assembled – once again following the maxim *tua res agitur*.

The walls of the stage were of a dull silvery sheet metal, creating a cold atmosphere. The wall stage-right, however, resembled a faded Renaissance fresco. A few objects lay around the space, suggesting the idea that some actions would soon be performed on or with them. They did not call to mind a particular space: stage-right was a small water basin and a bridge, stage-left a staircase, leading to nowhere in particular. The seats for the spectators were aligned with the staircase, on the left side of which stood a huge garbage can. Before it, near the front of the stage, a carpet. To its right was a large wooden table with metal fittings on top. Spread out on the tabletop were a towel, a knife, a loaf of bread, a bottle of vodka, a helmet, and a sword. In the background, white sand covered the floor.

In the beginning there was no light and the space lay hidden in darkness. Very gradually, the new god emerged from it, dressed in a white sweater, trousers, and sneakers. His birth took place in the way described in the opening quotation to this chapter. From the beginning, the audience was faced with the question of what kind of a god this might be, oscillating between animal, child, and man, yet to learn speech. This was not a preexisting god arriving from elsewhere, e.g., Lydia, but a new god, born at this very moment.

Although just come into existence, the ways in which this newly born god was worshipped seemed quite familiar to the spectators. Three elderly women (Stanisława Celińska, Magdalena Kuta, Marta Maj) appeared on stage dressed in black fur coats and holding prayer books in their hands. One of them was holding a statue of the new god. At first glance, they brought to mind the three Marys at Jesus' tomb, as Jan Kott had interpreted the bacchants after Dionysus' "resurrection" from the "tomb" of his prison. The women's first appearance also suggested this idea, despite the colorful ribbons and roses in their hair and the strange makeup on their faces. Their appearance was accompanied by low, entrancing music (composed by Paweł Mykietyn). The one carrying the statue put it on the floor near the water basin and covered it with a glass shrine. Deliberately and trancelike, the three walked to the empty chairs at the staircase and sat down, their gaze fixed on the statue. A very bright light emanated from the statue, which seemed to light up the whole space as in an apotheosis. The women took turns reciting the first chorus song in a low voice, still transfixed by the statue.

Regardless of whether or not the women were supposed to represent the three Marys, any spectator would have been able to identify them as Catholic devotees, adoring a statue of their god in a shrine, saying prayers from their holy book, and entering some kind of an ecstatic trance. The rituals were undoubtedly Catholic in nature. One critic wrote about this scene:

> The daily order to which the spectators belong is dominated by the Christian worldview of a just and merciful god and a sense of sacrifice. This god is opposed to the wild ethic of *The Bacchae*. Warlikowski, knowing this very well, drew on this contrast for the first strong sensation of the spectators. Where had our merciful god gone? Had he been transformed into Dionysus?
> (Gruszczyński 2001)

Tiresias (Lech Łotocki) and Cadmus (Aleksander Bednarz) joined the worshipping of the new god and introduced some new rituals in a rather grotesque scene. Tiresias appeared with a black blindfold, a bottle of vodka in his hand. Cadmus was dressed in a white shirt, black trousers, and a black hat. After both took a gulp from the bottle, they stripped down to their white boxer shorts and knelt down on the carpet. Tiresias took some necklaces made of gigantic wooden beads out of a cardboard box held by Cadmus and hung them around Cadmus' and his own neck. He opened a can and began to apply dark cream on his forehead, chest, and arms, then handed it over to Cadmus, who did the same but extended the application to his bald head. Both began shaking their heads, pretending or attempting to enter a state of ecstasy. They did headstands and remained in this position for a while – two old hippies, left over from the 1960s, i.e., the era of *Dionysus in 69*, reviving these old times and their rituals in order to worship the new god. A slightly different interpretation could be found in another review, which connected Cadmus and Tiresias to more contemporary changes of custom in writing that they were "reminiscent of contemporary Europeans who seek out Far Eastern religions" (Pawłowski 2001). Another critic saw them "transformed into Hindu yogis" (Węgrzyniak 2001).

These two scenes focused the audience's attention on the question of religion and faith. An unknown god was born, but nobody asked who he might be or what kinds of rituals would be appropriate. Instead, the rituals of the Catholic Church in the case of the elderly women, the "mothers," and the rituals of the hippie and flower power movement of the 1960s in the case of the two old men, were used. The discrepancy between the unknown god and the rituals performed for his worship thus came to the fore. While the allusion to the hippie movement remained an isolated reference, the Christian iconography prevailed almost until the cruel end, bringing into focus its inadequacy.

The encounters between Pentheus (Jacek Poniedziałek) and Dionysus were staged as power struggles that mirrored and reversed each other. Pentheus, wearing a bright-red down jacket with a hood, made his first appearance via the auditorium, addressing the audience when he spoke. It seemed that he wrote the names Agave, Ino, and Autonoe on the opened lid of the garbage can for the spectators to memorize them. Before throwing Cadmus' and Tiresias' clothes into the garbage can, he looked at the audience for approval. He clearly felt that he was acting as the spokesperson for the spectators and their own common sense.

Later, Dionysus crawled across the bridge on all fours until he reached the statue. Pentheus went up to him, walking very upright. He looked at and then squatted down beside him. Dionysus answered his questions in a soft tone of voice, smiling at him and playfully twisting his fingers around strands of his curly hair. When Dionysus refused to say "what form he [the god] did assume" (v. 477), Pentheus grabbed a handful of sand, threw it into his face, and jumped up. He went to the table, cut off a slice of bread with the knife and ate it while continuing to interview Dionysus. The encounter ended in a wrestling match. After Pentheus had taken off his red jacket, Dionysus playfully jumped on him. They wrestled. Finally Pentheus lay down on top of Dionysus, bumping his abdomen against him several times, their faces almost touching until Pentheus suddenly leapt up. The sexual undertones of this first encounter, particularly the wrestling match, were emphasized by most of the critics. In his review Grzegorz Niziołek writes: "He (Dionysus) plays with his hair and responds to all of Pentheus' actions empathetically. A child, an animal, a bit coquettish like a homosexual" (Niziołek 2001). And in his book he explains: "Pentheus is convinced that he is confronted with a homosexual who is trying to seduce him" (Niziołek 2008: 79). Rafał Węgrzyniak (2001) identified "a sexual subtext" in the wrestling match.[2]

The first and third encounters were devised symmetrically. After the dressing scene, Pentheus appeared in a white embroidered dress to the muffled sound of church bells, no wig on his bald head.

Dionysus, now wearing the red jacket, stood leaning on the table and cutting a slice of bread. Pentheus walked slowly towards him, barefoot and smiling, holding one hand to his bald head lacking curls. With his other hand he spread open his embroidered dress, presenting himself to the god. When he reached Dionysus, the latter slapped him hard in the face. Pentheus stumbled back, then slapped himself. He knelt, lay down on his back, and stretched out before Dionysus, rubbing his head on Dionysus' foot while clutching the other leg with his hand in an allusion to sadomasochistic sex practices. A strange noise swelled up, increasing in volume and resembling the sound of a roaring, frenetic crowd in a soccer stadium. Dionysus jumped up all of a sudden, grabbed Pentheus by the arm, and dragged him over the sand at the back of the stage, whirling up a cloud of sand in the process. The three devotees stood by the bridge, shouted the words of the chorus song, and laughed loudly, almost hysterically. The noise from the stadium reached its peak. Red light spread over the background. Silence. It was finished. A critic comments: "Does the

FIGURE 6.1 Pentheus (Jacek Poniedziałek) and Dionysus (Andrzej Chyra). Photo: Stefan Okolowicz.

sacrifice end here? Does it entail a transformation? My body, chalice of my blood? The cultural–religious paradigm of the spectators was twisted in the theatrical machinery of deconstruction" (Gruszczyński 2001).

The reversals in the two scenes were obvious. Earlier, Pentheus in his red jacket had loomed over the crouching Dionysus dressed in white, while Dionysus, wearing the red jacket, now stood over Pentheus, clad in white. Pentheus had thrown sand into Dionysus' face. Now Dionysus slapped him. Pentheus had cut a slice of bread and eaten it before the wrestling match. Dionysus did the same before dragging Pentheus to his death. However, while Dionysus was not submissive but rather coquettish and playful in the beginning, e.g., when caressing his curls and starting the wrestling match, Pentheus handed himself over unconditionally to Dionysus, who was going to crush him. In fact, they appeared as each other's monstrous doppelgängers, although by the end there was no doubt as to who was the more monstrous of the two.

Although at this point we can still not be entirely sure who the new god might be, it can be determined with certainty who this god is not. He is by no means Christ resurrected as in the production in Częstochowa six years earlier, nor is he one of the "gods" worshipped in the hippie movement. One critic suggested he was no god at all but only "an idol, invented by the crowd" (Rataj 2001). In any case, he is not a redemptive god but a god of revenge and destruction – a twin brother of the former authoritarian ruler, only mightier and more cruel.

Agave appeared on stage, her face and dress smeared with blood, holding a huge trunk of a fir tree in her hands – probably the tree on which Dionysus had placed Pentheus. She threw herself on it, dragged it over the sand, and sat down on it as if she wanted to ride it. Her belly was round. A moment later, she gave birth to the bloody head of her dead son. She placed the newborn head on the phallic thyrsus-like trunk. In the opening scene, Dionysus was born without a head. Now it is only a head that is squeezed out. While Dionysus' birth took place in darkness and semi-darkness, the birth of Pentheus' head occurred in full light.

During the report of the messenger, the bacchants had sat at the table drinking milk and eating bread, sharing it with the messenger. They wiped off their makeup and put on their shoes. Now they got up from the chairs, picked up the table, and set it down front stage in the middle. While Agave crawled in their direction, they placed two chairs on the left side of the table, put on their fur coats and left, accompanied by a strange rattling sound coming from the back.

Agave dragged the tree trunk with Pentheus' head on top to the table and sat down on the tabletop. She still held the trunk in her hand and caressed it as if it were a human body. Cadmus appeared, his white boxer shorts smeared with red blood. He had on the red jacket, first worn by Pentheus and then by Dionysus. He held a metal bucket in each of his hands, which he set down behind the table.

During the recognition scene Agave lay stretched out on the table as if she was about to be operated on, the trunk still between her legs. Cadmus sat down on one of the chairs, holding Agave's hand and then caressing her hair. He got up, removed the trunk from her legs and the head from the trunk. Agave, still on the table, curled up in a fetal position. When Cadmus stood before her, Pentheus' head in his hands, she smiled at it. As he put her hand on the severed head he asked her: "And whose head do you hold in your hand?" (v. 1276). She grasped at it, looked closely at the very realistic head, and touched it. She turned her head in agony, groaning, screaming, and making animal sounds. While Cadmus held her head, she continued to scream. When he returned to his chair, Agave sat up slowly and placed Pentheus' severed head between her knees, after which she continued to caress it. After a while, she slid down from the table, placed the head at its center and emptied the two buckets Cadmus had brought with him to the left and right of the head. Two large shapeless pieces of raw meat came into view – more of Pentheus' remains. A torn-up human body was displayed on the table and there it would remain, never to be made whole or brought to life again.

The dimming light was focused on Agave and Cadmus, sitting side by side at the table in silence. Finally they both disappeared in the darkness, from which the new god had been born in the beginning. He did not reappear. All that remained was darkness.

The production was received mostly but not entirely with enthusiasm. One critic, for example, called it a "scandal," for "in the performance there are words but there is no content, there are ideas but there is no form, there are actors but no roles" (Kowalczyk 2001). Another complained: "The least we should be able to expect from theatre is that it speaks about faith in general, a faith independent of time and space, and also about the fate of man, incapable of recognizing God . . . As it turns out, no conflict takes shape in Warlikowski's production, no clear question is posed . . . To present chaos and no world in the theatre is the latest fashion" (Rembowska 2001). A third hopes that no one will go to see *The Bacchae* but will instead remind themselves of what "Jan Kott wrote in his essay 'The Bacchae or the Eating of the God' on the mystery of Euripides' play" (Waker 2001). It is noteworthy that Kott is often cited as a reference in these reviews.

With the exception of the first, these negative reviews seem to suggest that this production addressed the question of faith and religion (if in an inappropriate and highly unsatisfactory manner). This basic assumption was also shared by most of those critics who praised and celebrated the production. Łukasz Drewniak began his review with the statement: "Krzysztof Warlikowski speaks about who God is, how we know Him and to whom He shows himself. And he does so with a passion which I have not seen in Polish theatre for a long time." Later he explained: "He interweaves Greek and Christian threads, showing what the next appearance of Christ will be like. In his vision, this will be another Christ – Christ-Dionysus . . . God's image disappears and reappears" (Drewniak 2001). Another critic called the production "a drama of today's faith and doubt" (Pawłowski, 2001) and a third asked "where the delicate demarcation line between faith and madness" was and "whether it is really possible to sacrifice everything for your faith" (Rataj 2001).

The critics quoted above who were in favor of the production discussed the question of faith in the performance with a view to the situation in contemporary Polish society. Pawłowski (2001) understood it as "a voice speaking for tolerance and a warning against sects" and related it to "the ambivalent attitude of contemporary culture towards faith. It also demonstrates that we are not the first to be torn between faith and doubt." Gruszczyński explores the relationship between theatre and faith in more depth:

> Is it theatre's purpose to touch on the sacrum without reverting to kitsch or banality, the purpose of knowledge and consecration still fulfilling the demands of the sacrum? . . . Should we reflect on whether *The Bacchae* is to be regarded as a commentary on today's spiritual situation? Are we being warned not to submit to fanatic emotions too easily? . . . The production is another step

towards expanding the limits of theatre. Used as a tool for knowledge and in agreement with the demands made by the sacrum, theatre is capable of igniting a deep intellectual discourse, based on the profoundest emotions.

(Gruszczyński 2001)

Warlikowski's *The Bacchae* appears to have defined the relationship between theatre and society in such a way that theatre was accorded the license, indeed the duty, to address questions of faith and religion in a society soaked in but still uncertain about religion and its role. With Warlikowski, theatre was once again invited to deal with the sacred. Despite the various possible readings of the production, this particular interpretation, favored by the critics, is substantiated by the consistent use of Christian iconography. Even objects that did not trigger any obvious Christian associations at first had to be seen in that context as the performance progressed. This was certainly true of the table, which initially might have only brought to mind a garage, rural kitchen, or slaughterhouse (Niziołek 2006). However, after the three bacchants made their entry, sat down on the chairs next to the table, and sang their first song, the table began to resemble an altar. This sense was enhanced when Pentheus went to the table, cut off a slice of bread, and began to eat it before the wrestling match. Although an everyday action, the Christian context and the role of the bacchants called to mind the Last Supper, in addition to foreshadowing Pentheus' cruel death. The loaf of bread of course symbolized the human body: "Take; eat; this is my body" (Matthew 26.26). Dionysus repeating the action further emphasized this relationship and reversed the Christian paradigm. It could no longer be overlooked that here, "in the truest communion of man with God, it is man, not God, who is eaten up" (Drewniak 2001). The table, now a slaughter-bench as well as an ancient altar, displayed the raw flesh of the sacrificial "animal" to be consumed by the community of believers.

In Soyinka's version the relationship between Dionysus and Jesus was established via the symbolic wine. The dressing scene was replaced with one of the two Jacobean mask scenes, which showed the wedding in Cana where Jesus transformed water into wine. The wine spurting from Pentheus' head thus alluded both to Dionysus, the god of wine, and to Jesus, who likened the wine to his blood at the Last Supper. In Zé Celso's *The Bacchae* the wine also figured prominently, although the allusion to Jesus was already made when Zeus said on the occasion of Dionysus' birth: "Drink the blood, eat this raw flesh." In both these cases, the bread, which Jesus called his own body and raw flesh at the Last Supper and shared with his disciples, was not referenced directly – neither in the dialogue nor as a prop. In Warlikowski's production, however, it figured prominently. But while the bread was eaten – by Pentheus, Dionysus, and his followers – the raw flesh on the table remained untouched, not followed by a *omophagia*, neither affirming a community nor restored to wholeness and life. Maybe, as one critic suggested, it would later be thrown into the garbage can that stood behind the table (Niziołek 2006).

In contrast to the performance in Częstochowa six years before this production, Dionysus did not reappear here nor was there an end to the crisis. The final image of Agave and Cadmus sitting on the chairs beside the table with their heads hanging, Pentheus' remains laid out before them as they gradually dissolved in the darkness, suggested that the crisis was still raging. This impression was not diminished by the fact that Cadmus appeared for the final scene in the red jacket, the symbol of power. It only hinted at the possibility of the former representative regaining control, which was certainly not a promise of renewal.

Despite the exhaustive use of Christian iconography, it should not be taken for granted that Warlikowski's production was related to issues of religion or the sacrum at all. Starting with Grotowski, Polish theatre has been enjoying a long tradition of dealing with the sacred beyond Christianity.[3] In transferring the messianic idea of the romantic paradigm from society to the theatre, from politics to acting, Grotowski developed the idea of the "holy" actor and of acting as "a serious and solemn act of revelation" (Grotowski 1968: 210).[4] His notion of the holy actor was best approximated by Ryszard Cieślak in Calderón's *The Constant Prince* (1965) in Słowacki's adaptation. The critic Jósef Kelera wrote about his acting: "A sort of psychic illumination emanates from the actor ... At any moment the actor will levitate ... He is in a state of grace" (cited in Grotowski 1968: 109).

In 1977 Grotowski's former collaborator Włodzimierz Staniewski founded his own theatre group in Gardzienice, a small village in the southeast of Poland, 100 miles from the Ukrainian border. This group, the Gardzienice Theatre Association, developed another form of "holy" theatre based on their research among rural people for "native culture," focusing on voice, music, and sound. Their performances grew out of songs in Polish, Yiddish, Greek, Latin, and other languages. *Avvakum* (1983), developed while martial law was in effect, drew heavily on the Russian Orthodox context, while *Carmina Burana* (1990) referred back to the thirteenth-century Carmina Burana song cycle. All of the group's performances speak to their search for a new spirituality without their members necessarily practicing any particular religion (Allain 2004).

In 1996 Grzegorz Bral and Anna Zubrzycka-Gałaj left the group and founded their own, Pieśń Kozła (Song of a Goat – τραγῳδία). Their first and eponymous production premiered in 1997 in Wrocław. It was a particular version of *The Bacchae*, highlighting the dithyramb and the lament and inspired by folk songs and dances from Greek Epirus, Romania, and Albania. The singing and dancing were at the heart of the performance, pointing back to the ancient Greek chorus while also conjuring up a new spirituality in the actors and spectators.

Another group with a similar approach is Teatr Zar, founded by Jarosław Fret in 2003. The performances are all based on song. The members did not belong to any particular religious group. Teatr Zar also strives to put across a particular spirituality. In this sense all the groups in the genealogy that began with Grotowski deal with the sacred (Innes and Shevtsova 2013).

The work of these groups makes it difficult to give sole credit to Warlikowski's *The Bacchae* for reintroducing the sacred to Polish theatre and society. It should instead be seen as a searing critique of religion, pseudo-religion, and the transfer of religious attitudes to other fields of society. The new god – Dionysus – should not necessarily be conceived of as the founder of a new religion or sect. He also symbolizes deified ideologies, beliefs, convictions, or values of all kinds, even individuals. In other words, mass phenomena such as nationalism, capitalism, or consumerism, to name just a few, take the place of religion or even individual apotheosis, although in the end they turn out to be as devastating as Dionysus, the god of revenge and destruction.

The relationship between theatre and society as established in *The Bacchae* can be described as a demystifying agent, not celebrating the mystery but tearing away the obscuring shroud surrounding it. The production showed deification and the religious attitude towards new trends in society as disastrous, promising the people happiness and redemption but in reality leading to catastrophe. In fact, in *The Bacchae*, theatre turned into "a tool for knowledge . . . capable of igniting a deep intellectual discourse" without pretending to know "the truth" that the spectators should learn as their lesson.

The intellectual discourse is deepened by the ambiguity of the production. Since it invited the spectators to interpret it each in their own way, it challenged their reflection. Discussing the performance potentially led not only to a new understanding of the play but also to a new common self-understanding of all those involved. Theatre is unable to outline, let alone define, a new cultural identity. Rather, it is engaged in the ongoing critique of society and the search for new identities, made possible by the critique. Theatre – like Dionysus and his followers – is able to let the crisis that haunts society emerge from under the surface and take a clear shape, without, however, being capable of overcoming it by itself.

Warlikowski's *The Bacchae* bestowed the function of social criticism on theatre, almost forcing the spectators to recognize the dangers of lionizing people and ideologues and eliciting strong emotions from them, potentially leading to catharsis. Aesthetic experience as liminal experience here was not meant as an encounter with the sacred. Instead, it had to be sensed as a painful wound that would continue to hurt for a while. Religions of all kind and the worship of all gods was dismissed as the basis of a common self-understanding and cornerstone of cultural identity. The production raised the question whether there could ever be something like a clearly defined cultural identity which did not automatically lead to crisis and destruction – an "empty city," as Jan Kott put it.

The issues Warlikowski addressed in *The Bacchae*, however, were not relevant to the Polish context alone. Moreover, by staging a second Greek tragedy, he continued the dialogue with other European/Western cultures that regard Greek tragedies as their common cultural heritage but which can still be applied to each context separately. This possibility was explored in more depth in Warlikowski's *(A)pollonia* (Warsaw 2009), which was widely celebrated in Warsaw and abroad, e.g., at the Avignon Festival in 2010, where it was hailed as the best production of the entire festival by *Le Figaro*. It dealt with the problem of (self-)sacrifice by drawing on fragments from the *Oresteia*, Euripides' *Iphigenia* and *Alcestis*.

Others soon followed Warlikowski's example in internationalizing Polish theatre.[5] During the theatre season of 2006/2007 the Stary Teatr at Cracow organized a festival with the title "Re-Visions/Antiquity," presenting Staniewski's *Iphigenia* and *Electra* (Gardzienice, Lublin), Jan Klata's (born 1973) production of the *Oresteia* and Maria Spiss' (born 1977) production of Sophocles' *Ajax*, and Dimiter Gotscheff's *The Persians* (Deutsches Theater Berlin), along with productions of Jan Kochanowski's *Discharge of the Greek Envoys* (Michał Zadara – born 1976), Racine's *Phèdre* (also Michał Zadara), and Krystian Lupa's *Zarathustra* (adapted from Nietzsche's *Thus Spoke Zarathustra* and Einar Schleef's Nietzsche Trilogy). The festival aimed to reflect on the common cultural heritage of European countries and the possibilities, indeed necessity, of constantly appropriating and transforming it, e.g., through processes of rewriting. The announcement of the festival read: "The question faced by today's theatre with regard to a conscious dialogue with ancient Greece is not only a question about heritage and continuity but first and foremost a question of our identity . . . Exploring ancient Greece in today's theatre must therefore be seen as an attempt to construct a perspective through which we can look upon ourselves."[6] With Warlikowski's *The Bacchae* it seems that Polish theatre returned to the common European context where Poland traditionally had its place before it was carved up by the Russians, Prussians, and Austrians, as the Kochanowski (1530–1584) staging confirmed. By using this Greek tragedy in his unique way, Warlikowski contributed to the ongoing discussion of how to productively apply this common heritage to today's societies.

Notes

1. I have not seen the performance myself. The material I am analyzing includes a video recording of the performance, some reviews, the book by Niziołek (2008); and an interview I conducted with the director on February 29, 2012 when, on the

occasion of his most recent production, *African Tales*, he was a guest at the Schaubuehne Berlin.
2. However, he only touches upon it there, his focus being the question of power.
3. The fusion of antiquity and (Slavonic) Christianity and of Dionysus and Christ has a long-standing history in the Polish theatre tradition. It can be traced back to Stanisław Wyspiański's *Akropolis*, in which the Wawel Castle took the shape of Troy, and the Vistula river was identified with the Scamander. In the finale, the triumphant figure of Dionysus–Salvator emerges on the ruins of the Wawel Cathedral out of the dialectic between ancient Greece (thesis) and Christianity/biblical tradition (antithesis). This heavily symbolic image reappeared in the staging of *Akropolis* (1962) by Jerzy Grotowski and Józef Szajna, who showed Auschwitz as an integral part of the Greco-Christian legacy. Recently, the fusion of these two traditions was reinterpreted by Leszek Kolankiewicz in his book on the ritual of Dziady. Kolankiewicz (1999) connects the Greek veneration of the dead (and tragedy) with old Slavonic rites of communion with the dead called Dziady (and Adam Mickiewicz's *Dziady*).
4. See chapter 2, this volume.
5. This internationalization did not occur solely by means of recourse to Greek tragedies. That same year, Warlikowski himself staged Sarah Kane's *Cleansed*, which was just as controversial as *The Bacchae*. In fact, the two plays were seen and interpreted in conjunction with each other. *Cleansed* also became a significant moment in the reception of Western plays and staging techniques, as there soon followed a wave of interest in foreign, mainly German theatre styles, a tendency which continues even today. Both *The Bacchae* and *Cleansed* fulfilled an important function in initiating the process of mediation between Polish and foreign theatre forms.
6. At http://www.stary.pl/pl/re_wizje/_antyk (accessed June 21, 2013).

References

Allain, Paul. 2004. *Gardzienice: Polish Theatre in Transition*. New York: Routledge.
Blażewicz, Olgierd. 1979. "Eurypides w Gnieznie" [Euripides in Gniezno]. *Tydzień* 21. May 27.
Drewniak, Łukasz. 1995. "Czarny mesjasz" [Black messiah]. *Teatr* 3. March 1.
Drewniak, Łukasz. 2001. "Goście wieczerzy Panskiej" [Guests at God's supper]. *Przekrój* 11. March 18.
Drewniak, Łukasz. 2006. "Tsunami Młodości" [Tsunami of Youth]. In *Strategie Publiczne, Strategie Prywatne. Teatr polski 1990–2005*. Edited by Tomasz Plata, 102–119. Warsaw: Świat Literacki.
Drewniak, Łukasz. 2007. "Serce w celofanie" [Heart in cellophane]. *Przekrój* 6.08. February 8.
Dziewulska, Małgorzata. 1997. "Po premierze" [After the premiere]. *Didaskalia* 17: 7.
Grotowski, Jerzy. 1968. *Towards a Poor Theatre*. New York: Simon and Schuster.
Gruszczyński, Piotr. 1997. "W poszukiwaniu własnego języka" [In search of a language of his own]. *Tygodnik Powszechny* 6. February 9.

Gruszczyński, Piotr. 2001. "Obcy Bóg" [Strange-God]. *Tygodnik Powszechny* 9. March 4.
Innes, Christopher and Maria Shevtsova. 2013. *Introduction to Theatre Directors*. Cambridge: Cambridge University Press.
Kolankiewicz, Leszek. 1999. *Dziady. Teatr święta zmarłych*. Gdańsk: Słowo/Obraz Terytoria.
Kowalczyk, Janusz. 2001. "Tania jatka" [Cheap butchery]. *Rzeczpospolita* 36.
Mogilnicka, Krystyna. 2010. "Sophocles' *Electra* by Krzysztof Warlikowski: Transgression of the Hero." In *Tragic Heroines on Ancient and Modern Stages*. Edited by Mariade Fátima Silva and Susana Hora Marques, 75–86. Coimbra: University of Coimbra Press.
Niziołek, Grzegorz. 2001. "Muzyka 'Bachantek." *Didaskalia* 42. April 1.
Niziołek, Grzegorz. 2006. "Historia stołu" [History of the table]. *Didaskalia* 71/02. April 3.
Niziołek, Grzegorz. 2008. *Warlikowski. Extra ecclesiam*. Cracow: Homini.
Nowak, Maciej. 2005. "My, czyli nowy teatr" [We, or a new theatre]. *Notatnik teatralny* 35.04. January 28.
Pawłowski, Roman. 2001. "'Bachantki' Eurypidesa w teatrze Rozmaitości" [Euripides' *The Bacchae* in the Teatr Rozmaitości]. *Gazeta Wyborcza*, February 13.
Plata, Tomasz. 2006. "Osobiste Zobowiązania." In *Strategie Publiczne, Strategie Prywatne. Teatr polski 1990–2005*. Edited by Tomasz Plata, 217–238. Warsaw: Świat Literacki.
Rancière, Jacques. 2004. *The Politics of Aesthetics: The Distribution of the Sensible*. Edited and translated by Gabriel Rockhill.New York: Continuum.
Rataj, Agnieszka. 2001. "Przedstawienie nie dla czytelników 'Mitologii' Parandowskiego" [A production not meant for the readers of Parandowski's *Mythology*]. *Rzeczpospolita*.
Rembowska, Aleksandra. 2001. "Po co komu tragedia?" [Why and for whom this tragedy?]. *Więź* 4.
Szablowski, Stach. 2006. "Spektakle z rzeczywistości." In *Strategie Publiczne, Strategie Prywatne. Teatr polski 1990–2005*. Edited by Tomasz Plata, 182–201. Warsaw: Świat Literacki.
Waker, Jacek. 2001. *"Zjadanie własnego ogona" [Eating up one's own tail]*. Życie.
Wanat, Andrzej. 1997. "Po katastrofie" [After the catastrophe]. In Wanat, Andrzej, *Pochwała teatru* [In praise of theater]. Warsaw: Oficyna Wydawnicza Errata.
Węgrzyniak, Rafał. 1997. "Czystka w Argos" [Cleaning up in Argos]. *ODRA* 5. May 1.
Węgrzyniak, Rafał. 2001. "Dionizos Nadchodzi" [Dionysus arrives]. *ODRA* 5. May 1. At http://www.stary.pl/pl/re_wizje/_antyk. Accessed April 12, 2012.

BLACKWELL BRISTOL LECTURES ON GREECE, ROME AND THE CLASSICAL TRADITION

Part III

Productive Encounter or Destructive Clash of Cultures?

Dionysus arrives in Greece from Asia as a stranger in order to introduce his cult. This provokes a productive encounter – as with Tiresias and Cadmus – as well as a clash, leading to the dismemberment of his opponent Pentheus. When Greek tragedies began to be performed with regularity at theatres in India, Japan, and China in the 1960s, this also resulted both in productive encounters and clashes between Greek/European/Western and the Japanese, Indian, or Chinese/Asian cultures. This was especially true for performances of *The Bacchae*.

In each of the productions discussed in the third and final part of this book, the difficulty was not only how to combine elements from two different theatre cultures. The challenge was not just to bring together Greek tragedy with another performance style, e.g., different traditional theatre forms as in Suzuki Tadashi's productions or a single one such as Kathakali in India or

---

Dionysus Resurrected: Performances of Euripides' The Bacchae in a Globalizing World, First Edition. Erika Fischer-Lichte.
© 2014 Erika Fischer-Lichte. Published 2014 by John Wiley & Sons, Ltd.

Beijing Opera in China. That is to say that the hurdle to be overcome was not just aesthetic in nature. The challenge, in each case, went hand in hand with very specific cultural as well as political problems. Aesthetic responses had to be identified in conjunction with solutions for certain cultural and political problems.

The performances under discussion deal very differently with these issues. For instance, there is a differentiation between the level of the represented and that of representation. While the first highlighted a clash of cultures, e.g., state vs. religion, male vs. female, democratic vs. authoritarian, Japanese vs. American, the second accomplished a productive encounter. In the Kathakali case, the production was seen by the artists involved as the result of a productive encounter, while the Greek critics in Delphi regarded it as the manifestation of a clash of cultures. In the third example, the dominance and demands of the American side led to the dismemberment of Beijing Opera as a particular theatre form.

The productions of *The Bacchae* to be discussed, i.e., as interpreted in Suzuki's performance style and through Kathakali and Beijing Opera, adapted different shapes and functions of Dionysus. They brought about a union and a restoration of wholeness out of fragmented or diverse elements in a manner similar to the god when he united not only the citizens of the polis but also all of its inhabitants into a festive community. On the other hand, they led to the dismemberment either of the tragedy or of the theatre form, depending on the perspective and perception of the parties involved. In all three versions the performances showed Dionysus as the god of productivity, of destruction, and of synthesis and, thereby, as the god befitting a paradoxical world.

7

Dismemberment and the Quest for Wholeness
Suzuki Tadashi's *The Bacchae* in Japan and on World Tour (1978–2008)

The 1960s in Japan were marked as much by rebellion, upheaval, and change as in Europe and the United States. The modernization of the country that began after the opening up of Japan (1853) during the Meiji era (1868–1912) had been continuously pushed by the government after World War II until it reached a peak in the 1960s. Because of the US occupation a new wave of modernization swept the country, permeating it so thoroughly that no aspect of Japanese life remained untouched, be it politics, law, the economy, education, or the arts. Modernization at that time was not seen from the perspective of "multiple modernities," a term coined many years later by the sociologist Shmuel N. Eisenstadt (2003). It was instead perceived as Westernization based on pure imitation, which soon brought about the devaluation and negation of traditional Japanese values, customs, habits, and ways of life – a "dismemberment" of traditional Japanese culture and self-understanding. Westernization had resulted in a loss of self through the all-encompassing identification with the Other. In the 1960s and early 1970s the young generation of Japanese rebelled against this situation and demanded decisive cultural changes.

The protests first erupted in 1960 and were directed at the planned US–Japan Mutual Security Treaty. They intensified when the United States entered the Vietnam War and went on for fifteen years, thus continuing

---

Dionysus Resurrected: Performances of Euripides' The Bacchae in a Globalizing World, First Edition. Erika Fischer-Lichte.
© 2014 Erika Fischer-Lichte. Published 2014 by John Wiley & Sons, Ltd.

even after the treaty had been signed and implemented. Over the course of these years they exerted an enduring effect on Japanese society.

In the late 1960s, new theatre forms sprang up – the so-called *angura*, meaning underground theatre, and, later on, the *shogekijo*, meaning Little Theatre Movement. These new theatre forms, which were to be subsumed under one of these labels, were opposed not only to the social and political situation but also to Shingeki, the "modern" Japanese theatre. Founded during the Meiji era, it was created to allow for encounters with European drama and its realistic–psychological approach to performance. The first European plays to be shown, e.g., Shakespeare's *The Merchant of Venice* and Schiller's *Wilhelm Tell*, were adapted for the Japanese stage in Kabuki style. In 1909, however, Tsubouchi Shoyo, the founder of the Bungei Kyokei (Literary Society, 1906), which had been conceived to promote Western literature in Japan, opened an acting school to train men and women in realistic–psychological acting. Shakespeare, Ibsen, and Chekhov were taught. The aim of introducing Western drama was to bring about the literarization of theatre, which provided the basis for this new form of spoken theatre.

The proponents of Shingeki found traditional forms such as Noh and Kabuki aesthetically outdated and sterile. They believed that these forms of expression were unable to respond to and deal with the changed conditions of Japanese society, especially when it came to the problems of modernization. Through recourse to realistic–psychological theatre from Europe, they attempted to develop modern Japanese society and present it with a model.

Based on André Antoine's Théâtre libre in Paris and Otto Brahm's Freie Bühne in Berlin, Osanai Kaoru and the Kabuki actor Ichikawa Sadanji II founded the Jiyu Gekijo (Free Stage) in 1909. Its first performance took place on November 27, 1909, in a theatre modeled after Max Reinhardt's Kammerspiele (Chamber Theatre). It opened with *John Gabriel Borkman*, the first Ibsen play ever performed in Japan. The production intertwined elements of realistic–psychological theatre with those of classical Kabuki. Here, for the first time, the play seemed to have been more important than the acting. One critic wrote: "It is the play that matters, not the actors. Don't be so proud of yourselves, Actors!" (SM 1909, cited in Mori Mitsuya 2010: 76). The performance marked the beginning of Ibsen's widespread popularity in Japanese theatre, which was highly important because of its great impact on the history of theatre and society.

The early high point of Shingeki, which proved its capacity to intervene in current social debates, was the first production of *A Doll's House* in November 1911. Directed by Shimamura Hogetsu, it starred Matsui Sumako, a young actress who had received her training at Tsubouchi's school. At that time it was still unusual to see actresses on stage, since the law of 1630 prohibiting women from performing in public had only recently been rescinded. Matsui Sumako was indeed the first to practice a completely new style of acting. Her realistic–psychological performance enabled the spectators to identify with regular people facing common problems that were relevant to their own lives. According to the critics, she succeeded in emotionally drawing the audiences into the performance.

With this performance, theatre practitioners and audiences joined the discussion on the role of women in Japanese society, which had become salient following the Russo-Japanese War in 1905 and centered on the concept of "the new woman" as promulgated by the "Bluestockings" women's movement. Shingeki proved its ability to take on a social and political function that traditional forms of theatre did not seem capable of fulfilling.

Shingeki, by virtue of its realism and – as far as the leftist movements were concerned – its socialist realism, continued to serve important social and political purposes during the Meiji era and well into the 1930s. By the 1950s, however, it was Shingeki that seemed aesthetically outmoded and sterile. This meant the end of realism in Japanese theatre, which had initially been intended to further the process of modernization in Japan through the imitation of Western models. Shingeki tried to eschew the crisis by staging Western plays that were not considered realistic theatre. In 1960 Beckett's *Waiting for Godot* premiered in Japan, staged by the Shingeki group Bungaku-za and directed by Ando Shinya. The same year Ionesco's *Rhinoceros* was shown, followed one year later by *The Chairs* and Beckett's *Act Without Words* and in 1962 by Edward Albee's *Zoo Story*. Although the performances of the so-called Theatre of the Absurd were received by the rebellious younger generation as a source of inspiration, this did not prevent them from founding their own theatres set to launch a radically new beginning.

The Little Theatre Movement was, in fact, partly informed by translations of absurdist and other contemporary Western plays, among them Arthur Miller's *The American Dream*, Tennessee Williams' *Suddenly Last Summer*, Harold Pinter's *The Dumb Waiter*, and Tankred Dorst's *Die Kurve* (The Curve). It was also influenced by contemporary Japanese plays, such as Mishima Yukio's Noh adaptation *Yoroboshi* (The Tired Boy) or Fukuda Yoshiyuki's *Omoidashicha Ikenai* (Do Not Remember). However, it differed significantly from Shingeki in that it shifted the focus from the text to the body of the actors/performers.

Among the new groups that emerged in the second half of the 1960s in opposition to Shingeki were the Waseda Shogekijo, which grew out of a students' theatre group and was led by Suzuki Tadashi, and the group Gendaijin Gekijo (Contemporary Theatre), founded by Ninagawa Yukio and others. These groups disapproved of Shingeki as a mere imitation of Western theatre and instead drew heavily on traditional Japanese theatre forms. Yet they, too, strove to create a new modern theatre better attuned to Japanese sensibilities than Shingeki. From the 1970s onwards Suzuki and Ninagawa became internationally known for their productions of Greek tragedies – Suzuki, in particular, for *The Trojan Women* (1974) and *The Bacchae* (1978); Ninagawa for *Oedipus the King* (1976) and *Medea* (1978).[1]

Greek tragedies had never formed a constituent part of the repertoire of Shingeki. There had been a few isolated productions during the Meiji era and shortly thereafter. In 1894 Kawakami Otojiro staged *Oedipus the King*. A reformer of Kabuki, he belonged to the so-called Shinpa, a "new Kabuki," which staged new plays, written according to modern European dramatic standards. Between 1899 and 1902 he toured the United States and Europe with his troupe. He chose traditional Kabuki plays for his tour but changed them significantly to suit what he believed was Western taste. Since the 1630 prohibition against women on stage was still in effect, Kawakami's wife Sada Yakko, a trained dancer and geisha, only took over the leading roles once they had embarked on their international tour (which began in San Francisco in 1899), where she immediately became the star of the company. In France and Germany, where theatre artists were fed up with all forms of realistic theatre, particularly naturalism, the troupe's performances were celebrated as a model for the theatre of the future, which European avant-gardists had been looking for. A Berlin newspaper commented:

> What we are able to see, conceive and understand – the outer appearance, the physical – . . . is anything but naïve, undeveloped, juvenile, an art form of the past, which lies behind us and which we surpassed. It is still before us, it is imminent, perhaps we are steering towards it . . . We are looking at the future.
> (*Der Tag*, quoted in N. N. 1902; see also Fischer-Lichte 2009)

While the Japanese turned toward realistic–psychological theatre as practiced by Stanislavsky in search of a modern theatre, the European avant-gardists considered traditional Japanese theatre as their model.

Since the production of *Oedipus the King* was staged five years before the tour, it can safely be assumed that it was adapted in the Kabuki style of Shinpa. In 1916 Kawakami once again staged the tragedy, this time together with the Geijutsuza theatre company founded by Shimamura Hogetsu and Matsui Sumako, the director of the first Japanese production of *A Doll's House* and the actress who played Nora in the realistic–psychological style. In this production Matsui Sumako played the part of Jocasta. It is very likely that this second production of *Oedipus the King*, twenty-two years after the first, adhered to the realistic style. A history of Japanese theatre further mentions a production of Sophocles' *Elektra* (in Hofmannsthal's version), staged in 1913 by the Koshu gekidan company led by Matsui Shoyo. Kawai

Takeo, a famous *onnagata* of the Shinpa, played Electra (see Ozasa Yoshio 1985: 155–156, quoted in Ruperti 2011: 140). There is no mention of other performances of Greek tragedies.

Two developments led up to Suzuki and Ninagawa's productions of Greek tragedies. The first sprang from university activities, as did Suzuki's theatre work. At the end of the 1950s a group of professors and students at Tokyo University founded the Girisha-higeki-kenyûkai, the "Seminar on Greek Tragedy." It proceeded from an academic, historical interest and aimed at reconstructing the performance style prevalent in Athens in the fifth century BCE. The students were encouraged to translate the texts themselves and then reconstruct the staging, including the costumes, as "faithfully" as possible. The result of their efforts was shown in a production of *Oedipus the King* in 1958. Other productions followed on a yearly basis – *Antigone*, *Prometheus Bound*, *Agamemnon*, *Philoctet*, *The Trojan Women*, *Heracles*, *The Persians*, *The Bacchae*, *The Suppliant Women*, and *Seven Against Thebes*.

The performances usually took place in June at the open air theatre of the concert hall Hibiya-ongaku-dô in a park in central Tokyo. The chorus songs were sung and accompanied by dancing. Although the cast consisted mainly of students, it also included a few professional actors and dancers (in the chorus). At the performance of *Agamemnon* (1961), masks based on ancient Greek models were used for the first time. Mori Mitsuya, who directed *The Bacchae*, introduced the ancient Greek convention of using only three male actors. Because of the enormous size of the space, which encompassed 2,500 seats, the actors performed exaggerated gestures and employed microphones, as their voices were not yet sufficiently trained. The performances became very popular. Since *Prometheus Bound* they were regularly sold out. In 1968 the last performance, *Seven Against Thebes*, took place. The performances of the Seminar on Greek Tragedy seem also to have inspired some professional theatres to stage Greek tragedies. In 1959, the same year as the Seminar on Greek Tragedy, the Engekiza Theatre in Tokyo presented *Antigone*, and, in the late 1960s, in the context of the protests against the Vietnam War, several theatres performed *The Trojan Women*, albeit in Sartre's version.

The other series of events goes back to the Noh actor Kanze Hisao and his cooperation with Jean-Louis Barrault, made possible by a scholarship from the French government. In 1963 Kanze lived in Paris for six months and studied the local theatre scene. This included Barrault's 1955 "Brazilian" *Oresteia* into which Pierre Boulez had incorporated Noh music. It is very likely that this performance suggested to him the idea of a certain kinship between Greek tragedy and Noh. This idea was probably further substantiated when Kanze arranged a program consisting of Noh pieces for the Herodes Atticus Theatre in Athens in 1965, where almost exclusively Greek plays had been performed up to that point. In 1971 Kanze, together with his younger brother Kanze Hideo and the celebrated Kyogen actor Nomura Mansaku, founded the theatre company Mei no Kai (Society of Darkness), which staged several Greek tragedies in the style of Noh, Kyogen, and Kabuki: *Oedipus the King* (1971), *Agamemnon* (1972), and *Medea* (1975). In the program notes to *Oedipus the King*, Kanze Hisao explained that "the reason we picked a Greek play is possibly because of Jean-Louis Barrault. Noh and Greek drama have common ground between them because their original theatrical characteristic is the confrontation between Man and Fate" (cited in Carruthers and Takahashi Yasunari 2004: 28). This once again confirmed the kinship between Noh and ancient Greek tragedy.[2]

It is not certain whether Suzuki had seen any of the performances staged by the Seminar on Greek Tragedy, in particular their *Trojan Women* and *The Bacchae* or some of the productions of *The Trojan Women* (in Sartre's version) of the late 1960s. However, his connection to Kanze Hisao, who appeared as Old Man and Menelaus in Suzuki's *The Trojan Women* and as Dionysus in his *The Bacchae*, is well documented.

In 1972 Barrault invited Suzuki to participate in the Festival Théâtre des Nations in Paris with a workshop and a presentation of parts from his production, *On the Dramatic Passions II* (1970). The Japanese delegation also included Kanze Hisao, his brother Hideo, and the Kyogen actor Nomura Mansaku, i.e., the three founders of the Society of Darkness. It further comprised Watanabe Moriaki, Professor of French at Tokyo University. The topic "The Theatre and Body Movement" was assigned to them.

On the Dramatic Passions II starred Shiraishi Kayoko, who had received neither traditional nor any "modern" training but turned out to be a powerful "shamanistic" actress. The production was an adaptation of Japanese classics, mostly from the Kabuki repertoire, all revolving around a mad woman (played by Shiraishi Kayoko) and juxtaposed with Vladimir and Estragon from Beckett's *Waiting for Godot*. Suzuki called the two productions "an attempt to examine the roots of stage acting, the impulses which people have deep inside their minds" in the preface to the performance text of *On the Dramatic Passions I and II* . He hailed an "actor-centered" approach and asserted that they "have all been changed during the rehearsal. The lines themselves may have the feeling of the original plays, but the situation of this play was very different" (cited in Carruthers and Takahashi Yasunari 2004: 100). With these two productions, which made "a selective and critical use of traditional performance techniques" (Carruthers and Takahashi Yasunari 2004: 98), Suzuki began his systematic research into the possibility of a new theatre based on particular body techniques.

On the Dramatic Passions II was exceedingly successful. The planned four-week run in Tokyo was extended by another three so that at least four thousand spectators must have seen the show in the end. The great success of the production in Paris, where Shiraishi's acting was "one of the most

DISMEMBERMENT AND THE QUEST FOR WHOLENESS 165

talked-about subjects of the festival" (N. N. 1973b) and Suzuki was hailed as the "Japanese Grotowski" (N. N. 1973a), might have strengthened Suzuki's conviction that the new theatre he was striving for should be rooted in Japan but, at the same time, enable cultural encounters and exchanges due to a common basis.

In Paris Suzuki saw Kanze Hisao and his brother performing the Noh play *Dojoji* (Dojo Temple) on a stage that was a far cry from a traditional Noh stage. As he later reported, it left a deep impression on him and encouraged him in his search for a basis of theatre common to all cultures:

> As presented in Paris . . . nō gave an altogether different impression. When Kanze Hisao and his brother put on *Dojoji*, the crowds swelled around the stage, more and more people pouring in until they had crowded right up to the raised stage itself, so that the playing space was narrowed considerably.
>
> As presented in this fashion, nō revealed a strength it never exhibits in Japan, and I remember how deeply moved I was by what I saw. Surrounded by spectators, Hisao, in his mask and costume, performed the final scene with all his might, to thunderous applause. In the midst of his huge audience, sitting, crouching, sprawling, witnessed by Frenchmen, Chinese and Indians, this nō actor matched his voice to the rhythms of the music as he played on through the voices thundering their appreciation. I became conscious all over again of both the mystery and the force of nō.
>
> (Suzuki Tadashi 1986: 71)

After his return to Japan, Suzuki developed a new kind of physical training which was meant to provide this common basis and came to be known as the Suzuki Method. When he was appointed artistic director of Iwanami Hall, Tokyo, two years later, he decided to stage a Greek tragedy – *The Trojan Women*, starring Shiraishi Kayoko as Hecuba, Kanze Hisao as Old Man and Menelaus, and the Shingeki actress Ichihara Etsuko as Cassandra and Andromache. This cast meant that he had brought together actresses and an actor from three different "schools": Noh, Shingeki, and his own method.

Why did Suzuki choose a Greek tragedy, specifically *The Trojan Women*, for the presentation of his new theatre, which was meant to enable cultural encounters and exchanges? Greek tragedy was commonly considered the origin of all European/Western theatre. Moreover, a certain kinship between Greek tragic theatre and Japanese Noh was repeatedly stressed. *The Trojan Women* was already well known because of the many performances at professional theatres in the late 1960s. Here, for the first time, Suzuki displayed his new theatre as double-edged: on the level of representation, an encounter, exchange, and even interweaving of the different performance cultures took place. On the level of the represented, however, a clash of cultures occurred – the clash between the Trojans and the Greeks in the Trojan War or between the Japanese and the Americans in World War II.[3]

The productive encounter and creative exchange between different performance cultures – between those of the West and Japan as well as within the Japanese – was based on two theorems; the supposed kinship between Noh and ancient Greek tragic theatre and the human body as the common ground of all theatre.

Suzuki developed a particular philosophy of the human body for his training method. In his essay "Culture is the Body!"[4] he proceeds from the assumption that "one of the resulting evils" of the modernizing process in theatre, which in Europe and Japan tended "to use non-animal energy in every facet of its activities instead of the animal energy of the human body," is to be found in the fact that

> the faculties of the human body and physical sensibility have been overspecialized to the point of separation . . . Modernization has "dismembered" "our physical faculties from our essential selves" . . . What I am striving to do is to restore the wholeness of the human body in the theatrical context, not simply by going back to such theatrical forms as nō and kabuki, but by employing their unique virtues, to create something transcending current practice in the modern theatre. We need to bring together the physical functions once "dismembered" to regain the perceptive and expressive abilities and powers of the human body.
>
> (Zarrilli 1995: 164)

Suzuki goes on to explain that the stomping practiced in Noh and Kabuki conjures up energy and evokes the feeling that the feet are firmly planted on the ground. Although derived from traditional Japanese theatre forms, Suzuki believed that the stomping and the effect it provoked were not culturally specific, i.e., exclusively Japanese. Rather, it had to do with

> the discovery of an inner physical sensibility or with the recognition of an inner and profound memory innate to the human body . . . Whether in Europe or in Japan, stomping or beating the ground with the feet is a universal physical movement necessary for us to become highly conscious of our own body or to create a "fictional" space which might also be called a ritualistic space, where we can achieve a personal metamorphosis.
>
> (Zarrilli 1995: 166)

Suzuki was well aware that there are cultural differences determining the use of the body not only in everyday life but also in theatre. He does not deny the fact of cultural differences with regard to how we make use of our bodies. What he was after was a method of using the body in order to restore its perceptive and expressive abilities – a method that could be acquired by anybody irrespective of their cultural background. Such a method would focus on movements of the feet, e.g., stomping. For

> perhaps it is not the upper half but the lower half of our body through which the physical sensibility common to all races is most consciously expressed; to be more specific, the feet. The feet are the last remaining part of the human body which has kept, literally, in touch with the earth, the very supporting base of all human activities
>
> (Zarrilli 1995: 167)

The training method Suzuki developed was based on these insights.[5] It formed the basis for the approach to acting in *The Trojan Women*. The performance privileged and emphasized a particular body posture – the squat. The critic Senda Akihiko regarded it as "a critique of the modern." Having cited literature that explained squatting as a typically Japanese posture, in particular for the lower classes, he states that it "represents a basic bodily stance not only for the Japanese but for all Asians, including the Chinese," he describes how in the performance "this basic posture is never abandoned." He comes to the following conclusion:

> It seems to me that Suzuki's experiment has taken the stuff of Greek tragedy (which constitutes, after all, the source of all Western drama) and "reread" it altogether in terms of the Japanese national sensibility and body movements, creating in the process what is essentially a new form. Further, such a production constitutes a strong critique of the kinds of productions of Western drama presented until now in Japan, productions that privilege traditional, European interpretations of the texts, thereby denying any role to authentic Japanese (indeed Asian) sensibilities. The very appearance of this "squatting" posture constitutes one vivid model of such a critique . . . While he has retained the basic framework of *The Trojan Women*, he has added a new element: an old man (played by Kanze Hisao), struck down and burned out of the house and home at the end of the Pacific War, spinning out his own "vision of Troy." By this device, the tragedy of Troy is personalized, extended into the historical moment, indeed the very physical sensations of those who experienced the . . . realities of the immediate postwar period in Japan . . . So it is, then, that we are able both to witness this tragedy of ancient Greece and to have the rare experience of a drama set in contemporary Japan.
>
> (Senda Akihiko 1997: 50–52)

Senda sees Suzuki's production as a searing critique of modernization as Westernization as practiced in Shingeki. He praises the director for staging a "Western" play, i.e., an ancient Greek tragedy, as "a drama set in contemporary Japan" and for privileging a body posture that, in his opinion, is typically Japanese, if not pan-Asian. In his view, the production accomplished the Asianization of a Western play. When *The Trojan Women* was presented at the First International Meeting of Ancient Greek Drama in Delphi in 1985, Terzopoulos singled out the squat as an ancient Greek body posture used in age-old healing rituals and concluded that this testified to the human body as the common ground of theatre all over the world.

Senda's response to *The Trojan Women* stands in contrast to that of Western critics, whose reactions were nevertheless in line with Suzuki's convictions. In the years following the premiere and before Shiraishi's departure from the company in 1989, the production was shown in Paris, Rome, Lisbon, Berlin, Bonn, Milwaukee, and New York, as well as in many other places in Europe, the United States, Australia, and Asia (e.g., Seoul and Hong Kong). In all of those places the critics' and audiences' responses were wildly enthusiastic and deeply emotional. The Paris performances were praised as "a tragedy of an exceptional force and beauty, a summit of theatre art of all times and places" (Tunc 1977). At the Los Angeles Olympics in 1984 it was described by the press as "one of the single greatest nights in the whole sweep of theatre," for "Suzuki has so concentrated his approach that there's truly no language barrier" (Kelly 1984). Another critic stressed that the production was "agonizingly true to the original precisely because everything in the play has been boldly revised and recreated . . . His characters are both modern and ancient at the same time" (Saville, cited in Carruthers and Takahashi Yasunari 2004: 128). In London Michael Billington (1985) similarly saw "Suzuki's achievement" in that he had "forged a style that unites past and present." Shiraishi's use of her voice, in particular, earned her the admiration of the spectators. Michael Ratcliffe (1985) remarked that "the acting of Shiraishi – voice wrenched from the belly and rising through fearful colours and strains unthinkable under Western training, face gleaming with the triumph of indestructible despair – is by any standards, astounding." And John Barber (1985) even described her voice as "the conscience of mankind in contemplating the holocaust."[6] None of these critics regarded the production as an Asianization of the tragedy, although they did note that some of the techniques were unusual, even "unthinkable under Western training." Mostly, however, they received it as "true to the original" and as a performance that "after all is what Euripides' play is all about" (Billington 1985) – in other words, it was seen as a productive encounter, indeed as an interweaving, of Western and Japanese performance cultures. In view of these reactions by the Western press it seems justified to conclude that Suzuki's training method succeeded in making the bodies of the actors "speak" not only to Japanese but also to different Western audiences, thus "restoring to wholeness" their "dismembered bodies."

Based on this premise Suzuki staged *The Bacchae* in 1978, setting out on a journey that would continue for approximately thirty years, reworking and reviving the production several times. The choice of the tragedy seemed consistent, as it tells the story of the dismemberment of a human body and the impossibility to restore it to wholeness. It also deals with the arrival of a stranger in the city-state of Thebes and its resulting destruction – that is to say it deals with a clash of cultures. Yet, by the time Suzuki began to direct *The Bacchae*, he had further refined his training method so that no such clash would happen on the level of representation. It seems that staging this particular tragedy opened up new possibilities for experimenting with the double-edged character of Suzuki's theatre, i.e., striving for an encounter or the interweaving and even fusion of different cultures (e.g., modern–traditional; Japanese–Greek; Eastern–Western; religious–political; male–female) on the level of representation while exposing their clash on the level of the represented. It therefore does not come as a surprise that Suzuki stated: "*The Bacchae* is one of my favorite plays because it deals directly with such problems as religion, politics, family and gender."[7] While the production was entitled *The Bacchae* until 1989, Suzuki renamed it *Dionysus* in 1990.

The approximately thirty years of work spent on this production yielded many different versions with innumerable important and fascinating aspects – too many to discuss within the framework of this chapter. I shall restrict my analysis here to what I have called the double-edged character of Suzuki's theatre – the attempt to develop a theatre aesthetics rooted in the human body as the common ground of all cultures and therefore appealing to the – in each case particular – sensibilities of members belonging to the most diverse cultures, while exposing the cyclical nature of political history as a repeated clash of cultures leading to death and destruction.[8]

In the program prepared in 1985 for an international tour that was to last for several years and presented the productions of Greek tragedies and Chekhov's *Three Sisters* in different locations in Europe, the United States, and Asia (e.g., in Seoul for the Asian Games Art Festival and in Hong Kong for the International Theatre Festival, both in 1986), Suzuki described the level of the represented in his first version of *The Bacchae* as follows:

> This production is performed as a play-within-a-play, or to be more exact, a play-within-a-play-within-a-play. The basic story has been restructured into a fantasy embodying the hopes and aspirations of people oppressed by a totalitarian and despotic ruler. Thus Dionysus makes his appearance as the symbol of the dreams and desires of people deprived of their freedom by such a ruler (with nothing left to wait for but death). In order for them to express their desires for vengeance, they perform Euripides' *The Bacchae*. But I have further added another frame to "distance" the story. At the very end, precisely when the oppressed people have begun to think that their revels are ended, Pentheus comes back to kill them. This is a nightmarish vision but a brutal fact repeated ever since the beginning of political history – a moment of festive liberation cruelly crushed down by the despot.
>
> (SCOT 1985: 13)

The clash between the oppressor and the oppressed dominated this production, turning the "festive liberation" celebrated so ecstatically in Schechner's 1968 version into its opposite and revealing it as a delusion. The critic Senda, comparing Suzuki's production from 1978 with Schechner's, wrote in favor of Suzuki's:

> Naïvete [in Schechner's production] is replaced with cruel convolution . . . Instead of a Dionysian praise of revelry the cynical line of vision employed here aims rather at a portrayal of those humans who find themselves forced to seek out such a dark vision.
> (Senda Akihiko 1997: 85)

Concerning the level of the represented, Senda distinguished two groups within those who "seek out such a dark vision":

> One turns away from everyday reality, becoming "vagrants" who rush to seek the revelry of the Dionysian space. In Suzuki's view, however, these vagrants also possess a spiritual and an intellectual dimension. By this I believe that he means to suggest a double image in which he portrays intellectuals altogether fascinated with Western ideologies.
> (Senda Akihiko 1997: 87)

In order to substantiate his "reading" Senda adds that all of them "wear the kind of eyeglasses preferred in Japanese intellectual circles" (Senda Akihiko 1997: 87). According to Senda, the performance of a Greek tragedy and the escapism into Western ideologies does not protect them from the violence done to them by the oppressor who, as Pentheus, surprisingly comes from the world of their "vision." Even with regard to the level of representation, Senda's comparison between Schechner and Suzuki's production is in favor of the latter: "Rather than a show of the firm, gymnastic flesh seen in the earlier production [Schechner's], there was an intensity, both emotional and physical, concealed beneath a calmer surface" (Senda Akihiko 1997: 87).

Kanze Hisao played Dionysus and Shiraishi had the parts of Pentheus and Agave, thus blurring the boundaries between the male and the female. As an example of the "intensity, both emotional and physical," Senda referred to the encounter between Pentheus and Dionysus, "faced off each other on opposite sides of the stage . . . Seething emotions seemed to boil up from unseen depths as the two faced each other. Shiraishi squatting down to bring her center of gravity closer to the earth, Kanze Hisao filled with a deep joy, with a look stretching to the heavens" (Senda Akihiko 1997: 86–87).

Moreover, Senda addressed the central problem of Suzuki's aesthetics by stating that most of his productions up to that point "have provided a sort of bouillabaisse of various elements and ingredients" whereby the encounters and slippages between them "give off a certain creaking sound." This seems to have been quite different in *The Bacchae*:

> In the case of this performance, however, Kanze Hisao brings to his performance his great abilities as a nō actor. Along with his beautifully rhythmic performance . . . comes that of Shiraishi Kayoko; and they in turn are supported by the skilful effort of the other members of the Waseda Little Theatre . . . At first I thought that Suzuki was using the wild music of Perez Prado, but it turned out to be the music of Mori Masako and the Nippon Ondo – 'Everyone is looking for the road to tomorrow, shaba, shaba, shaba . . . ' – and to an operetta melody from Diabolo, Mori Shin'ichi bowls out the finale in a husky voice . . . Yet, on this occasion, such diverse ingredients did not produce any sense of disharmony; rather, they contributed to the performance of a theatrical structure here scrupulously woven together . . . In that sense, in terms of the kind of forms . . . [Suzuki] wishes to create, this production serves as an interim report, if not indeed a final balance sheet.
> (Senda Akihiko 1997: 85)

According to Senda, Suzuki succeeded in creating a seamless fusion of "traditional" and "modern" in *The Bacchae* – whereby the Japanese elements were traditional as well as modern and so were the Western elements. While on the level of the represented history was shown from a pessimistic perspective, on the level of representation its aesthetics realized the utopian vision of a harmonious encounter, even fusion, of different cultures.

The Bacchae in its first version had a very short run because of Kanze Hisao's illness (he was soon to die of cancer at the age of 53). After his death Suzuki recast *The Trojan Women*, assigning the role of the Old Man to Shiraishi, so that she as the Old Woman in her vision of Troy on the ruins of World War II would change into Hecuba. This meant that *The Bacchae*'s run was terminated. It was not until 1981 that Suzuki revived it and in a way that differed significantly from the first version. Many other versions followed – some with only slight alterations, others remarkably different. I shall consider only those versions that are particularly relevant to my overall question regarding the double-edged character of the production: the versions from 1981, 1989, 1995, and 2006.

In 1980 Suzuki had begun to teach his method at the University of Wisconsin, Milwaukee. The following year he continued to do so and also taught at the Juilliard School in New York. His teaching provided him with a unique opportunity to test his claim of "universalism" for the principles on which his training method was based. The first result of this experiment was a bilingual version of *The Bacchae* with two choruses consisting of twelve American and twelve Japanese members. Shiraishi played the parts of Dionysus and Agave, while Pentheus was played by an American actor, Tom Hewitt, who had completed Suzuki's training along with the twelve American chorus members.

By letting Japanese and American actors with the same training act side by side, Suzuki tried to verify the hypothesis underlying his method, i.e., that it was able "to bring together the physical functions once 'dismembered'; to regain the perceptive and expressive abilities and powers of the human body" and thus "to restore the wholeness of the human body" (Suzuki 1984: 164), irrespective of ethnic background. The training method was supposed to allow anyone to "speak" to spectators of another culture – the Japanese actors to the Western spectators (as already evidenced by his production of *The Trojan Women*) and the American ones to Japanese audiences. While two different languages (Japanese and English) were indeed spoken despite what would have been largely monolingual audiences in either case, the actors were supposed to "speak" a body language understood by all spectators. This production was shown the same year in Milwaukee, Toga,[9] and Tokyo in order to validate this underlying assumption.

In this version the performance began with a narrator speaking the last words of the tragedy in Japanese: "The gods have many shapes./The gods bring many things/to their accomplishment. And what was most expected/ had not been accomplished./But god has found his way/for what no man expected./So end the play" (v. 1387–94). After the "vagrants" made their entrance, Pentheus appeared and raged against "that effeminate foreigner who plagues our women with new disease."[10] As recounted by Carruthers, "the opening of Scene 2 discloses this 'disease' as the male vagrants 'start to mutter' and 'take off their clothes to reveal women's underwear'" (Carruthers and Takahashi Yasunari 2004: 159). Thus, the male–female relationship was highlighted, which was further stressed by the fact that a woman played Dionysus, the "effeminate foreigner." On the other hand, by casting the American actor Tom Hewitt as Pentheus, the Japanese–American connection was also foregrounded.

Following the recognition scene between Agave and Cadmus and their preparations to leave Thebes, the performance came to an end with the joint return of Pentheus and Dionysus reciting their opening speeches.

On the level of the represented, thus, the clash of such categories as male–female, religion–state, and Japanese–American was here displayed along with the cyclical nature of history. But what about the level of representation? What about the new aesthetics of this bilingual performance? Was it, in fact, capable of speaking to Japanese and American audiences in the same manner because of the identical use of the performers' bodies despite the differences in language?

While the chorus songs were delivered in both languages, first by one and then by the other chorus, so that audiences in Milwaukee as well as in Tokyo were able to understand them, this was not the case with the lines recited by the protagonists. The long report of the herdsman about the women in Cithaeron was spoken in English; the even longer report by the messenger about Pentheus' death was delivered in Japanese. Since this content could not be communicated by body language alone, it must have remained largely a mystery to the other segment of the audience.

While the Japanese critics complained about the long English report of the herdsman, they received the experiment favorably overall, recognizing that the protagonists had, in fact, been able to communicate through physical means. Okazaki Ryôko "admired . . . the mixing of English and Japanese" because it prevented the spectators from slipping completely into one set of cultural assumptions or another and required them to direct their attention to "the more direct effect" of bodily communication. She felt "very moved by it". Miyashita Norio surmised that most Japanese spectators received and responded to the energies and tensions transmitted by the actors, "even if they couldn't understand a word" of the English spoken parts. She concluded that "the effect is remarkably like watching Noh" and felt that through this use of the two languages "the world of theatre had really been enlarged" (Miyashita and Okazaki Ryôko 1981, cited in Carruthers and Takahashi Yasunari 2004: 159). Following the reviews we can deduce that, as far as Tom Hewitt's acting was concerned, the Japanese spectators had the feeling that it spoke to them. In this regard, the experiment was successful. It proved that Suzuki's training method was capable of "restoring to wholeness" not only Japanese bodies, alienated from their own traditional culture due to the prolonged period of Westernization, but also American bodies, largely unfamiliar with any but the Western traditions. It enabled them to adopt expressive faculties and qualities that let them "speak" to Japanese audiences as well. After the bilingual *The Bacchae*'s guest performances in New York in May the following year, the first International Toga Festival opened in July, presenting productions by Robert Wilson, Terayama Shuji, Tadeusz Kantor, Meredith Monk, and others, thus extending Suzuki's concerns about a common basis of theatre to include international encounters and exchanges of different theatre cultures.

In 1989, ahead of the production's planned Australian tour to the Spoleto Festival in Melbourne (now known as the Melbourne Festival) and to Canberra, Shirasishi Kayoko decided to leave the company. This meant that the parts of Dionysus and Agave had to be recast, but Suzuki also used this as an opportunity to reconceptualize the whole production. On the level of the represented, the focus now shifted to religion and its clash with an existing political and social order. A number of sects, many related to New Age cults, had mushroomed all over the Western world after the 1970s, some of them openly criminal. With Asahara Shôkô's AUM Supreme Truth Cult this trend also reached Japan. While Asahara's criminal past and AUM's blood initiations were discussed in the newspapers and parents "charged the cult had taken their children away" (Kaplan and Marshall 1996: 24), AUM battled Tokyo City Hall in 1989 for recognition under Japan's Religious Corporation Law. Shortly thereafter, in February 1990, "AUM was contesting no fewer than 25 seats in the Lower House" at national elections (Kaplan and Marshall 1996: 47).

Suzuki now read the plot of the play as the cover-up of a political assassination by a power-seeking religious cult and interpreted what was happening as "the way society responds to the introduction of a strong alien cultural or religious presence" (cited in Carruthers and Takahashi Yasunari 2004: 161). The recasting as well as the changes in the plot were undertaken according to this central idea. Pentheus was played by Nikishibe Takahisa, a Japanese member of the company who had already taken over the part from Tom Hewitt in 1987. The American Jim De Vita played Dionysus. The famous dancer Ashikawa Yôko, who had played Sonia in Chekhov's *Uncle Vania* that summer in Toga, agreed to play Agave. This recasting worked well with Suzuki's new idea. It had an impact on the level of representation as well as on that of the represented.

In this new version it was not Agave but Dionysus and his priests who killed her son, even though she was made to believe that she had committed the act. In line with Suzuki's idea that "a struggle of state and religion" lies at the heart of the tragedy, he explained the myth of Agave's dismemberment of her son as "a fabrication intended to cover up what amounts to an assassination of the king of Thebes by a religious group" (1989 program, quoted from Carruthers and Takahashi Yasunari 2004: 160). The play's chronology was broken up in order to stress the irrationality of the narrated events. As Carruthers reports, Agave already appeared with Pentheus' severed head in Scene 4; the confrontation between Dionysus and Pentheus took place in Scene 5; Agave argued with Cadmus over the slain Pentheus in Scene 6; in Scene 7 Pentheus appeared dressed as a woman and was slaughtered by the priests and Dionysus.

In this version the frame with the "vagrants" was gone: the performance opened with "a chorus of six men, the followers of Dionysus (god of wine) . . . , [dressed in priestly white vestments and carrying staves], Kadmus asks them if they are the only followers among the citizens of Thebes. They bemoan the lack of believers and state their interest to spread the teachings of Dionysus" (program synopsis for Scene 1, cited in Carruthers and Takahashi Yasunari 2004: 161).[11] From the very beginning there was no doubt that the focus would be on the clash of state and religion.

On the level of the represented, it was of utmost importance that in this version Pentheus was played by a Japanese and Dionysus by an American actor. The performance was again bilingual. However, here it was the god

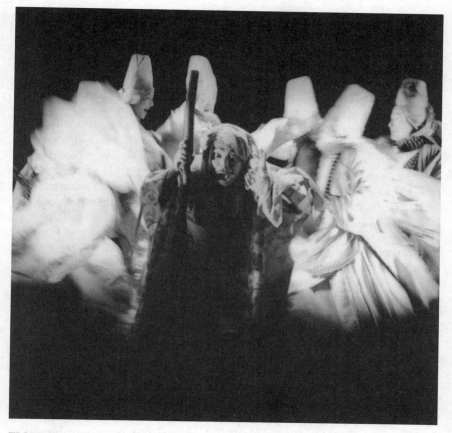

FIGURE 7.1 The priests of Dionysus stab Pentheus (Nishikibe Takahisa) to death in a swirl of motion. Photo: Mori Yasuhiro.

who was English-speaking, even if he was not introduced as such before his encounter with Pentheus in Scene 5. In Scene 3 Dionysus "spoke" Japanese:

> The voiceover is in Japanese, high-pitched, rapid, and stridently amplified, like AUM's political electioneering loudspeaker-announcements. Kadmus and the six priests sit and listen to it impassively, as if receiving the word of God:
> "To these people who stand against my godhead . . . I must manifest my real divinity. If it goes well here, then I shall pass on to other countries to let them know my divine power. If, by some one-in-ten-thousand chance, government officers try to chase my women from their mountain by force, I will stand in their vanguard prepared to fight. For that reason I have hidden my god's form and appear here in human shape. Come my worshippers, . . . reveal my real power to Kadmus' kinfolk."
>
> (Carruthers and Takahashi Yasunari 2004: 162)

Since this version was first shown in Australia, this meant that most of the spectators would not have understood anything – maybe not even that this was the god's voice. For them he first appeared as part of Agave's vision in the next scene. In later performances in Japan, however, the voice did remind the spectators of AUM.

Before Agave has the vision of Dionysus in human form at the end of Scene 4, she meets the maenads and dances with them. "Ashikawa Yôko . . . is an apparently cowed, unprepossessing woman in middle age with untidy, loose hair. She wears a large brown priest's begging-bag over a white kimono with long sleeves, and in her right hand, carries before her the severed head of her son. She stops center stage and begins falteringly with . . . 'Honourable angels' rather than 'Women of Asia'" (Carruthers and Takahashi Yasunari 2004: 163). The four maenads were dressed in voluminous costumes with red and white stripes – the colors of the Japanese flag – and ending in a long train of cloth, which they dragged behind them. They danced with Agave to Tenteken music, used in Suzuki's training for a variety of "slow walks." "It starts with drums and metal banging and scraping and music by Serge Aubrey, interspersed with labored, amplified horse-snorting which sounds as if a great weight were being dragged up a steep hill by spirited animals" (Carruthers and Takahashi Yasunari 2004: 164). When Agave moves away from the dancers to a tatami mat next to Cadmus, the maenads slowly rotate, their arms raised high above their heads. This is the moment when Dionysus makes his "hieratic slow motion entry to a grunting squeaking saxophone" (Carruthers and Takahashi Yasunari 2004: 164). The god that came to her in a vision turned out to be an American with "Afro-style dreadlocks, hippy beads, and a long loose purple- and crimson kimono stitched with gold needle work" (Carruthers and Takahashi Yasunari 2004: 164). The clash of state and religion here also revealed itself as the clash of Japanese and – deified – American culture, worshipped by Japanese priests and maenads.

The long reports by the herdsman and the messenger were left out in this version. Instead, there was a victory dance by the priests and the maenads to the music of Perez Prado's *Voodoo Suite* (after Pentheus had left to change into women's clothes) and the killing of Pentheus on stage by the priests and Dionysus.

Pentheus, dressed in a female kimono with a fan pattern, a light-brown pilgrim's begging-bag slung over one shoulder and a woman's head-covering of the same material adorning his head, appeared to Noh music from the climax of a ghost play, but played on tape at half speed.

> The High Priest stalks from behind and drives the samurai sword concealed in his staff up through the ribs and lung of his victim . . . Each priest comes forward in turn to stab or clash the terror struck Pentheus in slow motion and, as he collapses to his knees, still clinging to his staff, they circle him counter

clockwise with drawn swords in a motion as disorienting as the music. The circling gradually intensifies into a dizzying billowing of white garments.
(Carruthers and Takahashi Yasunari 2004: 166)

When the priests withdrew to their seats, Pentheus dragged himself to Dionysus' feet and the god raised his staff in slow motion and clubbed him on his head and stomach "as if crushing a large insect."

De Vita then turns to face the audience and raises arms and staff in a hieratic gesture of victory more cruelly powerful for being so facially impassive, paradoxically it carries strong overtones of the Resurrected Christ of religious iconography. The maenads perform ecstatic "moving statues" to the ancient Bugaku music of the shô, and, while the American God stands there in beautiful/terrible glory, the amplified multiple voices of Dionysus are heard as voiceover in a stereophonic, echoing overlapping babble of Japanese. Agave, mouth agape on her Asian mat, and Kadmus tight-lipped on his Greco-Roman chair, sit behind the exultant God like 'empty shells'/program description.
(Carruthers and Takahashi Yasunari 2004: 168)

The play ends with the light on Agave and Cadmus, with the latter delivering a choral epode:

> Oh blessed is the man
> Who escapes the winter sea
> And wins his haven
> Free above his own striving.
> Let other men on other ways
> Other men surpass in wealth or power.
> He who lives each day
> For the happiness each day offers
> Him I call blessed.
> (Cited in Carruthers and Takahashi Yasunari 2004: 169)

The most important change in this version did in fact refer to the level of the represented. While the shift in focus toward the clash of state and religion was obvious, the shift resulting from the recasting of a Japanese actor to play Pentheus and of an American actor for Dionysus was more ambiguous. In this version Dionysus was the only part played by an American. Yet Dionysus was first heard as a voice speaking Japanese in a way that would remind local audiences of the AUM sect; spectators with no knowledge of Japanese would in any case identify it as Japanese. When the god took on human form, he did so with the outward appearance of a Westerner, and when, in Scene 4, he spoke for the first time, he used American English. This possibly hinted at the proliferation of sects in the United States and at the deification of American ideologies and ways of life. On the other hand, his outlook after the brutal killing of Pentheus alluded to Christian iconography. In this case the religious cult coming from abroad seemed to refer to the Christian religion. It is therefore not entirely convincing to identify unequivocally the casting purely as a clash of Japanese and American culture, but it should instead be seen as the clash of a given community with a foreign religious cult. In this context it makes sense that in the versions to follow the god of the new religion no longer appeared on stage.

On the level of representation new "ingredients" were added regarding body movement techniques and the music. With Ashikawa Yôko, a dancer figured prominently. She used the Butoh technique to great effect in Scene 6 when she danced "a Butoh dance of utter darkness" (Carruthers and Takahashi Yasunari 2004: 165) to the music of Vangelis in front of the maenads. The score was composed of modern and pop as well as of Noh, Kabuki, and even Bunraku music. What Senda had already said about the first version was perceived even more intensely now. Elements from a wide range of performance cultures were brought together in a seamless fusion. The aesthetics of the performance were obviously able to appeal to very diverse sensibilities.

On March 3, 1990, Suzuki opened his new ACM Theatre in Mito City (Acting Company Mito), a former rich feudal fief belonging to the Tokugawa Clan during the Edo period and now in search of a new image as a lifestyle alternative to Tokyo on the Pacific Coast. To celebrate this occasion, *The Bacchae* was performed in yet another new version, which was called *Dionysus* even though the god did not appear on stage at all. The chronological order of the plot was restored, and Agave killed her son on stage. A new frame was added, consisting of three men in wheelchairs singing a children's song in a childish way. After them the Cult Leader made his entrance, also in a wheelchair but pushed by an assistant, singing "Farewell to all Histories and Memories"; each line was repeated by his three followers. This setting created a Beckettian atmosphere from the very beginning, which allowed for no uncertainty about the tendency of this cult. The three imbeciles in the wheelchairs reappeared twice, once chanting the "Tomorrow, and tomorrow, and tomorrow" line from *Macbeth* – recalling the song from the first version "Everyone is looking for the road to tomorrow . . . " – and the second time repeating their opening song.

This version, too, was reworked several times. At the Toga Festival in July of the same year actresses took over the role of the Cult Leader and of his assistant – the latter played by the same actress who appeared as Agave. In this version *Dionysus* was conceptualized as the first play in a trilogy, followed by *Macbeth* and *Ivanov*. The trilogy was entitled *The Farewell Cult*. The frame was extended in order to "aid the cross-relation of the themes of these plays (the rise of power, the overarching, and the decline of Western culture)" (Carruthers and Takahashi Yasunari 2004: 170).

Over the next few years other changes followed, mostly due to the recasting process, which included bringing in more American actors. In the 1992 version all the main parts, including those of the wheelchair believers, were played by Americans. Only the priests and the maenads were played by Japanese actors from Suzuki's company. This engendered a number of new readings of the cultural clashes between the Japanese and the Americans. The same effect was achieved in 1994 by recasting John Nobbs, an Australian dancer, in the role of the Cult Leader and giving the role of Agave to Ellen Lauren. This combination lasted for four international tours until Takemori Yoichi, a male actor of the company, took over the part of Agave in 1998, playing her in the style of a Kabuki *onnagata*. This change not only affected the level of the represented but also that of representation because it brought in some new movements and speech patterns, which were in line with the overall aesthetics of the performance.

In 1995 the first International Theatre Olympics took place in Athens, Epidauros, and Delphi, initiated two years earlier by Theodoros Terzopoulos, Heiner Müller, Suzuki Tadashi, Robert Wilson, Yuri Lyubimov, Tony Harrison, and others. The festival was inaugurated with a new version of *Dionysus* at the Herodes Atticus Theatre in Athens, where thirty years earlier Kanze Hisao had shown his Noh program. It starred Ellen Lauren as Agave beside John Nobbs as Cult Leader within an otherwise all-Japanese cast. Nishikibe, who had played Pentheus for so many years, had to be replaced by a young member of the company, Kijima Tsuyoshi, due to severe illness. Suzuki's new idea underlying this version was that "a group with a communal need for unity and the will to spiritually influence the masses created a 'story' named Dionysus". This was not meant as a new reading of the tragedy, rather the point was "to use Euripides' play to stage my world view" (Suzuki in his director's notes in the program, cited in Carruthers and Takahashi Yasunari 2004: 173), i.e., to dismember the text of the play in order to create the wholeness of a new performance. In this version it was again the priests – not Agave – who killed Pentheus in a similar way as in the 1989 version, without needing the god to finish the job.

The performance opened with the three Farewell Cult believers in wheelchairs singing a children's song. The Cult Leader again declared "Farewell to all Histories and Memories," repeated by the believers. As in the earlier version they reappeared after the confrontation of Pentheus and the priests, saying their "Tomorrow, tomorrow and tomorrow," and again after the recognition scene between Cadmus and Agave, first repeating the words of the Cult Leader – "Farewell to all Histories and Memories" – and then the line from *Macbeth* before finally exiting. Then the maenads exited followed by the priests. The performance ended with the Old Man/Cadmus in a wheelchair pushed on to the stage in the beginning by the Cult Leader's assistant, musing on the wondrous and immaculate nature of the god's will.

Paul Allain remarked on the wheelchair believers:

> The energetic physicality and complex use of rhythms supported the classical material. The Believers' rapid scurrying as they perched on the edge of wheelchairs shattered the otherwise vibrant stillness, contrasting with the slow, elegantly robed white-faced priests of Dionysus. The image of the wheelchair men was absurd and comic, a vision from Beckett's *Endgame* multiplied. With their feet barely touching the floor but sweeping themselves swiftly along, the physicality was demanding, however at ease the performers seemed. Suzuki's constantly reiterated metaphor of man's sickness and the world as a hospital were embodied in the wheelchair-bound performers/ characters.
>
> (Allain 2002: 164)

The two high points of the performance were the killing of Pentheus, followed by the swirling around of his corpse by the priests, and Agave's appearance on the stage stepping over the corpse, holding Pentheus' severed head in her left hand, followed by the recognition scene. A critic wrote about Ellen Lauren's performance at the Teatro Olimpico in Vicenza, where the production had been shown one year earlier (and would again be presented the following month):

> The actors were all outstanding for their charismatic, focused energy. To mention only the entrance of Ellen Lauren's Agave, she comes down from the back of the central perspective holding Pentheus' head in her hands . . . , she reaches the body of Pentheus lying at centre stage and then gives vent to her wild grief with such power that the audience is left breathless for the whole scene.
>
> (N. N. 1994; cited in Carruthers and Takahashi Yasunari 2004: 179)

The fact that Agave was played by an American actress and the Cult Leader by an Australian dancer did not seem to have affected the level of the represented anymore. It was the destructive force of religion that lay at the center. The clash happened between believers and non-believers, no matter where they came from. Religion, in this scenario, did not unite different people into a community but split it up. As Allain concludes: "The piece indicated not only the deep schisms that can separate groups but also reinforced how one set of ideologies are merely replaced by another when communities subdivided" (Allain 2002: 163).

This version of *Dionysus* stood in stark contrast to the productions discussed in the first part of this book. It did not celebrate communality brought about by a god but demonstrated the schism of a community as a consequence of blindly believing in this god. It is not surprising, then, that the production's topicality was seen as shocking when it was performed in the

United States in late 2001, when the country was still reeling from 9/11 and its aftermath.

On the level of representation, however, the production seemed to have ideally realized the utopian vision of an interweaving or even of a seamless fusion of very diverse performance cultures. Regardless of whether the performers were Japanese, American, or Australian, whether their background was in dance or theatre, whether they referred to different traditional or modern theatre, music or dance forms, their acting spoke to audiences all over the world. Suzuki's training method, which he had begun to develop over twenty years earlier, had indeed enabled actors from different cultures to appeal to a wide range of sensibilities with their acting. The above-quoted critic wrote about the production of *Dionysus* in Vicenza:

> For an hour and a half the audience at the Olimpico was transfixed, such was the tension and magnetism of the actors, as well as the stage actions, atmospherics, musical effects and lighting. The play was performed in Japanese and, in part, in English. Everything about it was superlative . . .
>
> The production lived thanks to actions and movements whose rhythms and articulations . . . affect the audience viscerally. The words of the Japanese text . . . became highly charged . . . No nonsense with subtitles or a simultaneous translation . . . The message was entirely clear because emotionally clear. Wherein lies the strength of Suzuki's theatre? . . . He pushes his actors to a concentration, which is totally unrelenting. Even if the actor isn't the focus of attention, he or she is still "tense", present and dynamic in his or her immobility.
> (N. N. 1994)

When this version was revived at the International Festival of Toga in 2006 the frame of the wheelchair believers had been cut. Six beige chairs were lined up along the back wall of the stage for the priests to retire to from time to time. The focus lay on the priests' greed for power and their clash with the ruler Pentheus. It was an all-Japanese cast – Cadmus played by Takahashi Hitoshi, Pentheus by Niibori Seijun, and Agave by Kuboniwa Naoko. The changes resulted in an even greater denseness in the performance, a more focused concentration on the central clash without, on the level of representation, losing any of its strengths of interweaving elements from different performance cultures.

Two years later, this version was shown at the Daendo Theatre belonging to the Shizuoka Performing Arts Centre. It was built in 1997 by the architect Isozaki Arata, who had designed all the theatres for Suzuki. Isozaki took the Teatro Olimpico as a point of departure for his design and was thus able to make some significant transformations that resulted in the Daendo (literally "Elliptical Hall"). More than thirty years after the first performance of Suzuki's *The Bacchae* in Iwanami Hall, *Dionysus* took place in a space designed specially for the production and keeping its performance in the

Teatro Olimpico in mind. The critic Watanabe Tamotsu compared both performances:

> Comparing it to the first performance, as theater, the register changed completely. Today, the performance I saw was just like Noh drama. Anything unnecessary was pared away, leaving it terse and limpid. Moreover, the stage was brimming with an extraordinary tension and concentration, from which the skeletal structure of drama arose clearly . . . Throughout Japan's history, Noh theatre told of the relationship between human beings and their world, and reached its fundamental culmination. The reason it seemed as though I were watching Noh in *Dionysus* was because of the contrast between the first and second acts, the pseudo-composition of the script, and the sensuality hidden within the actors' expressions . . . However, the greatest reason for thinking it was Noh was because this play told of the relation between human beings and the cosmos, and exhibited the most fundamental profundity that Noh had achieved. It seemed to me that there was nothing more that theater might need to say. Building on *The Bacchae*, Tadashi Suzuki had for the first time arrived at the origins of theater.
>
> (Watanabe 2009: 34)

Participating in the performance taking place in a space which, by itself, resulted from a productive encounter, the critic received it as a kind of "homecoming" when citing the Noh theatre, as well as arriving at a transcultural point, located beyond as well as in any specific culture – at the origins of theatre.

It was a long journey from the first production of *The Bacchae* foregrounding the never-ending repression through a political ruler to the last ones centering on the destructive forces of religious cults. However, all the versions, as different as they were in their concepts and also in their impact on audiences of various cultures, displayed the double-edged character from which I proceeded in this chapter: representing history as a never-ending struggle for power between different destructive and deadly groups by presenting an aesthetics that realized the utopian vision of a peaceful and productive encounter or even interweaving of utterly diverse performance cultures. Therein lies the "magic" and "miracle" of Suzuki's theatre and, in particular, of *The Bacchae/Dionysus* productions. It is a case of *coincidentia oppositorum*: the pessimism concerning history as an ever-recurring power struggle between different forces leading to the "dismemberment" of the communal and the individual human body coincides with the optimism of a utopian vision of the "restoration to wholeness" to be realized in the performance. Even if history will never bring about such a restoration to wholeness, theatre can do so – not by creating an illusion on stage but through its particular aesthetic means that highlight the human body as the common ground of culture and theatre, wherever it takes place.

Notes

1. Another representative of the angura theatre to later win international acclaim was Terayama Shuji (Sorgenfrei 2005).
2. This kinship had already been asserted by Ernest Fenollosa who, perhaps in the context of the craze for Sada Yakko, made comparisons between Noh and Greek tragedy in a manuscript edited by Ezra Pound (Fenollosa and Pound 1916). This kinship is further explored in Smethurst (1989).
3. For more on this production, see the review by Senda Akihiko (1997: 49–53) and the description in McDonald (1992: 21–44), as well as in Carruthers and Takahashi Yasunari (2004: 124–153).
4. First published in English in *Performing Arts Journal* 23 (1984), cited in Zarrilli 1995: (163–167).
5. For further reading on this method see Brandon (1978: 29–42) and Carruthers and Takahashi Yasunari (2004: 70–97).
6. All of the reviews above are quoted from Carruthers and Takahashi Yasunari (2004: 127–128).
7. Suzuki Tadashi in an interview recorded by NHK TV following a performance of Dionysus in Mito in 1992; cited in Carruthers and Takahashi Yasunari 2004 (154).
8. Of all the different versions that were staged I saw only the one shown at the Festival of the Theatre of the World in Stuttgart in 1987. I have a video recording of the performance presented in 2006 at the International Theatre Festival in Toga. For the other versions I refer to descriptions in McDonald (2004: 59–74 – version of 1981), Carruthers and Takahashi Yasunari (2004: 160–169 – version of 1989), Carruthers and Takahashi Yasunari (2004: 169–179 – version of 1990 and thereafter), and Sampatakakis (2005: 211–220). For the first version, I refer to the review by Senda Akihiko (1997: 83–87). I saw *The Trojan Women* with Shiraishi as Hecuba, Cassandra, and the Old Woman (instead of the Old Man, first played by Kanze Hisao who died in 1978, shortly after the premiere of *The Bacchae*) as well as the bilingual *Clytemnestra* starring Shiraishi and Tom Hewitt as Orestes, and Chekhov's *Three Sisters* at the Festival Theatre of the World in Frankfurt, 1985. I also had the opportunity to interview Suzuki and observe one of the training sessions at the festival. For the *Three Sisters*, see Fischer-Lichte (1997: 158–168).
9. From 1976 onwards Suzuki's company was based in Toga, Japan, and renamed the Suzuki Company of Toga (SCOT).
10. Philip Vellacott's translation was used here for the English lines, Euripides (1954: 203).
11. For more on this version, see the extensive and detailed description by Carruthers and Takahashi Yasunari (2004).

References

Allain, Paul. 2002. *The Art of Stillness: The Theatre Practice of Tadashi Suzuki*. London: Methuen.

Barber, John. 1985. No title. *Daily Telegraph*, April 11.
Billington. Michael. 1985. No title. *Guardian*, April 11.
Brandon, James. 1978. "Training at the Waseda Little Theatre: The Suzuki Method." *Drama Review* 22 (4): 29–42.
Carruthers, Jan and Takahashi Yasunari. 2004. *The Theatre of Suzuki Tadashi*. Cambridge: Cambridge University Press.
Eisenstadt, Shmuel N. 2003. *Comparative Civilization and Multiple Modernities*. Leiden: Brill.
Euripides. 1954 (rev. 1973). *The Bacchae and Other Plays*. Translated by Philip Vellacott. London: Penguin.
Fenollosa, Ernest and Ezra Pound. 1916. *Noh or Accomplishment: A Study of the Classical Stage of Japan*. London: Macmillan.
Fischer-Lichte, Erika. 1997. "Intercultural Aspects in Postmodern Theatre: The Japanese Version of Chekhov's *Three Sisters*." In Fischer-Lichte, Erika, *The Show and the Gaze of Theatre: A European Perspective*. Iowa City: Iowa University Press.
Fischer-Lichte, Erika. 2009. "Interweaving Cultures in Performance: Different States of In-Between." *New Theatre Quarterly* 25 (4): 391–401.
Kaplan, David and Andrew Marshall. 1996. *The Cult of the End of the World*. London: Arrow.
Kelly, Kevin. 1984. No title. *Boston Globe*, July 1.
McDonald, Marianne. 2004. *Ancient Sun, Modern Light: Greek Drama on the Modern Stage*. New York: Columbia University Press.
Miyashita Norio and Okazaki Ryôko. 1981. "Engeki jihyo" [Theatre criticism page]. *Higeki Kigehi* 12: 101–109.
Mori Mitsuya. 2010. "Women's Issues and a New Art of Acting: *A Doll's House* in Japan." In *Global Ibsen: Performing Multiple Modernities*. Edited by Erika Fischer-Lichte, Barbara Gronau, and Christel Weiler, 75–88. New York: Routledge.
N. N. 1902. "Die Kawakami-Truppe (Sada Yakko) in Berlin." *Ost-Asien* 4 (46): 450.
N. N. 1973a. No title. *Le Point* 31: 64.
N. N. 1973b. No title. *Drama Review* 22 (December).
N. N. 1994. "Dionysio, Suberbo." *Sipario*, October 10.
Ozasa Yoshio. 1985. *Nihon gendai engekishi*, Vol. 1. Tokyo: Hakusuisha.
Ratcliffe, Michael. 1985. No title. *Observer*, April 14.
Ruperti, Bonaventura. 2001. "Greek Tragedies in/and the Productions of Ninagawa Yukio." In *Japanese Theatre Transcultural: German and Italian Intertwinings*. Edited by Stanca Scholz-Cionca and Andreas Regelsberger, 138–156. Munich: Iudicium.
Sampatakakis, Georgios. 2005. *Bakkhaimodel: The Re-usage of Euripides' Bakkhai in Text and Performance*. London: London University Press.
SCOT: Suzuki Company of Toga. 1985. Tokyo: The Japan Performing Arts Center.
Senda Akihiko. 1997. *The Voyage of Contemporary Japanese Theatre*. Translated by Thomas Rimer. Honolulu: University of Hawai'i Press.
SM. 1909. "Haiyu muyo ron" [Actors are unnecessary]. *Tokyo Asashi Shinbun*, December 1.

Smethurst, Mae J. 1989. *The Artistry of Aeschylus and Zeami: A Comparative Study of Greek Tragedy and Nō*. Princeton: Princeton University Press.
Sorgenfrei, Carol Fisher. 2005. *Unspeakable Acts: The Avant-Garde Theatre of Terayama Shuji and Postwar Japan*. Honolulu: University of Hawai'i Press.
Suzuki Tadashi. 1984. "Culture is the Body!" *Performing Arts Journal* 23.
Suzuki Tadashi. 1986. "The Toga Festival." In *The Way of Acting: The Theatre Writings of Tadashi Suzuki*. Translated by J. Thomas Rimer, 69–97. New York: Theatre Communication Group.
Tunc, André. 1977. No title. *La Croix*, June 2.
Watanabe Tamotsu 2009. "'Who is the Criminal?' SPAC Shizuoka Performing Arts Center's 'Dionysus, God of Wine.'" *Teatro*, July: 34. Quoted in an unpublished internal manuscript by Isozaki Arata, *Dionysus: The Teatro Olimpico and the Daendo Theatre*. Translated by Jon Brokering.
Zarrilli, Phillip B., ed. 1995. *Acting (Re)Considered: Theories and Practices*. New York: Routledge.

Further Reading

Fischer-Lichte, Erika. 2005. *Theatre, Sacrifice, Ritual: Exploring Forms of Political Theatre*. New York: Routledge. For an analysis of the first performance of Hofmannsthal's version, see "Electra's Transgression," pp. 1–14.

8

Transforming Kathakali
The Bacchae by Guru Sadanam P. V. Balakrishnan in Delphi and New Delhi (1998)

In the 1990s the Greek Embassy in New Delhi approached Guru Sadanam P. V. Balakrishnan, the director of the International Centre for Kathakali in New Delhi, on behalf of the Committee of the Greek Drama International Meetings at Delphi with the suggestion to stage *The Bacchae* in traditional Kathakali style for the Delphi Festival of 1998. Such a suggestion seems surprising considering the highly codified performance tradition of Kathakali with its strict rules and conventions that allow little room for experimentation. This is not to say that Kathakali is immune to change. As will be explained later, it has undergone a number of changes throughout its long history, which mostly, however, remained within the range of the "appropriate" as judged by the connoisseurs (Zarrilli 1992).

Although there is no consistent performance tradition of Greek tragedies in India, a few remarkable productions were staged after the country gained independence in 1947: *Medea* at the Theatre Unit in 1961, then still located in Bombay (now Mumbai), and *Oedipus the King* at the National School of Drama in New Delhi in 1964. Both productions were staged by Ebrahim Alkazi (born 1925), one of India's greatest stage directors, who served as director of the National School of Drama from 1962 until 1977 and who not only supported the growth of contemporary Indian drama in the 1960s but also staged Greek tragedies. Another well-known director, Shambu Mitra (1915–1997), staged *The Trojan Women* with the great actress Tripti Mitra in the lead role, and *Oedipus the King* with his Calcutta-based company

---

Dionysus Resurrected: Performances of Euripides' The Bacchae in a Globalizing World, First Edition. Erika Fischer-Lichte.
© 2014 Erika Fischer-Lichte. Published 2014 by John Wiley & Sons, Ltd.

Bohurupee in the late 1960s. After the German director Hansgünther Heyme had staged *Antigone* in Calcutta in 1980, Kavalam Narayana Panikkar directed another production of *Antigone* at the Avadh Theatre, which was invited to Delphi in 1986. In the 1980s the self-proclaimed Brecht disciple Amitava Dasgupta (born 1947) also began to stage Greek tragedies with his company Brechtian Mirror based in New Delhi; in 1982 he put Euripides' *Electra* on stage, followed three years later by *Iphigenia in Aulis*. In 1993 he even did a production of *The Bacchae*, which toured Himachal Pradesh, Lucknow, and Calcutta. The question arises, then, why the Greek Embassy did not ask one of the well-known directors of contemporary Indian theatre to stage *The Bacchae* but approached the International Kathakali Centre instead.

Since most of the above-mentioned productions were conceived and/or shown in New Delhi, it is to be assumed that the Greek Embassy might have known or could easily have found out about them. This is most likely the case with Dasgupta's *The Bacchae*, for it was staged in response to a bloody clash between religions, much talked about in India and abroad. In December 1992 the Babri Masjid, a sixteenth-century mosque located in the town of Ayodhya, also known as the location of important Ramlila performances – plays on the life of the god Rama as narrated in the epic *Ramayana* – was destroyed by a mob of Hindu fundamentalists, who believed that the mosque had been erected after the destruction of a Hindu temple on the same site marking the birthplace of Lord Rama. Hundreds of people were killed as the tensions between Hindus and Muslims escalated in the aftermath of the demolition so that other riots broke out, leading to many more deaths and horrendous destruction.

Dasgupta chose to stage *The Bacchae* because, similarly to Suzuki in his versions from 1989 onwards, he felt that the play told a story of communal, religious riots instigated and stoked by politicians. In his production he emphasized the similarities and references to contemporary Indian politics. He regarded Pentheus as "a right honest person. He was killed. Like Dhirendra Brachmachari. He used to give all sermons to Indira Gandhi. So, these godfathers, they have tremendous strength over politicians. And in India, the influence of godfathers is very strong" (Dasgupta 2009). Accordingly, in his production, Dionysus was not conceived of as a god but as a politician exploiting religion to achieve his cause.

Since the production was staged shortly after the destruction of the mosque and the riots following it and clearly addressed these events, it seems to have exerted a strong impact on its audiences in India.

The performance lasted one hour and forty-five minutes – not longer, because "people do not have time otherwise" (Dasgupta 2009). To achieve this goal, the text had to be shortened considerably. However – as in Zé Celso's production – Semele was included and her death enacted on stage. The central conflict was the triangle between Semele, Agave, and Dionysus.

Throughout the performance the stage was almost empty. A big oven, meant and probably understood by the audience as a sacred object with fire coming out of it, stood slightly off-center. A single pillar hinted at the palace. Dasgupta employed two effective staging strategies, the first of which aimed at emphasizing the reference to contemporary politics. This was further enhanced by the text. In between, one of the characters remarked: "Just see what actually happened in the name of religion, 200 persons were killed." After the final scene, Agave said, "Please my father, let us go somewhere where the dirty politics is not there." Mainly, however, it was achieved by some kind of "Brechtian" device. "In one performance we did captions and slides, where we showed headlines from the time, something documentary, for example Babri Masjid, then somebody committed suicide, then Rajiv Gandhi was murdered, then Sheikh Abdullah in Kashmir . . . We stopped the play and this was shown, and then we continued the play" (Dasgupta 2009). According to the director, the audience responded enthusiastically to these slides, with some spectators returning only in order to see them again and complaining when they were removed. For, meanwhile, the police had interfered, clearly informed of the play's potentially incendiary content by someone in the audience. This strategy demonstrated that it was religion, abused and exploited by politicians, that dismembered communities and perhaps even the whole nation.

The other strategy was the inclusion of different folk and classical dances. When Semele wanted the sun to shine on her love, the sun came out accompanied by Chhau dancers and their music, as was the case when she died. By contrast, Cadmus and Tiresias were accompanied by Yakshagana dancers, drums and violin. The chorus consisted of fourteen Kathak dancers. The level of music and dance allowed for the inclusion of different performance traditions and therefore communities, which were united into one aesthetic "whole." This strategy was in some ways reminiscent of India's Republic Day Parade, held annually in New Delhi and featuring, besides a military display, a cultural pageant representing the different folk traditions of the states of the Indian Union and thereby speaking to the Nehruvian ideal of national unity in cultural diversity (Jain 2002: esp. 62–75). While the representational politics and territorial agenda at work in the parade would have been absent in Dasgupta's production, the latter did lay claim to bringing together diverse dance traditions ostensibly to form an aesthetic whole, irrespective of ideology and the perhaps inevitable tendencies toward romanticism. Thus, on the level of the represented in his production, religious politics was shown as dismembering the community/state/nation, while on the level of representation two different strategies were employed. Firstly, the Brechtian devices that "dismembered" the "unity of action" by interrupting it, underlined, explained, and contextualized what was shown on the level of the represented. Secondly, the diverse dance traditions juxtaposed on stage to form an aesthetic unity that not only appealed to the particular sensibility of the spectators but also created a certain sense of harmony.

More than fifteen years after the production Dasgupta reiterated his belief that there was and still is a great relevance for Greek tragedy because of the political situation in India. He explains: "Today's rulers are greedy, just like Agamemnon who sacrificed his own daughter: His ambition was greater than affection. It is here, now also" (Dasgupta 2009).

The topicality of Dasgupta's *The Bacchae* and the enthusiasm with which it was received in New Delhi and elsewhere in India makes one wonder why the Committee of the Delphi Festival did not show any interest in a contemporary production dealing with the political and social situation "here and now," but instead asked for a Kathakali adaptation. The only viable reason that presents itself seems to be festival politics. One critic wrote after the festival of 1998 that the Greek audiences were weary of "the dangers of having the poetry and tragic wisdom of the ancient texts strangled through the sociopolitical burden of contemporary Western adaptations . . . No one wants such sterile top-heaviness any more, the over-consumption of psychological interpretations and the reductionist optical decoration of Western revivals." She concludes that it was "not a bad idea to devote this year's Festival to the traditions from the East, from Asia and Africa, since the avant-gardist experiments of the West are exhausted and now live off recycling the 'new'" (Matziri 1998).[1]

This is not a convincing argument. For, as mentioned before, performances from Japan, China, and India were invited to the Greek Drama Internationals Meetings in Delphi from the very beginning. These were "modern" performances, i.e., realistic, spoken theatre, as in the case of the Chinese *Oedipus* and the Indian *Antigone*, both invited to Delphi in 1986. The Chinese and Indian productions invited for the Meeting in 1998, however, were staged in "traditional" styles – the Chinese *Bacchae* as Beijing Opera (although, as will be explained in the next chapter, it did not actually follow that particular operatic style) and the Indian *Bacchae* in Kathakali. In the case of the Indian performance it was even commissioned by the Committee of the Meetings. Moreover, two of its representatives were present at the rehearsals and did not refrain from interfering in relevant directing decisions.

Keeping this state of affairs in mind, the utterance of the quoted critic reveals a dichotomous thinking, the prevalence of which at international theatre and arts festivals well into the 1990s might come as a surprise. On the one hand, there is "the West" with its vested interest in enabling performances of Greek tragedy to speak about topical sociopolitical issues. That there could be a similar interest in "the East" – in India, Indonesia, China, and Japan, for example – is not even considered. Instead, "the East" is charged with the preservation of traditions. This East–West dichotomy is unabashedly equated with that of the traditional vs. the modern. Instead of investigating the particular interest generated by Greek tragedies in India today, the reasons for and means with which they were performed or their reception by the audience, it was suggested to stage one particular tragedy – *The Bacchae* – in the traditional style of Kathakali. The choice of this tragedy, however, was not random. Its protagonist is, after all, a god from the "East," inclined to irrationality and destructive ecstasy and "tamed" in the tragedy by the Greek form. It might have interested the Greek side to see what happens with their dangerous god when he adopts an Eastern, "oriental" form. Will the "oriental" form be able to "tame" the god of Greek tragedy and Greek theatre, so that he adapts to it or will he resist and finally cause a dismemberment of Kathakali? Was an agon intended between Greek and Indian antiquity?

Such suspicions, however, seemed to have been far removed from Guru Sadanam P. V. Balakrishnan's mind when he accepted the project. He responded to the suggestion rather generously by telling the Greeks that he would do it only if it would not "spoil" the tradition. After having read the text and discussed the difficulties of such a project with Akavoor Narayanan, an eminent scholar of Kathakali from Jawaharlal Nehru University, he decided to embark on it. As Balakrishnan emphasized even ten years later, this production was not against the tradition. However, because of the encounter between two great theatre cultures in this production, both had to be changed to a certain extent:

> There are some changes but . . . that . . . is not spoiling our tradition . . . It must be Kathakali and Greek, it cannot be one side only . . . only Kathakali or . . . only Greek because we are bringing two completely different cultures together. So, you must have some positive, in-between approach, not be partial to Kathakali or Greek . . . I am a Kathakali artist, I am very committed to Kathakali but then we are bringing such a great culture to our own, we must also adapt.
>
> (Balakrishnan 2009)

According to Balakrishnan, his production/choreography of *The Bacchae* changed both: the text of the tragedy was curtailed considerably; some of the performance conventions of Kathakali were suspended, some newly added, without, however, "spoiling" the tradition. Kathakali was transformed but not "dismembered."

In order to understand and appreciate how this was accomplished, we must at least briefly consider the history and chief characteristics of Kathakali (see also Zarrilli 2000). In the late sixteenth and early seventeenth centuries Kathakali ("story play") emerged under this name as a distinct performance genre in Kerala in southeastern India. The performances enacted episodes from regional versions of the Indian religious epics *Ramayana* and *Mahabharata*, as well as from the Puranas, the holy book of popular Hinduism. The plays were written by playwright composers in highly Sanskritized Malayalam, the language of Kerala. The performances usually take place before a temple, beginning at dusk and ending at dawn. In the 1930s, when the old patronage structure had crumbled due to British colonialism, the Kerala Kalamandalam was founded as a new organization meant to safeguard the future of Kathakali. It is still the most important institution for teaching and performing Kathakali. In 1960 the International Centre for Kathakali was founded in New Delhi in order to "lift Kerala's Kathakali from its regional character, and to import it to a new dimension by making this unique art known to audiences drawn from not only the various States of India, but also from other countries" (International Centre for Kathakali 1968 New Delhi program, cited in Zarrilli 2000: 179).

Traditionally, Kathakali is performed by three groups of performers: the actor–dancers, who never speak; the two vocalists, who sing the entire text, the third-person narratives as well as the dialogues; and the percussionists, who accompany the vocalists as well as the actor–dancers. All performers are male.

The aesthetic of Kathakali is rooted in the *Natyasastra*, an ancient Indian treatise on the performing arts. It was written in Sanskrit between 200 BCE and 200 CE and is traditionally attributed to the sage Bharata. In the eleventh century it was expanded by the commentator Abhinavagupta. It deals with all aspects of the performing arts, including space, dramaturgy and language of a play, gestures and other body movements, gaits, music, costumes and makeup and, most prominently, the relationship between the representations of emotional and other states of being (*bhavas*) and the responses caused by them (*rasas*).

For Kathakali, the eight *bhavas* and corresponding *rasas* are essential. They comprise eroticism, love, or pleasure; comedy, mirth, or derision; pathos, sadness; fury, anger, wrath; heroism, vigor; fear, terror; repulsion, disgust; and wonder or marvel. Abhinavagupta added the *bhava/rasa* of peace, atonement to these eight. A particular facial expression corresponds to each of the *bhavas/rasas*. The technical instruction for the representation of eroticism, love, or pleasure, for instance, says:

> Open the upper lids as wide as possible. Keep the lower lids slightly closed. With the lips make a soft, relaxed smile, but do not show the teeth. Keep the gaze focused straight ahead. Having assumed this position, begin to flutter the eyebrows. Keeping the shoulders still, and using the neck, move the head first to the right, and then the left – back and forth. While keeping the external focus fixed ahead on one point, move the head to a 45 degree angle to the right, continuing to flutter the eyebrows. Repeat to the left.
>
> (Cited in Zarrilli 2000: 79)

All the changes of a character's inner state of being/doing (*bhava*) are reflected in his face.

Besides the facial expression, the twenty-four root hand gestures (*mudras*) are of prime importance. They can be combined in different ways. A special meaning is attributed to each gesture and combination. When a hand gesture is performed, the eyes have to follow the hands. The hand gestures are to be performed in accordance with the character, played and adapted to the particular dramatic context of a scene. They can be understood as their own language. In fact, they are used to

> literally speak the text, and therefore, in delivery follow the word order of Sanskritized Malayalam . . . When serving this purpose they range from literal mimetic representation of an easily recognizable object, such as 'deer' or 'lotus', to signs for grammatical construction, tense, case ending, etc., such as the plural ending for a noun, or saying, 'etc.'
>
> (Zarrilli 2000: 77)

However, hand gestures can also be purely decorative, emphasizing the beauty and quality of a movement in the dramatic context, as is the case in dance. Here, they do not carry particular symbolic meanings.

Zarrilli lists eight categories and qualities of *mudras*:

1. heroic gestures;
2. gestures for something or someone away from the body of the speaker such as 'chariot', 'giving an order', 'refusing a request';
3. powerful gestures such as 'energy', 'destruction', or 'obstruction';
4. gestures associated with the furious state such as 'demon', 'cruel', 'anger';
5. gestures for personal relationships such as 'brother', 'sister', 'elder brother';
6. gestures which describe the qualities of what is seen, such as 'mountain', 'brightness', 'black', 'red', 'clouds';
7. gestures performed in the neutral, stationary position such as 'lotus', 'moon' 'sun';
8. gestures associated with the erotic and pathos in which the hands move from the left to the right as the leg is closed such as 'beautiful lady', 'face', 'lips', 'eyes'.

(Zarrilli 2000: 77)

Some hand gestures, particularly the descriptive ones, must be accompanied by a simultaneous movement through the space, which completes their meaning. Although all of them have to follow a given pattern for the meaning to be conveyed, the actor–dancer will interpret each hand gesture according to the specific state of the character, the mood of the scene, or the content of what he is expressing. One has to keep in mind that the actors–dancers never speak but only use gestures. The words are sung by the vocalists on stage.

The vocalists not only sing the narrative passages composed in Sanskrit metrical verse (the *sloka*). They also sing the first-person dialogue and/or soliloquy passages (the *padam*) composed in a mixture of Sanskrit and Malayalam as dance music for the actors–dancers. The narrative passages allow the vocalists great freedom of interpretation. They are predominantly sung without any actors on stage. They set the mood and provide the context for the scene to follow. In case any actors are on stage while the vocalists sing a *sloka*, "they enact the essence of what the singers are narrating" (Zarrilli 2000: 41).

When the *padam*, the dialogue or soliloquy, is performed, all three groups of performers are involved: the vocalists sing the lines, the actors "speak" each line with hand gestures, and the percussionists set and keep the basic rhythmic structures and times within which the lines are sung and enacted. "As a general rule, each line of a *padam* is enacted at least twice by the actor–dancer while the line is sung repeatedly by the vocalists" (Zarrilli 2000: 41).

This explains the extraordinary length of the performance. When Balakrishnan discussed the text of *The Bacchae* with the Kathakali scholar, they realized that a performance of the whole text would take at least eight hours. Since this was too long a time for the Delphi Festival, the text had to be shortened considerably. Reducing the length of the text was inevitable given the maximum duration of two hours prescribed by the Greek side. Evidently, it was not the highly codified acting or the particular cooperation between the vocalists and the actors–dancers that required the abridgement of the text but the conditions imposed on the company by the Committee and its representatives present in New Delhi.

Such a highly codified acting system is not to be misunderstood as a Brechtian (or any other kind of) alienation of the actor from the character he is portraying. Rather, he has to become one with his character as required by the *Natyasastra*:

> In theatrical performance, after proper consideration of age and dress, he who has the suitable form should resemble the role in nature too. Just as a man's soul, discarding its nature along with the body, enters a different body with its different nature, a wise man, exercising his mental faculties, makes other's nature his own, holding 'I am he' and along with his dress, speech and body, follows his actions too.
> (Kale 1974: 58–59; translation of *Natyasastra* XXIV: 15–18)

There are basic types of characters, easily recognized by spectators in Kerala or by connoisseurs of Kathakali with the help of the performers' makeup. However, even the subsumption of a character under a particular type does not prevent the actors–dancers from individualizing the characters they are portraying within a very wide range. As such, they are not stock characters. Since the character types are determined by the makeup, they are all named after it. There are seven basic kinds of makeup:

1. "green" (*pacca*)
2. "ripe" (*payuppu*)
3. "knife" (*katti*)
4. "beard" (*tati*)
5. "black" (*kari*)
6. "radiant" (*minukku*)
7. "special" (*teppu*)

Masks are used occasionally and only for select characters.

"Green" characters (the color here refers to the face paint) include divine figures, kings, and epic heroes, while "ripe" ones (here the faces are painted orange–red or golden yellow) are reserved for the four divine characters: Balarama, Brahma, Shiva, and Surya. "Knife" refers to "mixed characters" – they are arrogant and evil, yet still have a streak of nobility. They wear the same facial makeup as the "green" characters and also the same shape and size of crown. However, they also have two bulbous white protrusions on the nose and forehead, indicating their evil nature.

The color of the beards is decisive. While a white beard is worn by a higher, divine and wise being, the red beard is a sure sign of the evil and base nature of its bearer. A black beard indicates the same qualities as the red one but conveys the additional information that its wearer is by nature a schemer.

The female demons all wear black dresses, bucket-shaped headdresses, and oversized false breasts, which have a comic effect. They are by nature "lustful, sexually charged, ugly, hysterical, and are dangerous shape-changers able to transform themselves" (Zarrilli 2000: 56). A "radiant" appearance, by contrast, refers to the idealized female heroines and "pure" dutiful wives, as well as to the most virtuous and noble male citizens, holy men and sages. The basic makeup for this type is a warm yellow–orange.

A modest rectangular cloth curtain is held up by two people between the scenes in order to hide changes.

This brief survey of the most important features and conventions of Kathakali provides insight into the parallels, even similarities, to Greek tragedy and into what aspects might have posed problems. The most obvious correspondence is their common preoccupation with mythology, gods and heroic mythical figures as reflected in the traditional makeup and costumes.[2]

Dionysus, in this production, was not just a divine figure but a god resembling Shiva. He transformed into a bull, a snake, and a lion. The "principles represented by Shiva . . . correspond to the nature of the bull, the snake and the panther (occasionally replaced by the tiger or lion) . . .

The bull is the vehicle of Shiva. The bull is Shiva, and in the animal Kingdom, is the manifestation of the principle represented by Shiva–Dionysus" (Daniélou 1984: 112). As such, Dionysus belonged to the category of "ripe" characters in Kathakali, set apart by his golden–yellow face. He wore a headgear resembling Shri Krishna's; however, unlike the latter's, Dionysus' also had a wreath on top and the hood of a snake above that.

The character of Pentheus was the topic of spirited discussions between Rajendran Pillai, the actor playing Pentheus, Balakrishnan, and the Greek theatre people, who were present during the rehearsal process. "Through the choreography, done by Balakrishnan, it was decided that Pentheus is an anti-hero, partly good, partly bad, and therein similar to the character of Ravanna from the epic *Ramayana*" (Krishnan, in charge of makeup and costumes; Pillai, who played Pentheus, 2009). Following these discussions, a green face, red mustache, and red eyebrows were accorded to him in addition to the white protrusions on his nose and forehead.

Tiresias' characterization was partially consistent with the tradition. He wore a white beard, typical of a wise man, but much longer than usual. His white wig and walking stick were new additions which, however, did not contradict the underlying principle.

FIGURE 8.1 Encounter between Pentheus (Rajendran Pillai) and Dionysus (Guru Sadanam P. V. Balakrishnan). Photo: International Centre for Kathakali.

The soldiers were conceived in a completely different style. Kunhi Krishnan used Emperor Alexander the Great's helmet as a model and referred to photos from Greek theatre for their costumes.

The greatest problem arose with regard to the chorus. In Kathakali there is no group dancing. It is usually a solo performance, and there are never more than five or six characters in any play. Balakrishnan initially suggested leaving out the chorus completely and assigning its songs to the vocalists. Later he came up with the idea of reducing the chorus to a single character. Both solutions had already been explored and embraced by Western stage directors. When Max Reinhardt staged Sophocles' *Electra* (1903) in Hofmannsthal's version in Berlin, there was no chorus at all. When Dimiter Gotscheff put *The Persians* on stage at the Deutsches Theater Berlin in 2006, the chorus was embodied by one actress. Both of these examples were celebrated productions. However, in the case of Kathakali, the Greek theatre people objected. As both Balakrishnan and Kunhi Krishnan report, the Greeks insisted that a chorus was necessary as it represented the "essence" of Greek theatre. Keeping in mind that Kathakali costumes are elaborate and costly because they play such a significant role, it struck the group as wasteful to have several people playing a "single" character such as the chorus. Moreover, the chorus was seen as a distraction from the main character and his solo performance. Synchronization was difficult. But since the representatives of the committee insisted, Balakrishnan included a chorus of sixteen dancers – half male, half female – for the performance in Delphi. When they performed again later in New Delhi, this number was reduced to four.

What can we make of such an intervention from the representatives of the host? It is highly unlikely that a similar demand would have been made of Western stage directors such as Peter Stein or Peter Hall. On the other hand, it is very possible that the host providing the funding and the prestigious performance venue felt entitled to make demands that entailed the risk not only of "spoiling" the tradition of Kathakali but also of dismembering it. Judging from Balakrishnan's statements, it posed a challenge for the Kathakali artists to find out how their form could incorporate elements from one that was quite different while staying true to their traditions. While clearly a chorus is not an "essential" part of the Kathakali tradition, Balakrishnan and his group, out of respect for both traditions and their "essence," tried to accommodate what to Western theatre artists would have seemed an improper and completely unfounded demand, which they probably would have turned down. However, even if they accorded the Greek theatre people the right to determine what the "essence" of Greek tragedy might be, they made it very clear that they would never go so far as to sabotage their own tradition. If the committee, based on the ideological claim of the universal "truth" and value of ancient Greek tragedy and on their argument of the chorus as its "essence," felt not only justified but also entitled to demand the distortion, perhaps even dismemberment, of the other's traditional theatre, Balakrishnan and his group would never have agreed to such a "compromise."

The inclusion of the chorus required the introduction of new conventions. New movements had to be found, which were borrowed from existing dance traditions also rooted in the *Natyasastra*, such as Manipuri and Odissi dance. They were incorporated without much difficulty.

Other changes also became necessary, especially in terms of the dialogue (*padam*), which is sung by the vocalists and "spoken" in gestures and movements by the actors–dancers.

> In Kathakali for one *padam* there must be so and so many lines. But here, for Dionysus we often had one line or even just one word, and the response would also be one word. So in between it was very difficult to keep the rhythm. It changed the rhythm and the music tone. One line, and then one line in response between characters. The quarrel scenes, back and forth. In traditional Kathakali the interaction is longer, must always be two–three lines at a time.
> (Balakrishnan 2009)

Another new element was incorporated with regard to Dionysus. Kathakali usually only employs percussionists. For this production another instrument was added, a wind instrument called a *kumbh*, which is traditionally used in Kerala as a ritual instrument in temples. In this case it was played whenever Dionysus did "some extraordinary things ... so the audience could recognize" (Balakrishnan 2009).

There is some disagreement between Kunhi Krishnan and Balakrishnan about the blood on Agave's face. While the first maintained that it was new to Kathakali, the latter asserted that there have been scenes in Kathakali where blood is shown. "Normally, according to *Natyasastra*, there is no fight, no bloodshed allowed on stage. But in Kathakali from the beginning, there are fights, and blood is shown ... Bloodshed is not a problem for us but in Kathakali it is always an evil person who gets killed. Here it is not like that" (Balakrishnan 2009; on the question of blood, see Zarrilli 2000: 132–133). However, it seems that while the vocalist sang the messenger's report, the actor–dancer "spoke" and enacted it with his gestures and movements in such a way that it had a strong impact on the audience in Delphi as well as in Delhi. Yet from the interviews and one of the Greek reviews it is not clear whether only the messenger enacted Pentheus' death or whether he was accompanied by Agave.

The scene in which Agave enters with Pentheus' severed head posed another challenge. It was decided that Pentheus' mask would be removed backstage and brought before the audience by Agave. "This was also a first because in Kathakali the masks are never removed on stage or shown without its bearer" (Krishnan and Pallai 2009). Balakrishnan reports that this scene evoked complete silence in the audience, followed by thunderous applause.

The curtailing of the text meant focusing on certain aspects. Dionysus, Pentheus, and Agave appeared as the central characters. While the other characters remained, they were clearly secondary. The director/choreographer selected those scenes that he felt were important to this main conflict. Then the English text had to be translated into "Manipravalam," the Sanskritized Malayalam used in Kathakali. The resulting text had the same structure as traditional Kathakali plays, even though the story and many words were new. Based on this structure, the choreography and the music were chosen "and when we saw it was not fitting we changed it. Like that, by trial and error, we developed the whole play" (Balakrishnan 2009). That Pentheus disguises himself as a woman, for example, was something that did not fit at all. In the end, it was not realized as a change of costume but by adopting the gait of a girl – modifying the acting replaced the cross-dressing.

The rehearsals took place on an empty stage, as is usual for Kathakali, with a particular lamp positioned at center front stage. When the group arrived in Delphi, there was a set waiting for them in the classical Greek style, with columns, etc. The program notes fail to inform the spectators that this was unilaterally conceived and set up by the committee. Of course, when the group returned to Delhi, they performed on the empty stage again but added one small pillar made of thermocol to give the set a Greek flavor.

To the audience in Delphi a performance was presented that, in the self-understanding of the group, adhered to the traditional Kathakali style, albeit with some novelties. The set, however, was against the tradition.

It is difficult to find out more about the audience responses. Balakrishnan and Kunhi Krishnan remembered very positive reactions, for instance to the final scene with Agave. Balakrishnan states that, generally,

> the reception in Delphi was fantastic, the audience reacted . . . They completely wet their towels [handkerchiefs] with tears. One man especially, a Greek man, he hugged me at the end, he said "What is the magic? Our characters you raised to divine level" and he said actually our Greek tragedy fits *only* to Kathakali, that is what he suggested to me.
> (Balakrishnan 2009)

Such reactions affirm the particular transformation of Kathakali brought about by the group. Their production affected the audience and some spectators very deeply. Reading the reviews in Greek newspapers, however, conveys a completely different impression.

One critic voices the opinion that the Delphi Center's commissioning of the play at the International Centre for Kathakali in New Delhi demonstrated the impossibility of productively relating Greek and Indian culture to one another:

> The traditional Indian Kathakali theatre is a system that remains a mystery to the non-initiated. It is rooted in Indian mythology and employs a traditional, very strictly codified language of gestures, expressions, movements of the head and the body, but also of masks and costumes; it was incapable of speaking about *The Bacchae*. The message was not revealed. The Indians were unable to give their language to *The Bacchae*; moreover, there were a number of missteps: the permanently smiling faces of the women in the chorus, the noisy musical accompaniment, the complete absence of the bacchanal in the two-hour performance.
> (Kaltaki 1998)

Another critic complained that the Kathakali version preserved nothing of the Greek original. She poked fun at the production, thus demonstrating "Greek superiority" over "Indian childishness":

> A ridiculous Tiresias with a shepherd's stick and a toga and some "ancient Greek" helmets pointed to a childish fairy tale, just as the shrill masks, the colorful phantasmagoria, the pantomimes, the thunder, the dragons [?] and the one-dimensional movements of the 14 [sic] dancer–interpreters.
>
> The ancient myth was disguised as an Indian fairy tale in which the language, the text, hardly matter, and neither does the concept of the tragic, an element unknown to Indian culture. The will to probe into the ancient text was completely lacking.
> (Matziri 1998)

This critic began her review by emphasizing that "ancient tragedy deals with the eternal truths of mankind beyond geographical and time limits." We have to conclude that from this perspective the Kathakali group "failed" to understand the "eternal truths of mankind." Such reviews confirm the idea that from the committee's side the project was initiated as an *agon* between two ancient theatre forms – Greek and Indian. While Greek theatre laid claim on "universality," the Indian stage tradition was seen as limited in its particular appeal; while the Greek embodied values valid in all cultures across the world, its Indian counterpart enacted exclusively local values and could not claim any interest, let alone validity, beyond its local reach. Ancient Greek theatre, therefore, by far surpassed ancient Indian theatre, which would never be able to understand, much less rival, its greatness and universal truth. In the eyes of the quoted Greek critics, their own antiquity had won the *agon* hands down, as ancient Greek theatre revealed itself as clearly superior to ancient Indian theatre.

Such reviews speak to a certain arrogance and ignorance as well to the long-lasting conviction that ancient Greek tragedy will, to a certain extent, always remain the exclusive property of the modern Greeks, because it "is written into our DNA" (cited in Mavromoustakos 2009: 311), the implication being that only they would ever be able to fully understand and properly stage it. The insistence of the Greek host on the inclusion of a chorus as well as the reviews of the performance suggest that the purpose of inviting theatres from other cultures to stage Greek tragedies in one of their own traditional theatre forms is to reaffirm one's own ideological schemata. Ultimately, the reviews document a "clash of cultures" that took place in Delphi, provoked by the committee but hopefully not even noticed by the invited guests, who received the suggestion to stage a Greek tragedy as an invitation for a productive encounter between two very different performance cultures.

Despite the four, perhaps even six months of rehearsal (the number varies in different statements), the production was shown in New Delhi only once, which is quite normal for experimental performances. Moreover, the fact that Balakrishnan later staged another Greek tragedy, *Alcestis*, with his own resources invalidates the idea that the production of *The Bacchae* did lasting damage to the tradition or was a failure altogether. *Alcestis* was performed several times in New Delhi and was even included in the Kathakali Festival of 2006. Clearly, it had a greater appeal for the local audience.

In the interview Balakrishnan stressed that some of the elements first introduced in *The Bacchae* were kept and regularly used, e.g., the *kumbh* instrument. So it seems promising to investigate the particular transformations Kathakali underwent through this production. I will end this chapter with a comparison between former changes and this one against the background of the overall question of encounter or clash of cultures in order to assess the significance of *The Bacchae* in Kathakali's ongoing process of transformation. Balakrishnan addressed the issue of changes to Kathakali in a globalizing world matter-of-factly. He states: "With the whole world coming so close, we must be ready to accept changes" (Balakrishnan 2009). Evidently, the group itself regarded the transformations as "appropriate." While changes were formerly mainly brought about by the Kathakali artists themselves as they developed their art further, here the changes resulted from demands made by staging a play not only outside their tradition but also from a whole other culture. The stage designer Kunhi Krishnan therefore felt the need to explain why these changes could also be deemed "appropriate":

> The reason the fusion of Kathakali and a foreign play worked out here was because the play was also a classic. Modern characters like Hitler, Lenin, or even Gandhi would not work in Kathakali, only superhuman stories work in Kathakali, partly because the costumes match those characters. Shakespeare's drama, too, is not really suitable for Kathakali, even though it has been done in the past. Kathakali and Greek plays are both mythology and therefore the collaboration worked.
>
> (Krishnan and Pillai 2009)

Kunhi Krishnan here draws a clear line between earlier experiments involving Kathakali and their own *The Bacchae*. During World War II there had been a Kathakali piece entitled *The Killing of Hitler*. In it Hitler appeared in red-beard makeup as the evil demon king who had set out to conquer the world. His opponents, including Chiang Kai-Shek, Stalin (not Lenin), and Roosevelt, wore green makeup. At the end of the performance Hitler was killed in a fight (for more on this and the following examples see Zarrilli 2000: 177–205). A few years later *People's Victory* was performed as a Kathakali piece. Both pieces were performed only once. Alluding to the latter piece, *People's Victory* was performed on numerous occasions in 1987 "for often wildly enthusiastic left-front political audiences" (Zarrilli 2000: 198). Even if Lenin was missing from the cast, the Marxist-Leninist Kathakali piece included World Conscience (in green) and Imperialism (with a red beard) as dramatic characters. Conscience defeated Imperialism and, in the end, the red flag was brought on stage. *People's Victory* was not performed for the usual Kathakali audience but for "common people," e.g., members of the All-Indian Agricultural Workers Union and the local Communist Party of India. As an eyewitness told Zarrilli: "When the red flag came to the stage, there was a tremendous response because of the political commitments of the audience . . . The audience forgot themselves when they saw the red flag" (Zarrilli 2000: 198).

These politically motivated experiments were not meant to – nor did they leave – a lasting imprint on Kathakali in the sense of changing the tradition. When the International Centre for Kathakali was founded in New Delhi, it initiated experiments that were intended to "adapt Kathakali to the modern stage" (cited in Zarrilli 2000: 179). Among the experiments of the 1960s were *Mary Magdalene*, the 1965 adaptation of the poet Vallathol's poem Maddalena Mariyam, *David and Goliath*, *Buddha Caritam*, *Salome*, and adaptations of Tagore's plays *Chandalika* and *Visarjan* (Sacrifice). Other experiments followed in the 1970s, also by other companies. In 1977 the cultural organization Kaliyarang in Kottayam adopted and produced Aymanam Krishna Kaimal's version of Goethe's *Faust*, *Faust's Release*. This was a particularly important experiment since it was received enthusiastically by critics and audiences alike. The review in the *Indian Express* praised the production for the "appropriateness" of the theme, character, and musical modes and for "giving the spectators as much delight as they would have derived had they been witnessing a story from our ancient scriptures." It "proved, beyond doubt, that purely Western themes can form suitable material for a classical art like Kathakali" (cited in Zarrilli 2000: 179).

All these experiments addressed different regional Indian audiences, familiar or unfamiliar with Kathakali. They were attempts to increase the interest in a classical performance genre faced with the challenge of surviving in and therefore forced to adapt to a modern and modernizing society.

This focus on regional audiences changed with the two international stage collaborations of *King Lear* in 1989. The Australian playwright and director David McRuvie and the French actor–dancer Annette LeDay originally conceived *Kathakali King Lear*. The first production was co-produced by their Association Keli (Paris) with the Kerala State Arts Academy (Kerala Kalamandalam). Besides highly regarded senior Kathakali artists, the cast also included LeDay (as Cordelia). The performances were mainly for international audiences at festivals such as those in Rovero in Italy and Edinburgh in the United Kingdom, as well as international guest tours to the Netherlands, France, and Spain. However, the premiere was in Kerala and was attended mostly by a Malayali audience. Rehearsals took place in Kerala and were observed by connoisseurs, triggering a discussion on the "appropriateness" of some of the decisions, e.g., the choice of the knife makeup for Lear instead of the kingly green or the "realistic" removal of Lear's royal accoutrements and typifying makeup during the storm scene. The discussion thus became part of the ongoing debate on the appropriateness of such changes to the tradition.

The discussion in Europe centered on other issues. While the French dance critics received *Kathakali King Lear* with much praise, the other critics mostly responded in a manner quite similar to the Greek reviewers when writing about *The Bacchae* almost ten years later. They either stressed the difficulties of coming to grips with such an unfamiliar, "foreign" theatre form or lamented the particular reading of the play with which, by and large, they did not agree (Zarrilli 2000: 188–195). The British critics especially were unanimous in their opinion that *Kathakali King Lear* had "little to do with Shakespeare" (Morris 1990; cited in Zarrilli 2000: 188). It is important to remember that the production toured Europe at the end of the 1980s, i.e., the heyday of so-called intercultural theatre, when Peter Brook's *Mahabharata* (1985) was praised by the British and European press as the epitome of interculturalism. Against this background, the incapability or unwillingness of the critics to consider seriously a "foreign" theatre form that incorporated elements from the Western tradition in a collaboration that demanded changes from both sides seems almost incredible. No critic in the Western world asked whether Peter Brook's "reading" of the *Mahabharata* would have been acceptable to Indian spectators. Yet they expected to find their own reading of Shakespeare's play realized in *Kathakali King Lear*. While Peter Brook in their view opened up the possibility for an encounter between cultures – even as Indians regarded it as a clash (Dasgupta 1991) – they mostly dismissed *Kathakali King Lear* as a kind of blasphemy and as a clash of cultures.

If we situate the Kathakali production of *The Bacchae* within this genealogy, the same pattern was still at work almost ten years later. While the Kathakali artists dealt with both traditions with great respect and tried their best to reconcile both sides without going against the "essence" of either, the festival committee made demands with reference to the "essence" of Greek tragedy without really considering whether or not this gesture could possibly go against the other's tradition. Some Greek critics, in turn, assessed the success of the production only against their own understanding of the play, declaring that their counterpart had failed to grasp it even while they themselves clearly did not know much about the other's tradition. Their response was a "dismembering" of what they perceived, because they perceived it as a clash of cultures.

The transformation process undergone by the Kathakali form in the production of *The Bacchae* was, however, seen by the artists involved as being more or less in line with their tradition. Keeping in mind that the production/choreography was done by the director of the International Kathakali Centre in New Delhi, founded in order to open up Kathakali for new audiences and, in this sense, "modernize" it, his readiness to get involved in the project seems consequential. The participating artists clearly regarded the production neither as an improper appropriation of the heritage of another culture nor as a dismemberment of their own tradition caused by the demands of the committee. As can be guessed from Kunhi Krishnan's negative response to earlier experiments, they had clear criteria – implicit or explicit – when judging the appropriateness and validity of the changes they made. The key was not randomly to remove, add, or change certain elements but to do it in agreement with the central underlying principles. It seems that the artists were fully aware that a productive encounter with another tradition meant respecting certain limits that were not to be transgressed, thus safeguarding what each side regarded as the "essence" of its tradition. The production did not plunder, exploit, or "occidentalize" the other culture in the way that Brook's *Mahabharata* had "orientalized" India. Rather, it resulted from an attempt to do justice to both traditions.

In this sense, the Kathakali production of *The Bacchae* can be regarded as exemplary with regard to interculturalism in the performing arts – even if not in the sense of the term "intercultural theatre" as coined in the West in the 1980s (see the preface). The production came into being out of the respectful encounter of two different traditions, even if this did not prevent the Greek critics from seeing it as a clash of these two cultures based on the alleged inability of the other side to grasp thoroughly and truly the universal and "eternal truths" of the Greek cultural heritage. For the Greek critics, this version of *The Bacchae* proved once again that no other cultural form, be it modern or traditional, can seriously claim to be a match for ancient Greek culture. They still believed in Winckelmann's dictum that a productive encounter with ancient Greek culture will be possible only as its imitation, to which, ultimately, they alone as the "descendants of Euripides" were entitled (Elena Spandopoulos in her review on Ninagawa's *Medea* in Athens 1984). However, as Balakrishnan's account confirms, there were also spectators present at the performance in Delphi who not only felt deeply moved by it but also linked what they perceived to their understanding of their own tradition. They experienced it as an encounter between their own cultural heritage and the Indian tradition of Kathakali, an encounter that enabled them to see their own tradition in a new light and to appreciate the other. Against this background, the Kathakali production of *The Bacchae* must be deemed an exemplary intercultural performance also in this respect, even if this term was never applied.

Notes

1. This and all translations of Greek reviews are by Anastasia Siouzouli.
2. Material on this production is scarce. I have not seen the performance myself and there is no video recording available. I have referred to the program notes, photographs and transcripts of conversations between Saskya Jain and the director, the stage designer and the actor playing Pentheus. I did see a video recording of *Alcestis*, staged later by the same group, which allows for a more thorough understanding of such an interweaving of performance cultures.

References

Balakrishnan, Guru Sadanam P. V. 2009. In conversation with Saskya Jain at the International Kathakali Centre, New Delhi, January 28.
Daniélou, Alain. 1984. French 1979. *Gods of Love and Ecstasy: The Traditions of Shiva and Dionysus*. Rochester, VT: Inner Traditions.
Dasgupta, Amitava. 2009. In conversation with Saskya Jain at Sangeet Natak Akademi, New Delhi, February 16.
Dasgupta, Gautam. 1991. "*The Mahabharata*: Peter Brook's Orientalism." In *Interculturalism and Performance*. Edited by Bonnie Marranca and Gautam Dasgupta, 75–82. New York: PAJ.
Jain, Jyotindra. 2002. "India's Republic Day Parade, Restoring Identities, Constructing the Nation." In *India's Popular Culture: Iconic Spaces and Fluid Images*. Edited by Jyotindra Jain, 60–75. Mumbai: Marg Publications.
Kale, Pramod. 1974. *The Theatric Universe: A Study of the Natyasastra*. Bombay: Popular Prakasha.
Kaltaki, Matina. 1998. "'Drama' in Delphi . . . " *O Kosmos tou Ependiti*, July 25/26.
Krishnan, Kalamandalam P. Kunhi and Rajendran Pillai. 2009. In conversation with Saskya Jain, January 16.
Matziri, Sotiria. 1998. "The Myth is a Lie that Says the Truth." *Eleftherotipia*, August 7.

Mavromoustakos, Platon. 2009. "Das antike griechische Drama als nationale Frage. Kritiker- und Publikumsreaktionen auf moderne Aufführungen." In *Staging Festivity: Theater und Fest in Europa*. Edited by Erika Fischer-Lichte and Matthias Warstat, 303–316. Tübingen: Francke.

Morris, Tom. 1990. "A Midsummer Night's Dream." *Times Literary Supplement*, August 24.

Zarrilli, Phillip B. 1992. "A Tradition of Change: The Role of Patrons and Patronage in Kathakali Dance-Drama." In *Arts Patronage in India*. Edited by Joan L. Erdman, 91–142. New Delhi: Manohar.

Zarrilli, Phillip B. 2000. *Kathakali Dance Drama: Where Gods and Demons Come to Play*. New York: Routledge.

Further Reading

Bharucha, Rustom. 1990. *Theatre and the World: Essays on Performance and Politics of Cultures*. Delhi: Manohar. The problem of Indian "intraculturalism" and the discussion on intercultural performance.

Bharucha, Rustom. 2004. "Foreign Asia/Foreign Shakespeare: Dissenting Notes on New Asian Interculturality, Postcoloniality and Recolonization." *Theatre Journal*, March. Shakespeare in Kathakali.

Dalmia, Vasudha. 2007. *Poetics, Plays and Performances: The Politics of Modern Indian Theatre*. Oxford: Oxford University Press. For Brecht in India and the combination of Brechtian devices with forms taken from folk theatre, see pp. 153–282.

"Dialogue: Erika Fischer-Lichte and Rustom Bharucha." October 12, 2010. At http://www.textures-platform.com/?p=1667. Accessed June 11, 2013. The history and function of the term "intercultural theatre."

Fischer-Lichte, Erika. 2011. "Introduction." In *Global Ibsen: Performing Multiple Modernities*. Edited by Erika Fischer-Lichte, Barbara Gronau, and Christel Weiler, 1–16. New York: Routledge. Provides a more recent reevaluation of the term "intercultural theatre."

Fischer-Lichte, Erika, Josephine Riley, and Michael Gissenwehrer, eds. 1990. *The Dramatic Touch of Difference: Theatre, Own and Foreign*. Tübingen: Gunter Narr. Discussion on intercultural performance.

Fischer-Lichte, Erika, Saskya Iris Jain, and Torsten Jost (eds.). 2014. *Beyond Postcolonialism: The Politics of Interweaving Performance Cultures*. London: Routledge. Elaborates further on the shortcomings of the term "intercultural theatre."

Pavis, Patrice, ed. 1996. *The Intercultural Performance Reader*. New York: Routledge.

Williams, David, ed. 1991. *Peter Brook and The Mahabharata: Critical Perspectives*. New York: Routledge.

9

Beijing Opera Dismembered
Peter Steadman and Chen Shi-zheng's *The Bacchae* in Beijing (1996)

> In this collaboration the *xiqu* [Chinese opera] serves as a means for approximation [to ancient theatre]. There is no *xipi* nor *erhuang* (Beijing opera chanting), no gongs and drums or stylized representation. As an autonomous theatrical system, the *xiqu* was unable to maintain characteristic features of its own. It is not an "equal collaboration," since it was based on the assumption that the theatre form from the periphery, rather unfairly, should orient itself after that of the center [the West] ... In this process, we constantly have to take on a passive role and are unable to decide anything for ourselves. The West is cooking its own soup, in which the *xiqu* is thrown in as a well-prepared ingredient. (Tang 1996: 43; cited in Lin 2010: 304–305)[1]

> The production used a few technical elements from Chinese opera; the result, however, added up to little more than a performance of an ancient Greek tragedy with a Chinese cast. It maintained the structure of the work, the use of music was Western, the costumes resembled Greek – albeit very old-fashioned – ones and the difficulty of the undertaking was clearest when it came to the part of Tiresias: a caricature! The great art and technique of the Chinese actors, however, was evidenced by the renowned actor Kong Xinyuan, who played the parts of the messenger and of Cadmus. (Kaltaki 1998)[2]

The first of the two quotes above is from a review by a Chinese critic written after the premiere of *The Bacchae* staged by the China National Beijing Opera Ensemble in 1996, in which he deplored what he perceived as the

---

Dionysus Resurrected: Performances of Euripides' The Bacchae in a Globalizing World, First Edition. Erika Fischer-Lichte.
© 2014 Erika Fischer-Lichte. Published 2014 by John Wiley & Sons, Ltd.

dismemberment of Beijing opera caused by this production. The second review was written by a Greek critic after the performance in Delphi in 1998 (the same year the Kathakali *Bacchae* was shown). While mentioning the "few technical elements" from Beijing opera, this critic was surprised that the production looked very Greek overall – and in an "old fashioned" way. She even identified an element of "caricature." Only one actor was spared the criticism. While both critics reached different conclusions, they agreed that the performance of *The Bacchae* by the National Beijing Opera was a far cry from a performance in the Beijing opera style. The same critic who had complained that the Indian artists were unable to let *The Bacchae* speak through the language of Kathakali was now taken aback by the absence of elements from Beijing opera.

What had happened? Why had the National Beijing Opera decided to stage *The Bacchae* while renouncing their own constitutive performance style? This is all the more surprising considering that there had already been a successful example of staging a Greek tragedy in the style of a traditional Chinese opera. The performance history of ancient Greek tragedies in China is rather short. While the first, roughly ten, translations of tragedies had already been penned in the 1930s, the first performances did not take place until the 1980s. Luo Jinlin, son of Luo Nian-sheng, who was one of the three most important translators of Greek tragedy, put *Oedipus the King* on stage in 1986, with students of the Central Academy of Drama in Beijing as actors. This was followed by a production of *Antigone* in 1988. Both were staged in the so-called *huaju* style – a genre of spoken theatre introduced to China at the beginning of the twentieth century by students who had witnessed the creation of the new theatre form Shingeki in Tokyo. In 1906 Li Xi-shuang founded the Spring Willow Society in Tokyo, which endeavored to introduce spoken theatre to China. After a few performances in Tokyo, the Friends of the New Theatre opened the Spring Willow Theatre in Shanghai in 1914, which was dedicated to furthering the development of spoken theatre, huaju.

The two performances of Greek tragedy in this style by Luo Jinlin became quite popular in China. *Oedipus* was even broadcast by the television company CCTV, reaching a large audience. At the same time, an academic symposium took place that was devoted to the production. As such, the production enjoyed a broad resonance throughout very different milieus. The response to *Antigone* was also very positive. The critic Huang Wenjun commented:

> I sense the unique, mysterious, deeply moving and soul-cleansing force of the Greek tragedy. Such tragedy happens without tears and sadness, brings forth a kind of irresistible effect of ethical sublimity.
>
> (Huang 1988: 43; cited in Lin 2010: 252)

Regarding the integration of aesthetic principles from traditional Chinese opera forms such as the *xiqu*, Huang praised Luo's *Antigone* as "a brilliant and excellent performance that successfully brought together the Chinese character as well as the essence of Greek tragedy" (Huang 1988: 44). In his view it presented a productive encounter between the two cultures.

Both productions were invited to Delphi. However, it seems that they did not garner as much praise there as at home. Terzopoulos, generally in favor of the productions, suggested to Luo that he adapt a Greek tragedy in one of China's many local or regional opera styles. In 1989 Luo adapted *Medea* to the style of the Hebei Bangzi opera (from the province of Hebei), which was presented in Delphi in 1991. This production, by contrast, won international acclaim. The critic Kostas Georgoussopoulos praised it in the highest terms, even while belittling Luo's *Oedipus* and *Antigone*:

> The former "Oedipus" was a naïve-moving, Western-inspired melodrama. Meanwhile, there was a similar "Antigone" and now, this year, came the solution, matter-of-factly, natural, simple as a breath. Luo Jin-lin, in the strict but fertile tradition of his country, has breathed and sucked in the language and the traditional customs . . . Luo Jin-lin has found his way and his way is a teaching for us which says: the most successful way to express your innermost is to nurture oneself from one's own deepest roots.
> (Georgoussopoulos 1991; cited in Lin 2010: 267–268)

Ironically, while Luo's *Medea* was seen as a productive encounter of their two cultures by the Greek side, the "nurturing from one's own deepest roots" was not met with the same enthusiasm in China. The Hebei Bangzi *Medea* did not arouse much interest. There were not many performances or reviews. In fact, up to its revival in Beijing in 2002 it was presented only twice. The reasons for the lack of interest in 1989 and even after its great international success in 1991 were manifold and somewhat contradictory. The connoisseurs of the Hebei Bangzi opera style felt uncomfortable with the changes it had undergone in Luo's *Medea* – changes which had gone unnoticed by the international audiences. Another group of critics were the opponents of traditional opera forms in general. They vehemently fought any attempt at their revival, seeing them as firmly rooted in feudalism. There was also a third party, which preached "truthfulness to the text." Since the text had to be considerably changed in order to fit the demands of the opera form, they complained that the performance was not true to the text. By 2002, however, these reasons no longer seemed to matter that much anymore. This time, the performance was met with great interest, also from the media, which highlighted and praised the extraordinary performance of the actors.[3]

This brief overview of the short performance history of ancient Greek tragedy in China and its reception in Delphi is rather telling, especially with regard to the criteria for the assessment of such a production as a productive encounter between Chinese and Greek culture. While the performances in the style of spoken theatre were seen as bringing about such an encounter in China, they were sharply criticized in Greece. And whereas the *Medea* in the style of Hebei Bangzi opera was deemed a productive encounter in Delphi, it was deplored as being unfaithful to the traditional style and also to the text of the tragedy in China. However, even if we keep in mind the different criteria that determine whether a performance is considered a productive encounter between two sides, the reviews quoted at the beginning of this chapter are noteworthy because both judged the performance as a failure from that perspective. The Chinese critic Tang attacked the production because it "was unable to keep characteristic features of its own," i.e., of the Beijing opera style as an "autonomous theatrical system"; and the Greek critic blamed it for having so little to do with Beijing opera and for being spoken theatre – as Luo's *Oedipus* and *Antigone* had been. However, contrary to Luo's productions, she lamented that this was not even "melodrama" but partly even "caricature."

What went wrong with this production that it aroused such serious criticism from both sides? Tang mentions an "equal collaboration" which he felt did not happen in this case. The production, which was the result of a collaboration between the New York Greek Drama Company and the China National Beijing Opera Ensemble, was made possible by a very generous grant from the United States National Endowment for the Humanities (NEH) – in fact, it was the largest grant ever awarded to a theatre production by this organization. This raises a crucial question. What interest did the NEH pursue when awarding such a large sum to a collaboration between the New York Greek Drama Company and the Beijing Opera Ensemble?

It was Peter Steadman, the director of the New York Greek Drama Company, who applied for the grant. His company used to perform ancient Greek plays in their original language. Steadman found this to be not quite fulfilling. As he himself stated, his desire was to revive ancient Greek theatre in an "authentic" performance – an endeavor that seems to me contradictory in its very concept (Fischer-Lichte 2008). Moreover, in this specific case, such a goal strikes me as doomed to failure given the lack of precise knowledge about the Athenian performance practices of the fifth century BC.

According to Steadman, he already intended to combine Greek tragedy with Beijing opera in 1993 in order "to give new life to the ancient theatre through the fresh blood of a vital traditional theatre form" and, thus, "to convey its lyricism by uniting language, music and dances as well as to restore the lost pleasure granted by ancient Greek theatre's total work of art" (Steadman 1996: 25).[4] As Wagner had conjured up ancient Greek theatre one and a half centuries earlier in order to justify his idea of a *Gesamtkunstwerk*, a total work of art, which was to be realized by his new form of music theatre, Steadman justified his attempt to revive Greek theatre with a similar Wagnerian vocabulary. However, while Wagner clearly stated that we can never return to the Greeks but must instead invent a new form of theatre, Steadman proclaimed a return to "authentic" Greek theatre. It was to this end that he wanted to collaborate with the China National Beijing Opera Ensemble, which raises the question of what the two performance genres have in common beyond combining lyrics, music, and dance.

This was indeed Steadman's argument. He declared that many classicists specializing in ancient Greek theatre celebrated traditional theatre forms from Asia for being much closer to ancient Greek theatre than any form of contemporary Western theatre, since the ancient theatre was non-naturalistic and unified lyrics, music, and dance. He argued that therefore only actors of traditional theatre forms following age-old principles similar to those of ancient Greek theatre would be able to stage its plays "authentically." This is why he approached the China National Beijing Opera Ensemble for a collaboration.

> The collaboration between the China National Beijing Opera Theatre and the New York Greek Drama Company for the performance of *The Bacchae* marks a historic event. Our production is the greatest collaboration between American and Chinese theatre. The United States National Endowment for the Humanities has offered the largest sum ever to be awarded since its foundation to our project. It is the first time that these two archaic theatre traditions – ancient theatre and Chinese Beijing opera – enjoy the same status and unite their forces on equal footing for a true artistic creation.
> (Steadman 1996: 22; cited in Lin 2010: 298)

In the above quote Steadman describes the encounter as occurring on an "equal footing," which, according to Tang, did not happen. Steadman highlights three aspects: the collaboration between a Chinese and an American theatre as a historic event; the fact that the NEH awarded the largest grant ever to this project; and the balanced meeting of "two archaic theatre traditions – ancient theatre and Chinese Beijing opera." All three points raise certain questions and concerns. What made this collaboration between Chinese and American theatre artists a historic event? Surely, theatre artists from these two countries had worked together in the past? Moreover, it seems inappropriate to place the New York Greek Drama Company – a theatre by no means renowned or well known even within the United States – on the same level as such a widely acclaimed and internationally celebrated opera company as the National Beijing Opera Ensemble. It seems that the financial backing from the NEH had the effect of artificially inflating the reputation of Steadman's theatre and of giving legitimacy to a project which was unsound in its basic assumptions of reviving ancient Greek theatre on a Beijing opera stage. Lastly, it is not convincing to speak of a Greek archaic theatre tradition. All that we have at our disposal is a tradition of handing down, reading, and interpreting the extant texts, which is disconnected from its performance tradition.

The same applies to labeling Beijing opera an archaic theatre tradition. In contrast to ancient Greek theatre, Beijing opera is a living theatre tradition. While it has been continuous, it is merely a few centuries old and therefore cannot be called archaic (who, for example, would call Western medieval culture "archaic?"). I hope that an examination of the materials available on the production will shed light on why Steadman used this misleading vocabulary and also enable us to address our remaining questions.[5]

Steadman conceived all the plans for the production himself. He named Chen Shi-zheng, who had studied in the United States and had been living there for many years, as director. Existing knowledge on ancient Greek theatre conventions determines that the cast had to be all male. The chorus consisted of twelve members and three actors were supposed to take over the eight parts in the tragedy. Steadman insisted that the chorus be composed of members of his own company. They had to sing in ancient Greek in order to convey "the meaning and beauty of Euripides' lyrics," as he put it. This meant that only the three actors playing the eight roles were members of the China National Beijing Opera Ensemble. The chorus members as well as the actors all wore masks. This posed a problem for the actors because wearing masks is not part of the Beijing opera tradition.

Steadman argued that the Chinese actors would encounter fewer technical difficulties than Western actors, as they were used to playing female as well as multiple parts and employed masks, which is not true. Moreover, referring to depictions on ancient Greek vases, he stated that the art of acting in both theatre forms was very similar in terms of "body postures, attitudes and round, circular movements" (Steadman 1996: 24; cited in Lin 2010: 300). Steadman also had specific ideas about the music used in ancient Greek theatre, even though our knowledge of it is scarce. He distinguished it from "modern harmonious" music by stating that it was characterized by "shrill tones" and "crashing sounds" (Steadman 1996: 24; cited in Lin 2010: 300), which in his view could be best recreated by using traditional Chinese musical instruments and three musicians from the Beijing Opera orchestra. However, he commissioned an American composer, Eve Beglarian, to write the music. Due to substantial differences in the ancient Greek and the Chinese tonal systems, as maintained by Steadman, he insisted on adapting the Chinese oboe *suona* in order to produce two more half-notes, which allegedly were present in the ancient score. The costumes and – to a certain extent – the masks were also made in Greek style. What, then, remained of Beijing opera?

Steadman's statements about the movements, gestures, and music of ancient Greek theatre were all based on mere assumptions. We lack sufficient evidence to support them. The depictions on the vases do not give grounds for the conclusion that the actors displayed body postures, attitudes, and movements similar to those used by Beijing opera actors. Nor do the sources on Greek music provide adequate evidence for Steadman's justification for changing a Chinese musical instrument. His approach to this collaboration suggests that he was following a specific agenda here.

This suspicion is nourished by Steadman's choice of this particular tragedy "authentically" to revive ancient Greek theatre with the Beijing Opera Ensemble. Steadman argued that *The Bacchae* is the only Greek play that blurs the strict separation between tragedy and comedy, a feature typical of ancient Greek theatre but non-existent in the Beijing opera tradition. The choice of the tragedy, so it seems, was made in order to facilitate the enterprise for the Beijing opera artists by bringing it closer to their own tradition. This argument is unconvincing. In his article quoted above, Steadman uses a telling phrase in speaking of the "fortress of Beijing opera." As Dionysus planned Pentheus' dismemberment right from the beginning, so, it seems, Peter Steadman intended the conquest of the "fortress Beijing opera" right from the start. This sentiment reflects Tang's complaints in his review.

It seems that Steadman succeeded – even if not completely, at least to a remarkable extent. The stage did not resemble a Beijing opera stage even though it was empty, with a golden-brown backdrop painted as a circular diagram. None of the actors wore traditional Beijing opera costumes. They were dressed in chiton-like tunics of different colors – short ones for the male, long ones for the female characters. Accordingly, when Pentheus was persuaded by Dionysus to put on women's clothes, he changed into a long tunic. The older men, Cadmus and Tiresias, were dressed in long robes with a chlamys-like mantle over them. "The costumes were finely embroidered, but because the design was detailed rather than bold, it was barely visible, and the overall ornamentation was more suggestive of the Aegean than the Yellow River civilization," is how Catherine Diamond described them (Diamond 1999: 149).

Oddly, the masks of the three main actors were based mainly on Commedia dell'arte, with red ones for Pentheus, Cadmus, and the Thebans and a green one for Tiresias. Dionysus and the chorus wore white masks, the latter made to look slightly more feminine with a red flower above the ear and long locks on the sides.

According to Catherine Diamond, the three actors confessed "that using the masks, which allowed them to play all the roles, was the most difficult aspect of their experiment. Not being trained in masked performance, their body and head movements were rarely able to bring the masks to life" (Diamond 1999: 149–150).

Another problem was posed by the chorus members chanting in ancient Greek. Since the director Chen wanted to add a Chinese flavor to it, he

FIGURE 9.1 Dionysus (Zhou Long) and some maenads. Photo: Huang Hai-wei.

rehearsed synchronized movements and processions with them that derived from existing Chinese folk traditions. According to him, it was very difficult to coordinate the singing and the movements. Since Steadman insisted on preserving what he called the rhythmic integrity of the Greek, the movements had to be adapted to it. Chen said that he interpreted the nature of the bacchants as female Chinese shamans (*wupo*) and claimed to have integrated their movements into the chorus. However, as Diamond reports, "Peter Steadman contends that it was he who suggested the correlation of shamans to the bacchants to Chen as a way of explaining the chorus to the Chinese press. Chen makes much of his observing shaman trances and dances of the Miao minority, but no one has described or identified these in the performance. Some of their movements might have served as inspiration but this was not evident in the final result" (Diamond 1999: 164, n. 42).

Regardless of who had the idea of relating the bacchants to shamans, this could be interpreted as another attempt to include a "Chinese" element. Since the Miao minority has nothing to do with Beijing opera, however, this attempt, too, ran the risk of contributing to its dismemberment and, given that the bacchants were not recognizable as Miao shamans, seemed to have failed altogether.

According to Catherine Diamond, "the prevailing effect was more aligned with martial arts executed in close military formation." The chorus, not only in its tight movement but also in the chanting, was very masculine in her view "with very little concession to the Bacchae's female nature or any suggestion . . . of their wild ecstasies." Diamond laments that only the masks gave the chorus members womanly appearances, "but nothing in their gestures, female 'shamans' notwithstanding, denoted either abandon or a female identity. Given this style, their occasional tittering with their hands over their mouths, a cliché-gesture, supposedly connoting femininity, was a travesty" (Diamond 1999: 154). This impression is also evoked in the video recording.

However, at one point Chen – or rather the star actor Kong Xinyuan – deviated from Steadman's instructions. To deliver his two long reports – that of the herdsman and then that of the messenger – the actor took off his mask to better employ facial expressions. Moreover, the two speeches were completely rewritten in order to adapt them to two different styles of traditional storytelling techniques that provided precise regulations for the rhythmical delivery of the story as well as for gestures and movement.

> As the herdsman, Kong accompanies his narrative with the clapping of two large pieces of cow-bone. He uses a dialect and a peasant storytelling style called *su lai bao* to echo the low status and style of the speaker in Greek . . .
> As the messenger bringing news about Pentheus, he uses a different storytelling style, one traditional to Chinese tea-houses. Called *shuo shu*, it is a far higher form of narration than the *su lai bao* and more appropriate to the tragic content of the speech.
>
> (Kilroy 1996: n.p.)

Here the actor was, for the first time, able to utilize his Beijing opera training, even if the performance was of a different genre, in order to deliver a virtuoso performance that triggered immediate applause. As one critic reports on the performance in Beijing, "the audience roared with laughter when the Herdsman tore off his mask, and launched into a description of the Maenad's orgies, and applauded the speech enthusiastically" (Melvin 1996).

These, then, were the leftover fragments from Beijing opera – the skill with which the reports were delivered and a few acrobatic jumps and poses by Dionysus and Pentheus. It seems impossible to regard this production as a productive encounter between the Chinese and the American theatres or between Beijing opera and ancient Greek tragedy. Unlike Luo's *Medea*, the text of the Greek tragedy was not changed at all and partly not even translated into Chinese, so that the local audiences could not follow. Tang deplored the fact that there was no recognizable interpretation of the tragedy, so that the spectators could not understand the actions except for the fact that some god of wine arbitrarily took revenge – a critique also articulated by Diamond. Steadman claimed that the "universality" of Greek tragedy could only unfold its full potential when every word was spoken in ancient Greek, even if the spectators could not understand a single word. In contrast to Suzuki's use of a foreign language, for example, the American chorus members of Steadman's company clearly were unable to convey anything through their acting. The only adaptations – of the herdsman's and the messenger's speeches – were made because of a star actor's insistence, on whom neither Steadman nor Chen could exert any influence. He knew what would appeal to the audiences and went for it.

On the other hand, the Beijing opera style was changed to such an extent that it lost its particular identity. Its constituent features, praised by Steadman as being similar to those of ancient Greek theatre and therefore not only offering but guaranteeing the possibility of an "authentic" revival, were erased. Beijing opera, here, was not realized as a total work of art. This invalidated Steadman's main argument of combining Greek tragedy with Beijing opera in order to create an "authentic" performance. The claim to universality of Greek tragedy and, following from it, its absolute authority was instrumentalized for the conquest of the "fortress" Beijing opera.

By bestowing universality on Greek tragedy and, at the same time, appropriating it as a common heritage of Western cultures – thus including North America – Steadman succeeded in conquering the embodiment of Chinese culture. As such, it was dismembered: Steadman arrived as a stranger in the "fortress" Beijing opera and ended up destroying it. Initiating and realizing this production of *The Bacchae* can be regarded as an act of American cultural imperialism. The performance did not need to convey a particular "reading." Rather, it meant precisely what it did – the dismemberment of the Beijing opera.

Against this backdrop, the choice of the play makes sense, too. It also answers the questions raised by the three aspects highlighted in Steadman's essay. The collaboration can be seen as a "historic event" in that, from Steadman's perspective, it demonstrated the superiority of Western over Chinese culture. The emphatic proclamation of the integrity of a text that "embodies" the heritage of Greek, European and, by extension, American, i.e., Western, cultures, was made in order to use the text as a pretext for dominating a theatrical form that, in a way, can be regarded as the embodiment of the Chinese cultural heritage. This explanation provides an answer to the second question, as the NEH had a stake in the project and was thus willing to provide such a huge grant. It seems, then, that calling both traditions equal was nothing but pretense.

Suzuki incorporated American actors into his training and his productions in order to demonstrate that his new approach to acting, his "grammar of the feet," would coin a truly universal theatrical language in the sense that spectators in the most diverse cultures would be able to respond to it. By contrast, the universality as proclaimed by Steadman and accorded to texts written in a dead language served as a means to dominate another culture, in this case the Chinese, which in many ways has set out to rival the claim of the United States to be and act as the only superpower – "the leader of the West that has become the leader of the world" as George H. W. Bush put it in his "Address on the State of the Union" from January 28, 1992. Beijing opera, as an "autonomous theatrical system," had to be sacrificed on the altar of the United States' undisputed claim to leadership, causing a clash of cultures.

But why did the Chinese agree to this enterprise? Since the project was financed by the Americans and Steadman arrived with a fixed idea on how to realize it, the Chinese "partners" and, in particular, the China National Beijing Opera Ensemble should have known that they would be instrumentalized. However, they might have entertained certain hopes, even ideas, themselves to use this enterprise for their own purposes. In line with this, the reception of the production was by no means only negative, as the review by Tang might suggest. Rather, it was received as the realization of a new form that came into being. Especially younger spectators, who were not as well versed in ancient Greek theatre, found the performance quite exciting and celebrated it as an important innovation. The critic Ren Xiu-lin emphasized in her positive review that the production should not be judged according to the standards of Beijing opera. The connoisseurs who did do so unanimously rejected it. Ren Xiu-lin argued that instead it had to be seen and judged as a *huaju* performance which the Beijing opera actors embarked on here for the first time. Thanks to their special training, she said, they were superior to *huaju* actors in the dynamics of their movements. She regarded the production as enriching ancient Greek theatre and, in this respect, as a productive encounter. Therefore, she praised Chen Shi-zheng as a great director who deserved "gracious recognition" for such an "unprecedented attempt" (Ren 1997: 43; cited in Lin 2010: 304). She failed to mention the imbalance between the American and the Chinese sides. Instead, by stressing Chen Shi-zheng's directing, she placed emphasis on the achievements of the Chinese artists – the director, the actors, and the musicians.

Generally, then, there were two opposing views on the production. On the one side, there were the connoisseurs of Beijing opera, unwilling to accept any change to its conventions. Since they found these conventions to be mostly lacking in the production anyway, they were strongly opposed to it. On the other side, there were the younger spectators who were largely not even aware of these conventions. They did not receive the production as *xiqu* at all but as spoken theatre, as *huaju*, and as a novel form of it. As the critic Ren suggests, this impression was mainly due to the excellent acting of the Beijing Opera Ensemble members, which by far surpassed the faculties of *huaju* actors. Both parties, the disapproving connoisseurs and the enthusiastic spectators, based their opinions on their experiences of the performance without taking into account the background of the production.

Tang instead proceeds from the fact that the project was an American initiative and states that the Americans left China deeply satisfied. He raises the question: "Facing the applause we received and will receive [on the planned world tour to Hong Kong, the United States, and Europe, which, with the exception of Hong Kong and Delphi, did not materialize], should we not better keep our cool?" After harshly criticizing the project, e.g., in the quote at the beginning of this chapter, and emphasizing the imbalance, even unilateralism, of the enterprise, he tries to explain why the China National Beijing Opera Ensemble agreed to this collaboration:

> *The Bacchae*, apparently, exemplifies the fact that we are caught in a dilemma. On the one side, we yearn to participate, by all means possible, in the international cultural exchange and to enter a dialogue with the others in order to be acknowledged by them. On the other, we are so desperate that we have to accept Western money and are therefore involuntarily condemned to take over the passive role.
>
> (Tang 1996: 44; cited in Lin 2010: 305–6)

Tang names the hope to bring their own traditional theatre form to the world stage and win international recognition as the Chinese motive and justification for the collaboration. This hope, however, did not come to fruition, in his view. Beijing opera did not enter the world stage, mainly because the inequality of this collaboration meant that Beijing opera did not even survive as an autonomous theatrical form. As his argument indicates, he did not side with the connoisseurs either, who were against any kind of change. His point is quite another one:

> *The Bacchae* has arrived in China. We do not regard the *xiqu* as private property and therefore do not object when others want to absorb the artistic experiences of the *xiqu* collected over the last eight hundred years. We do not even mind if, every now and then, Beijing opera actors work for Western people who are in search of their roots. However, the key problem is that we began to be satisfied and proud when we heard the applause [of America]. Phrases such as "product of exchange" or "fusion of China and the West" which could be read in many newspapers, appeared as nothing but our illusions. The *xiqu* did not enter the world stage. Instead, the heterogeneous Western art forms and ideologies approached us at a fast pace. In the exchange between China and the West, we have such an inferior position that we are scarcely autonomous anymore.
>
> (Tang 1996: 44; cited in Lin 2010: 306–7)

As this paragraph suggests, there were indeed a number of people in China who regarded the production as the result of an exchange and a productive encounter, even "fusion," of Chinese and Western cultures. The focus was not so much on the Americans who initiated the project but on the fact that a

Greek tragedy was performed, presupposing that Greek tragedy actually is the root of Western culture. This, in Tang's view, is an illusion. His fear is that such kinds of so-called exchanges would ultimately lead to the total destruction and eradication of traditional culture.

> The inequality of today's cultural collaborations is often hidden, so that it can be recognized only with difficulty. The penetration by the heterogeneous Western cultural forms as well as their mild judgments and "soft" rhetoric result in the gradual loss of our indigenous traditions and in a weakening of our sense of responsibility to hand down our folk culture to the next generation. This is sad, but it teaches us to focus even more on developing the *xiqu* with passion and wisdom. In order to arrive at a dialogue on an equal footing, our last resort is to save ourselves. Only if we remain faithful to ourselves can we accept the cultures of others.
>
> (Tang 1996: 44; cited in Lin 2010: 307)

Tang does not mention the Cultural Revolution that also swept away the indigenous traditions and folk cultures so that, after its end, it was very difficult to save what was left and put them back together. Since the Cultural Revolution had already dismembered traditional Chinese culture to an extent that it could not be fully restored to wholeness, Tang clearly sees a similar danger lurking behind such kinds of collaborations: the danger of dismemberment not through open violence as in the Cultural Revolution but through the power, reinforced by generous funding, of "mild judgment" and "soft rhetoric." Tang's statement contains an implicit warning not to let capitalism destroy what communism had already damaged. At the same time, he stresses that he neither regards the *xiqu* as "private property" nor wants to freeze it in time, instead advocating to develop it "with passion and wisdom." His review is not to be misunderstood as a plea against any kind of collaboration. Rather, it is a plea for thoroughly reflecting on what should be adopted and how, in order to bring about a mutually productive encounter between different cultures.

His view is shared and supported by Liu Chong-zhong, a Chinese intellectual who strongly refutes the idea of the "universality" of Greek tragedy and Western culture in general and defies the notion of "particularism" attributed to all other cultures, which then have to be overcome by the "universality" of Western culture. This had been the case with the Beijing opera collaboration, which was made to dissolve in the "universality" of Greek tragedy. Proceeding from Said's concept of Orientalism, Liu argues:

> To idealize the culture of the "Other" in a selective and manipulative way, ostensibly acting in the interest of the people, is no privilege of the West. Occidentalism is its reversal, for it accepts the construction of Western cultural thought and the supremacy of the West. Western culture is regarded as a strong

and Chinese as a weak culture. This assumption means to authorize, centralize, and canonize the theory of Western thinking. Western culture is regarded as the reference system for Chinese theories on culture and art, so much so that they have become for us the system of theoretical coordinates. In this system, we can position ourselves at any point, since the evaluation of all our thinking on literature and art is based on Western scientific concepts and terminology. On the other hand, occidentalists present their own culture in a way that pleases the West by bringing it closer to Western culture, which sometimes is even called world or global culture, in order to gain recognition from it.

(Liu 1999: 18; cited in Lin 2010: 331)

The trauma of the Cultural Revolution seems to lurk behind Tang's deliberations and Liu's reflections. After it had almost completely erased all traces of traditional culture,[6] scholars and artists alike found themselves either trying to reconstruct or even reinvent it, or, as the so-called Occidentalists did, to adopt Western culture as the "stronger" one and therefore to change what was left from their own in a way that "pleased" the West. *The Bacchae* at the China National Beijing Opera is a good case in point here. From Steadman's point of view it was the – successful – attempt to conquer "the fortress Beijing opera," which was nothing more than an act of cultural imperialism financially supported by the NEH and quite in line with official American cultural politics. The Chinese side allowed for such a "conquest" because they hoped that this would bring about international recognition and acclaim for their own traditional culture. In order to "please" the other, i.e., the Americans and the West in general, they allowed Steadman to distort it in such a way that it could no longer be regarded as Chinese traditional culture at all. This created a scenario in which Chinese culture was shown as nothing but an imitation of Western culture.

This was exactly what happened in Delphi. None of the Western critics were aware of the political dimension; no one discussed the conditions of its coming into being. Peter Steadman's name was not even mentioned. The stage director Chen Zhi-zheng alone was blamed for the failure of this "modern production" (Kaltaki 1998). He was seen as a Chinese director because of his ethnicity, and no one ever mentioned the fact that he had studied, lived, and worked as a director in the United States for a long time. Instead, the impression was created that the China National Beijing Opera Ensemble had staged *The Bacchae*, directed by a Chinese director of their choice. The production, which some Chinese critics had hailed as a result of cultural exchange that would "please the West," was taken as an exclusively Chinese production by the Greek critics and unanimously condemned. "The spectators were disappointed when they saw to what extent the Chinese artists of *The Bacchae* of the National Beijing Opera had assimilated the Greek elements when we had expected more Chinese elements," the critic Dimitra Petropoulos wrote in a critique similar to the one quoted at the beginning of this chapter and to those of the other Western critics. The German critic Ernst Schumacher, professor of theatre studies at Humboldt University in Berlin at the time of the German Democratic Republic and by the 1990s retired, referred to an argument from an old debate and called the production an "appalling example of eclectic formalism" (Schumacher 1998). He did not link the all-male cast and the costumes to ancient theatre conventions. Instead, he likened the costumes to those bought at the store of the Oberammergau Passion Plays and condemned the use of masks as artificial. None of the reviews written by Western critics that I read recognized the production as a revival or an "authentic" performance of ancient Greek theatre. Unanimously, they blamed Chen for his "modern" and "eclectic" production, some at least praising Kong Xinyuan for his performance as herdsman and messenger. The dismemberment of Beijing opera as a consequence of Steadman's act of cultural imperialism in the name of universality accorded to Greek tragedy – a concept with which most Greek critics would have agreed and which the Chinese side did not contradict, let alone prevent – went unnoticed.

The reception of *The Bacchae* in Delphi clearly confirmed Tang's as well as Liu's concerns. It was not Beijing opera that entered the "world stage" and was recognized as such but an imitation of an old-fashioned Western way of staging Greek tragedies as had been prevalent in Europe until the end of the 1950s and in Greece even a decade longer. This production of *The Bacchae* was therefore unable to serve the purpose which the Chinese side had hoped for.

Even if these goals continued to be pursued in Chinese cultural politics, Tang's and Liu's concerns were taken into consideration. In 2002, on the occasion of the revival of Luo's Hebei Bangzi *Medea*, a symposium took place to debate these issues. On the one hand, the conditions for productive encounters through performances of Greek tragedies in the form of the *xiqu* were discussed. The renowned dramaturge Zhu Xin-yan concluded that it was impossible to "clone" the original, i.e., Greek tragedy, and that therefore it should not be allowed to set any restrictive demands (Zhu 2003: 53). The critic Ding Ru-jin further defined what it took to create a "meaningful adaptation": "Only when the original, notwithstanding its canonical status, is interpreted according to the Chinese logic and moral perspective, a meaningful adaptation comes into being" (Zhang 2003: 5; cited in Lin 2010: 259). Such a meaningful adaptation is regarded as the prerequisite not only for successful productions in China but also first and foremost for enabling the *xiqu* to enter the world stage. This was emphasized in the introductory remarks to the symposium made by the chair, Qin Hua-shen, director of the Beijing Research Institute of the Arts. He stated that "connecting the two theatre traditions in the new century is of utmost importance, especially because there has been a plea to bring Chinese culture into the world ever since China joined the World Trade Organization" (Zhang 2003: 1; cited in Lin 2010: 259).

The production of *The Bacchae* had been guided by the hope of internationalizing Beijing opera, which, however, did not happen on the stage at Delphi. This now became the official guideline of cultural politics in China. The vice chief editor of the journal *Zhongguo Wenhuabao* (Chinese Cultural Journal) Xu Shi-pei strongly supported the idea of such "meaningful adaptations" of Greek tragedy and defined their goals as follows:

> In view of China's opening up towards the global market and the intensification of multilateral trading processes as well as of cultural exchange, the new task will be to find out how theatre art as a kind of "global" language can further develop for the purpose of overcoming the barriers of cultural background and verbal communication and to present traditional Chinese art and culture in foreign countries so that the market for Chinese art products as well as the Chinese cultural influence can be expanded.
>
> (Xu 2003: cited in Lin 2010: 260)

It seemed to be the common belief that these goals could be better achieved when the *xiqu* enters the world stage not with performances of traditional Chinese plays but with those from the Western canon, such as Greek tragedies or Shakespeare plays. After returning from a guest tour to the Sixth International Ibero-American Theatre Festival at Bogotá in Colombia in 1998, the director of the Hebei Bangzi Company from the province of Hebei, Li Jiu-yuan, had already formulated such insights as follows:

> In order to carry Chinese theatre art into the world and to take a particular share on the global market, it is mandatory, wherever it is possible, to renounce local contents and instead, for an international guest tour, select such plays from the repertoire which are internationally influential and popular.
>
> (Li 1998: 57; cited in Lin 2010: 261)

Among these plays Greek tragedies stand out, although they are by no means as often performed as plays by Shakespeare, Ibsen, or Brecht. For, as the critic Xu Shi-pei emphasizes, Greek tragedy is regarded as the "gene bank of Western culture." Therefore, he advocates a "crossbreeding" of Chinese and Western culture from which, in his opinion, both sides of the audiences would profit:

> When the *xiqu* adopts and performs ancient Greek classics, which are long since restricted to the text form, it will transform them on today's stages into living art. This fusion has a much bigger chance to remain firm on the market than if we would present to foreign spectators our own works of art unmediated, because with regard to the cultural background, the action, the

worldview, etc. they are more accessible to them. In addition, there is the curiosity [of the foreign spectator] and the aesthetic expectation towards a foreign art.

(Xu 2003; cited in Lin 2010: 262–265)

On the other hand, Xu does not only mention the argument of the international market, which includes profiting from the West's exoticizing gaze. He also believes that such "meaningful adaptations" will enable a productive encounter between Chinese and Western culture, for it would provide "new nourishment . . . from the cultural roots of the West" (Xu 2003; cited in Lin 2010: 262–264) so that a new Chinese culture and art form could evolve. Therefore, he advocates "bilingual versions" – even if not in the sense of Suzuki:

> The version at home should take great care how to explain and interpret the historical Western background and the Western culture under consideration of the needs of the Chinese spectator. Regarding the version meant to be presented abroad the problem has to be solved how ancient Greek classics can be represented in the form of *xiqu*, so that this art can unfold its attraction for Western spectators.
>
> (Xu 2003; cited in Lin 2010: 263)

As we can conclude from the contributions to the symposium, the situation changed considerably over the six years since the performance of *The Bacchae*. Still, the goal is to present one's own traditional theatre forms on the stages of the world. Yet a discussion had in the meantime begun that took into consideration the concerns uttered by Tang and Liu. Moreover, confidence in the strength and potential of one's own culture, which went hand in hand with China's economic growth, had increased remarkably. The dismemberment of a traditional Chinese opera form, accomplished in order "to please the West," seemed inconceivable under these circumstances. At the symposium, the idea of Chinese culture as a strong culture was clearly prevalent – at least as strong as to be able to seek productive encounters with Western cultures. Six years after its production, *The Bacchae* could be regarded as a slip from the past, as a dead end, but not as a model for the future. It had its relevance in the warning it implied, made explicit by Tang. The program for performances of Greek tragedies to come, as formulated by the symposium considering the warning, pointed to the future.

In the so-called Beijing opera *The Bacchae*, Dionysus had appeared in Beijing as a stranger, coming in this case from the West and adopting the form of an American – comparable to Suzuki's version of 1989 – in order to cause a clash of cultures which resulted in the dismemberment of Beijing opera. At the symposium in 2002, Dionysus returned to Beijing, this time not as a human but as the god of theatre, to promote productive encounters between Chinese and Western theatre cultures and thus to enable the coming into being of new aesthetic "wholes" out of this encounter. However, this did not result so much in the spread of Greek tragedy in China – since 2002 only a few of them have been performed – but instead led to a flourishing industry of Shakespeare and Ibsen performances in the *xiqu* style, which followed this program.

Notes

1. All Chinese reviews referenced or quoted in this chapter are translated by Kuan-wu Lin and used by her permission. In writing this chapter I am greatly indebted to her study.
2. All Greek reviews referenced or quoted here were translated by Anastasia Siouzouli.
3. The Chinese reception and the reasons informing it are examined in detail in Lin (2010: esp. 251–265).
4. Translated into German by Lin (2010: 299). All the information on Steadman can be found there.
5. While I have not seen the performance, I was happy to be given access to a video recording. I also referred to Chinese and Greek reviews, a few essays and the chapter on the production in Lin (2010: 295–310).
6. That is to say, something remained: ten years after the end of the Cultural Revolution the old cultural traditions were revived. Quite a number of *xiqu* actors had survived and could hand down their knowledge to a younger generation. Very few, like the actress Pei Yan-lin, mounted the stage again themselves. Today, she is called a "national treasure" of China.

References

Diamond, Catherine. 1999. "The Floating World of Nouveau Chinoiserie: Asian Orientalist Productions of Greek Tragedy." *Theatre Quarterly* 15, part 2 (NTQ 58): 142–164.

Fischer-Lichte, Erika. 2008. *The Transformative Power of Performance: A New Aesthetics*. Translated by Saskya Jain. New York: Routledge.

Georgoussopoulos, Kostas. 1991. "The Chinese Paradigm: Medea has been liberated and revitalized by China's Style and Speech." Translated by Anastasia Siouzouli. *Ta Nea*, July 7.

Huang Wenjun. 1988. "Reuxin de lizan – wo kan 'Andigani'" [Praise for humanity – Seeing a performance of *Antigone*]. *Chinese Theatre* 7: 43–44.

Kaltaki, Matina. 1998. "'Drama' in Delphi." *Epediti*, July 25–26.

Kilroy, Charlotte. 1996. "*The Bacchae* of Euripides: Greek Tragedy Meets Beijing Opera." *Beijing Scene* 2 (7): 15–21.

Li Jiu-yuan. 1998. "Shije renmin xihuan Zhongguo xiju yishi" [Cosmopolitans love Chinese theatre art]. *Da Wutai* [The Great Stage] 3: 57.

Lin, Kuan-wu. 2010. *Westlicher Geist im östlichen Körper? 'Medea' im interkulturellen Theater Chinas and Taiwans: Zur Universalisierung der griechischen Antike*. Bielefeld: transcript.

Liu Chong-zhong. 1999. "Zhongguo xueshu huyu zhong de 'xifang zhuhi'" ["Occidentalism" as a Chinese scholarly concept]. *Foreign Literatures Quarterly* 2: 18.

Melvin, Sheila. 1996. "China: Euripides as Peking Opera." *Wall Street Journal*, May 9.

Ren Xiu-lin. 1997. "'Bakai': ba xiang jingju de jingju" [*The Bacchae*: A Beijing opera not resembling a Beijing opera]. *Xiju Zhijia* [The Home of the Theatre] 1: 43.

Schumacher, Ernst. 1998. "China und Indien in Delphi: Symposium über antikes Drama mit asiatischen Gastspielen" [China and India in Delphi: Symposium on ancient drama with guest productions]. *Berliner Zeitung*, July 31.

Steadman, Peter. 1996. "'Bakai': yanchu de yiyi" [The meaning of the performance of *The Bacchae*]. Translated by Yü-hua Lian. *China Peking Opera* 2: 22–25.

Tang Xiao-bai. 1996. "'Bakai-huanxian de qihe" [*The Bacchae* – the encounter of illusions]. *Chinese Theatre* 6: 42–44.

Xu Shi-pei. 2003. "Cong Hebei Bangzi shuokai qu" [The approach of the Hebei Bangzi "Medea"]. *Zhongguo Wenhuabao* [Chinese Cultural Journal], January 23.

Zhang Yan-yin. 2003. "Meideya Yanchu chengong yu yishu-baijing hebei bangzi jutuan 'meideya' yantao hui congshu" [The success and cultural importance of the *Medea* performance: Summary of the symposium on *Medea* of the Hebei Bangzi-Company from Beijing]. *Journal of College of Chinese Traditional Opera* 24 (1): 1–5.

Zhu Xin-yan. 2003. "Cong xila jitan feidao shenzhou wutai de 'Meidiya'" [*Medea* flown from a Greek altar to the Chinese stage]. *Journal of College of Chinese Traditional Opera* 24 (2): 53.

Further Reading

Min Tian. 2008. *The Poetics of Difference and Displacement: Twentieth Century Chinese–Western Intercultural Theater*. Hong Kong: Hong Kong University Press.

Epilogue
Dionysus – God of Theatre, God of Globalization

We proceeded from three problems which are inherent in the process of globalization according to most theoreticians:

1. Traditional communities dissolve and the question arises how to build new ones for which the old criteria of inclusion and exclusion are no longer valid and which are not meant to be long-lasting but fulfill their purpose on a temporary basis. In other words, how do we bond with each other in the "global village" (McLuhan)?
2. The dissolution of traditional communities inevitably leads to the destabilization of collective as well as individual identity. Is it even possible to acquire some kind of collective identity – maybe in a specific kind of "third space" (Bhabha)? Or must we see collective and all individual identity as fluid and continually undergoing transformations?
3. Today culture can no longer be perceived as a fixed or isolated entity. Members of one culture meet those of others, and they adapt to each other. Whether this happens between individuals or groups of any size, the question always arises whether this meeting will turn out to be a productive encounter or a destructive clash of cultures or a combination of both.

Strikingly enough, these problems refer to some of the different, partly even contradictory, purposes and functions Dionysus was believed to fulfill in

---

Dionysus Resurrected: Performances of Euripides' The Bacchae in a Globalizing World, First Edition. Erika Fischer-Lichte.
© 2014 Erika Fischer-Lichte. Published 2014 by John Wiley & Sons, Ltd.

antiquity. He was regarded as the god of liberation and communality. He freed his followers from all sorts of pressures and united them into a community. He transgressed or even dissolved the boundaries between male and female, man and god, man and beast, life and death. Thus, he destabilized given identities and initiated radical transformations. Encountering this foreign god could lead to a new form of being for his followers or turn into an unavoidable clash with his opponents, causing widespread death and destruction.

The performances discussed in the three parts of this book, each devoted to one of these problems, did not just *deal* with them. Rather, they acted as the god did: they *carried out* what they were dealing with – they liberated their spectators from certain pressures and united them into a community; they destabilized their identities and took place as a productive encounter or destructive clash between members of different cultures. In all of these cases, it was not the god as represented on stage who accomplished this but the performance itself.

In this respect the performances under discussion resemble each other, even though they otherwise differ remarkably. This holds true even for those grouped together. In each case, it is the sum total of the local conditions that made it unique.

The performances grouped together in Part I not only used very different means in order to bring about a community, as described in detail in each chapter. There was also a great variance in the kind of community that was established. In *Dionysus in 69* the community between the performers as well as that between performers and spectators was highly ambiguous. In the first case it was based on a kind of scapegoating related to the Shephard/Pentheus; in the second, there were some spectators who experienced the union with the performers in the dances as liberating, while others regarded it as a kind of violence done to them, which they resisted. In the London production of Soyinka's version a community among the spectators came into being as a relapse into a colonial situation. While the community as represented on stage was laughed at as that of a "savage tribe," the spectators felt united in their laughter and the sense of superiority from which it sprang. In the Teat(r)o Oficina the chorus acted as a community that was able to incorporate everybody – on the level of the represented even Hera, Pentheus, and the Cadmus family, and with regard to the audience everyone who was willing to join the bacchanal, the rituals or the common meals. In fact, they joined the community even just by getting up, applauding, and moving their bodies to the rhythm set by the chorus.

The destabilization of the spectator's cultural identity in the performances discussed in Part II refer to very different kinds of collective identities. In the Schaubühne performance the self-definition of a particular group of people, the so-called *Bildungsbürgertum* (educated middle class), was not only attacked but its very foundation shattered. Today, almost forty years after Grüber's production, it is hard to identify such a group as a distinctive social class. Terzopoulos' production in Delphi was received as an assault on the notion of Greekness, i.e., on the concept of national identity. Instead of hailing the idea of Greek culture's uniqueness, its distinction from other – in particular Asian – cultures, the production focused on the human body as the common basis of all cultures. Finally, Warlikowski's production, staged more than ten years after the fall of communism, not only questioned the idea of Poland as the Christ of all peoples, an idea cherished since Romanticism. Rather, it was a searing critique of the destructiveness of any clear-cut identity formation as a result of unconditional identification.

The productive encounters and destructive clashes between members of different cultures brought about by the performances making up Part III of the book are very diverse. However, in all three cases it depended on the perception of the performers and spectators whether they were received and regarded as a productive encounter or as a destructive clash. In all the different versions Suzuki staged over forty years, the destructive clash was localized on the level of the represented, whereas on the level of representation a productive encounter, even harmonious interweaving of elements from the most diverse contexts and cultures, took place. A utopian aesthetic was at work here. Whether the spectators focused on the one or the other level determined their experiences. As for the Kathakali version, we have to distinguish various perceptions. While the Kathakali artists, most of the spectators in New Delhi, and some spectators in Delphi regarded it as a productive encounter enriching both theatrical traditions, the representatives of the Delphi committee, who were present at the rehearsals, tried to force certain ideas on the Kathakali artists with no regard for their tradition. Many critics in Delphi, moreover, received the production as ridiculous, made fun of the Kathakali tradition, and brought about a clash. The Beijing opera production by Peter Steadman was planned as a conquest of the "fortress Beijing opera" and triggered a clash from the very beginning. Nonetheless, in Beijing it was received as a new form of theatre and a productive encounter by spectators who, however, neither knew Greek tragedy nor the conventions of Beijing opera. The connoisseurs of Beijing opera deemed it a destructive clash and a dismemberment of this theatre form. Other critics saw it as an attempt to fight traditional Chinese culture as a whole with the means of Western, mostly American, money and culture. In Delphi the production was accused of being a mere imitation of the Greek model. Ultimately, it was up to the different groups of spectators whether the performance was regarded as a productive encounter or a destructive clash of different theatre cultures.

Two conclusions can be drawn from this rough summary. On the one hand, the productions reflected the corresponding aspect of globalization and brought it to fruition. On the other, they each did this so differently and with such varied means that the results were far from homogeneous. The outcome was not homogeneity but the production of new differences. The ways in which the local and the global met and were interwoven was unique in each case.

If we take into consideration the time span between 1968 and 2008, other differences regarding the impact of the globalization process on theatre stand out. One of them is the permanently growing number of international theatre festivals all over the world, as well as of guest tours of single performances financed by different cultural institutions. It is quite telling that the performances discussed here that were produced before the end of the 1970s did not travel to other countries.

Yet the film versions of Schechner and Grüber's productions allowed for a wide dissemination, so that Zé Celso in his *Bacchae* could allude to some devices used in Schechner's, or Warlikowski to some scenic arrangements found in Grüber's production. A special case in point is Suzuki's theatre. While his *Trojan Women* had already traveled to Europe in the 1970s and was celebrated by international audiences, his *Bacchae*, because of Kanze's untimely death, did not tour before the 1980s. Although all of these performances dealt with questions arising from the process of globalization, they themselves did not "go global." They remained local in the sense that they were presented only in their native countries.

This changed with the productions of the 1980s and 1990s. Suzuki's various versions of the *Bacchae* as well as Terzopoulos' and Zé Celso's productions were indeed shown globally, while the Kathakali and the Beijing opera versions at least traveled to Delphi. This form of globalization clearly left an imprint on these productions, as can be guessed from Suzuki's bilingual versions, the commission of the Kathakali production by the Delphi Committee, and the large grant awarded by the United States National Endowment of the Humanities to the enterprise of reviving ancient Greek theatre through Beijing opera. In all of these cases the local eventually went global, even if for different purposes and with very different consequences.

In light of this permanent movement between the local and the global some more recent developments might seem rather surprising. Yerima's production of Soyinka's version was celebrated as an African homecoming: a Yoruba play by a Yoruba writer, performed by Yoruba actors before a Yoruba audience. Here, the global was localized in such a way as to appear completely local – as part of the Yoruba cultural heritage. A similar homecoming can be observed in Suzuki's last version, performed by an exclusively Japanese cast in a way that a critic thought "it was Noh" (Watanabe).

In all of these cases there was and is an ongoing movement between the local and the global set in motion by the process of globalization, sometimes approaching one pole, sometimes the other, and sometimes oscillating between the two. The performances of *The Bacchae* discussed in this book serve as exemplary models for the very specific movements between the local and the global.

In these performances Dionysus was resurrected as the god of globalization. The three characteristic features of the process of globalization highlighted in this study are identical with some of those traditionally attributed to Dionysus. Moreover, given that in these performances he is frequently likened to gods from other cultures – e.g., the Yoruba gods Ogun (Yerima) and Xango (Zé Celso), Jesus Christ (Warlikowski, Suzuki), or Shiva (Kathakali) – we might find such an epithet even more appropriate.

Dionysus' resurrection as the god of globalization was possible because he is also – if not first and foremost – the god of theatre. In all cases discussed here the conditions of theatre allowed for the absorption and fulfillment of his roles – even that of causing a destructive clash leading to dismemberment. As the god of theatre, Dionysus also does not cease to be ambiguous. In this sense, theatre appears to be the most appropriate site for enacting and

FIGURE 10.1 Black-figure Kyathos: Dionysus between eyes; roosters flanking handle. Source: Harvard Art Museums/Arthur M. Sackler Museum, Gift of a supporter of Sardis, 1970.34. Photo: Imaging Department © President and Fellows of Harvard College.

performing the different aspects and problems of globalization. Theatre can create communities, however temporary. It plays with and can destabilize identities, and it brings about transformations. It incorporates elements from the most diverse performance cultures, interweaving or making them collide.

It is perhaps no surprise, then, that Dionysus, the god of theatre, came back to life on a stage approximately forty years ago when the process of globalization was set in motion, which reached different cultures at different times and made itself felt in different ways. Since the process is still ongoing, we can expect to find Dionysus active and effective in many performances in various parts of the world, even if it is not *The Bacchae* that is being staged. Still, there is one thing we can be sure of wherever performances adopt and fulfill the functions dealt with in the three parts of this book: Dionysus is present.

Name Index

Abhinavagupta 191
Adua, Umaru Yar' 68
Aeschylus 12, 50, 97, 113
Aillaud, Gilles 101
Albee, Edward 161
Alexander the Great x, 196
Alkazi, Ebrahim 186
Althamer, Paweł 137, 140, 141, 143, 144
Ando Shinya 161
Aniszenko, Eugeniusz 142
Antoine, André 160
Aristophanes 86, 95, 121
Arrowsmith, William 31, 33, 51
Arroyo, Eduardo 101
Asahara Shôkô 6, 173, 174
Ashikawa Yôko 174, 176, 178
Aubrey, Serge 176

Bakhtin, Mikhail 75
Balakrishnan, Guru Sadanam P. V. 186, 190, 193, 195–198, 200, 204
Barber, John 64, 168
Barrault, Jean-Louis 163, 164
Bartoletti, Jessie 33
Beck, Julian 45
Beckett, Samuel 161, 164, 178, 180
Bednarz, Aleksander 146

Beglarian, Eve 211
Beuys, Joseph 19, 93
Billington, Michael 168
Bo Bardi, Lina 74
Bosseau, Damar 33
Bosseau, Jason 33
Boulez, Pierre 163
Brachmachari, Dhirendra 187
Brahm, Otto 160
Bral, Grzegorz 152
Brandt, Willy 94
Brathwaite, Kamau 50
Brecht, Bertolt xiii, 31, 10, 94, 116, 187, 188, 193, 221
Brecht, Stefan 36, 39, 40, 43, 44
Brook, Peter 49, 202, 203
Burkert, Walter xiv, 12–15, 18, 21, 22, 95–98

Cacoyannis, Michael 3
Cage, John 45
Calcanhotto, Adriana 83
Calderón de la Barca, Pedro 152
Caravaggio, Michelangelo Merisi da 52
Catirina, Mâe 84
Cavalli, Leona 72
Celińska, Stanisława 145

Dionysus Resurrected: Performances of Euripides' The Bacchae in a Globalizing World, First Edition. Erika Fischer-Lichte.
© 2014 Erika Fischer-Lichte. Published 2014 by John Wiley & Sons, Ltd.

NAME INDEX

Celso Martinez Corrêa, José 72–79, 80, 83, 87, 122, 129, 151, 169, 187, 228, 229
César, Chico 84
Chekhov, Anton 138, 139, 160, 169, 174
Chen Shi-zheng 206, 211–216, 219, 220
Chiang Kai-Shek 201
Christou, Yannis 126
Chyra, Andrzej 136, 148
Cieplak, Piotr 139
Ciéslak, Ryszard 152
Clark, John Pepper 50
Cooper, David 35
Csordas, Thomas 128
Cummings, Constance 59
Cunningham, Mercier Philip 45
Curtius, Ernst 112, 113

Dasgupta, Amitava 187, 188, 189
Dawes, Carol 3, 64, 66
de Andrade, Oswald 86, 87
De Palma, Brian 38
De Vita, Jim 174, 177
Dejmek, Kazimierz 137, 138
Diamond, Catherine 212–214
Ding Ru-jin 220
Dorst, Tankred 161
Drewniak, Łukasz 142, 144, 150, 151
Drummond, Marcelo 74, 76, 79
Dutschke, Rudi 5

Eisenstadt, Shmuel N. 159
El Greco 122
Enzensberger, Hans Magnus 94
Euripides ix, x, xiii, 2, 3, 12, 29, 37, 45, 48, 50, 52, 53, 55–59, 62, 63, 65, 68, 78, 82, 95, 116, 121, 141, 142, 150, 154, 168, 169, 179, 187, 203, 211

Feik, Eberhard 98
Finley, William 2, 28, 33, 37, 40, 43
Fitz, Peter 97, 102
Fleisser, Marieluise 94

Francisco, Pai 84
Fret, Jarosław 153
Friedrich Wilhelm IV 112
Fukuda Yoshiyuki 161

Gandhi, Indira 187
Gandhi, Mohandas Karamchand 200
Gandhi, Rajiv 188
Ganz, Bruno 96, 103, 104
Gassman, Vittorio xi
Georgoussopoulos, Kostas 208
Girard, René xiv, 14–19, 22, 35, 42, 43, 105
Giskes, Heinrich 97, 106
Gluck, Christoph Willibald 119
Goethe, Johann Wolfgang von x, 68, 95, 110, 112, 201
Gombrowicz, Witold 138, 139
Gorky, Maxim 94
Gotscheff, Dimiter 154, 196
Grene, David 31
Grotowski, Jerzy 31, 40, 139, 152, 153, 165
Grüber, Klaus Michael 3, 36, 93–95, 100, 109–111, 114, 227, 228
Gruszczyński, Piotr 150
Grzegorzewski, Jerzy 137–139, 141, 143

Hacker, Günter 106
Hall, Peter 106
Hanuszkiewicz, Adam 137, 141
Harrison, Jane Ellen xi
Harrison, Tony 179
Henze, Hans Werner 3
Herrmann, Karl-Ernst 95
Hewitt, Tom 172, 173
Heyme, Hansgünther 3, 95, 110, 187
Hitler, Adolf 113, 200, 201
Hobson, Harold H. 59, 63, 64
Hofmannsthal, Hugo von 162, 196
Holoubek, Gustaw 137, 138
Huang Wenjun 207, 208
Hübner, Zygmunt 141
Humboldt, Wilhelm von 112, 220
Hunt, Albert 59, 61

NAME INDEX

Ibsen, Henrik xii, 160, 221
Ichihara Etsuko 165
Ichikawa Sadanji II 160
Ionesco, Eugène 161
Isaiah 16

Jarocki, Jerzy 138
Jesus Christ 2, 122, 142, 145, 151, 220
Joffe, Roland 53, 59, 64, 87
John Paul II 143
Johnson, Lyndon Baines 5

Kaimal, Aymanam Krishna 201
Kajzar, Helmut 141
Kantor, Tadeusz 173
Kanze Hideo 164
Kanze Hisao 163–165, 167, 170, 171, 179, 228
Kawai Takeo 162, 163
Kawakami Otojiro 162
Kelera, Jósef 152
Kennedy, John F. 5
Kennedy, Robert 5, 27, 39
Kerr, Walter 39
Kijima Tsuyoshi 179
King, Martin Luther 5
Klein, Melanie 144
Kleist, Heinrich von 139
Kochanowski, Jan 154
König, Michael 119
Kong Xinyuan 206, 214, 220
Konstantinos, St. 122
Kott, Jan xiv, 16–19, 22, 95, 114, 121, 145, 150, 154
Kougioumtzis, Mimis 121
Koun, Karolos 4, 120, 121, 122
Krasiński, Zygmunt 138
Krishnan, Kalamandalam P. Kunhi 196–198, 200, 201, 203
Kuboniwa Naoko 182
Kuta, Magdalena 145

Lauren, Ellen 179, 180
LeDay, Annette 202
Lenin, Vladimir Illyich 200, 201

Li Jiu-yuan 221
Li Xi-shuang 207
Liu Chong-zhong 218–220, 222
Lösch, Volker 140
Lorca, Federico García 116
Łotocki, Lech 146
Luo Jinlin 7, 116, 207–209, 214, 220
Luo Nian-sheng 207
Lupa, Krystian 154
Łysak, Paweł 142
Lyubimov, Yuri 179

Macintosh, Fiona xi
MacIntosh, Joan 42
Maj, Marta 145
Malina, Judith 45
Mantegna, Andrea 122
Marcuse, Herbert 10
Matsui Shoyo 162
Matsui Sumako 160, 161, 162
Mauss, Marcel 127
McCarthy, Lillah 51, 52
McRuvie, David 202
Mercouri, Melina 116
Mickiewicz, Adam 137, 138
Mikhopoulou, Sophia 124, 125, 128, 130
Miller, Arthur 161
Minotis, Alexis xi, 120, 121
Mishima Yukio 161
Mitra, Shambu 186
Mitra, Tripti 186
Miyashita Norio 173
Monk, Meredith 173
Mori Masako 171
Mori Mitsuya 163
Mori Shin'ichi 171
Mrożek, Sławomir 138
Müller, Heiner 179
Murray, Gilbert xi, 17, 51–53, 55, 95, 129
Mykietyn, Paweł 145

Narayanan, Akavoor 190
Nietzsche, Friedrich x, xi, 32, 51, 53, 79, 106, 113, 154

Nikishibe Takahisa 174
Ninagawa Yukio 161–163, 204
Niziołek, Grzegorz 147
Nobbs, John 179
Nomura Mansaku 164

Offenbach, Jacques 143
Okazaki Ryôko 173
Osanai Kaoru 160

Panikkar, Kavalam Narayana 187
Patsas, Yorgos 123
Pawłowski, Roman 150
Paxinou, Katina 120
Petropoulos, Dimitra 219
Peymann, Claus 110
Pillai, Rajendran 195
Pinter, Harold 161
Plata, Tomasz 137–139, 141
Poel, William xi, 51–53
Polyzonis, Thodoros 124
Poniedziałek, Jacek 146, 148
Prado, Perez 171, 176

Qin Hua-shen 220

Racine, Jean-Baptiste 68, 154
Radulski, Wacław 141
Rancière, Jacques 140
Ratcliffe, Michael 16
Reich, Wilhelm 9
Reinhardt, Max 113, 160, 196
Ren, Ludwik 141
Ren Xiu-lin 216
Ronconi, Luca 3, 95
Roosevelt, Franklin D. 201
Rotimi, Ola 50
Rühle, Günther 94

Sada Yakko 162
Sakellariou, Akis 124, 130
Sampatakakis, Georgios 128
Sander, Otto 97, 102
Sangare, Omar 142
Santos, Silvio 74, 78
Sardinha, Pedro Fernandes 86

Sartre, Jean-Paul 74, 163
Schadewaldt, Wolfgang 109
Schechner, Richard 2, 3, 27, 29–32, 35–39, 41, 42, 49, 53–55, 60, 82, 109, 170, 228
Schiller, Friedrich 160
Schleef, Einar 154
Schlenther, Paul 119
Schmidt, Helmut 94
Schumacher, Ernst 220
Seidensticker, Bernd xiv, 12–14, 18, 22
Sellars, Peter 141
Senda Akihiko 167, 168, 170, 171, 178
Shakespeare, William xi, xii, 160, 200, 202, 221, 223
Shaw, Martin 59
Shimamura Hogetsu 160, 162
Shiraishi Kayoko 164, 165, 168, 170, 171
Siakaras, Dimitris 124
Sieradzki, Jacek 137, 138
Słowacki, Juliusz 138, 152
Smith, Ciel 42
Sophocles x, 12, 50, 95, 97, 137, 143, 154, 162, 196
Sotiriadis, Georgios 119
Soyinka, Wole 3, 48–51, 53–56, 58–66, 68, 73, 87, 109, 151, 226, 228
Spiss, Maria 154
Staniewski, Włodzimierz 152, 154
Stanislavsky, Constantin 162
Steadman, Peter 206, 209–216, 219, 220, 227
Stein, Peter 94, 99, 100, 110, 111, 143, 196
Stravinsky, Igor 101, 142
Sutherland, Efua 50
Suzuki Tadashi 4, 116, 117, 157–159, 161–174, 176, 178–182, 187, 215, 222, 227–229
Swinarski, Konrad 138, 141
Szcześniak, Małgorzata 144

NAME INDEX

Takahashi Hitoshi   164, 181
Takemori Yoichi   179
Tang Xiao-bai   209, 210, 212, 214, 216–220, 222
Terayama Shuji   173
Terzopoulos, Theodoros   116–120, 122, 123, 125–129, 132, 168, 179, 208, 227, 228
Theodorakis, Michael   60
Thomson, George   96, 98
Tsubouchi Shoyo   160
Turner, Victor   11, 27, 131
Tynan, Kenneth   60, 64

Vallathol, Narayana Menon   201
van Gennep, Arnold   11, 34, 96
Vangelis   178
Veloso, Caetano   83, 87
Vishnevsky, Vsevolod   94
von Drenkmann, Günter   94
Vostell, Wolf   19

Wagner, Richard   209, 210
Wajda, Andrzej   138, 141

Warlikowski, Krzysztof   18, 136, 137, 139, 141, 143, 144, 146, 150–154, 227–229
Watanabe Moriaki   164
Watanabe Tamotsu   182
Węgrzyniak, Rafael   147
Weiss, Peter   94
Wilson, Robert   173, 179
Winckelmann, Johann Joachim   100, 113, 203
Witkiewicz, Stanisław I.   138
Wittgenstein, Ludwig   103, 104, 109, 111
Wyoff, Elizabeth   31
Wyspiański, Stanisław   139

Xu Shi-pei   221

Yerima, Ahmed   66–68, 228, 229

Zadara, Michał   154
Zadek, Peter   110
Zhu Xin-yan   220
Zioło, Rudolf   138
Zubrzycka-Gałaj, Anna   152

Subject Index

absurd theatre 161
aesthetic experience 132, 153
agency 51, 141
alienation effect 31, 193
altar 12, 13, 21, 57, 96, 102, 103, 151, 216
anastenaria 122, 126, 128
angura 160
anthropophagy 86, 89
Asianization 167, 168
atmosphere 20, 32, 76, 77, 85, 101, 129, 145, 178

Baader-Meinhof gang 5, 94
bacchanale 28
    bacchanalia 15
bacchant 12, 16, 17, 29, 58–63, 66, 76, 78, 82–86, 103–107, 142, 145, 149, 151, 213
barbarism 59, 63, 86
bhava 191, 192
biodynamics 126
bugaku 128, 177
bu-no-mai 128

candomblé 79, 80, 81, 89, 129
cannibalism 48, 86, 87
capitalism 78, 153, 218
carnival 28, 72–77, 84, 87
    carnivalesque body 75–77

catharsis 153
    cathartic 15, 78
Catholic 5–7, 85, 144–146
Chhau 188
Christianity 152
Civil Rights Movement 5, 9
communalism 44, 54
communality xiv, 18, 22, 25–32, 34–36, 46, 65, 66, 75, 180, 226
communism xiii, 6, 137, 142, 143, 218, 227
community xiv, 4, 14–16, 19–22, 26, 30, 32, 35–39, 42, 44, 46, 48, 55–58, 61, 64, 66, 75, 79, 81, 87, 91, 92, 97, 98, 109, 125, 132, 133, 142, 151, 158, 178, 180, 188, 226
consciousness 31, 37, 51, 61, 79
corporeality 130
crisis 5, 11, 14–16, 91, 133, 142, 152–154, 161
culture xii–xv, 7, 9–11, 14, 21, 22, 27, 30, 34, 49, 50, 55, 56, 62–64, 66, 81, 86–88, 97, 100, 101, 111–114, 116, 117, 119, 120, 126–128, 133, 141, 144, 150, 152, 154, 157, 159, 165, 166, 168, 169, 171–173, 176, 178, 181, 182, 190, 199, 200, 202, 203, 208, 209, 211, 215–219, 221–223, 225–227, 229, 230

Dionysus Resurrected: Performances of Euripides' The Bacchae in a Globalizing World, First Edition. Erika Fischer-Lichte.
© 2014 Erika Fischer-Lichte. Published 2014 by John Wiley & Sons, Ltd.

SUBJECT INDEX 237

clash of cultures 22, 157, 158, 169, 200, 202, 203, 216, 222, 225
cultural revolution 7, 10, 11, 28, 29, 37, 44, 45, 49, 63, 64, 218, 219

dance of Pontos 126
dedifferentiation xiv, 15, 19
deification 153, 177
Democratic Convention, Chicago (1968) 5
demotiki 119
destabilization 62, 92, 129, 131, 132, 225, 226
diversity 139, 188
doppelgänger 15, 148

ecstasy 2, 27–29, 32, 36, 38, 44, 57, 59, 66, 76, 80, 93, 132, 146, 190, 214
erhuang 206
eroticism 17, 85, 191

fascism 29, 34, 43, 44
feminist movement 9, 11
festival xii, 3, 9, 15, 25–27, 37, 45, 50, 53, 55, 59, 72, 73, 75, 77, 78, 84, 86, 117, 119, 120, 126, 140, 154, 164, 165, 169, 173, 178, 179, 181, 186, 189, 193, 200, 202, 203, 221, 228
flower power movement 9, 146
formalism 220

Gesamtkunstwerk 209
gynophobia 44

Hebei Bangzi 208, 209, 220, 221
huaju 207, 216

identity 8, 10, 33, 34, 58, 87, 91, 92, 114, 118, 119, 130, 154, 214, 215, 225, 227
  cultural 22, 87, 92, 100, 101, 112–114, 118, 119, 123, 132, 152–154, 226
  individual 31, 34, 225
  national 100, 118, 139, 140, 227
imperialism 201, 215, 219, 220

incorporation 11, 34, 42, 79, 81, 87
individualism 27, 28, 30–32, 44, 54
instinct 31, 65, 117
interculturalism 202, 203
irrationality 174, 190

Kabuki 126, 128, 160, 162, 164, 166, 178, 179
kaiko 128
Kathakali 128, 157, 158, 186–191, 193–204, 207, 227–229
katharevousa 119
kotae ma 128

liberation xiv, 21, 22, 25, 26, 37–42, 46, 50, 54, 56, 61, 63, 68, 74, 78, 103, 142, 143, 160, 170, 219, 226
liminality 11, 27, 51, 54, 57, 75, 77, 92, 131, 132
literarization of theatre 160
LSD 28

madness 3, 18, 32, 101, 106
materiality 118, 129, 130
Meiji era 159–162
melodrama 98, 107, 208, 209
metamorphosis 166
modernism 86
  modernization 159–161, 166, 167
  postmodernism 87
monument 118, 119, 123
mudra 192

nature xiii, 8, 10, 26, 27, 40–42, 48, 53, 75, 77–79, 100, 103, 110, 132, 146, 158, 169, 172, 179, 193, 194, 213, 214
Noh 160, 161, 163–166, 173, 176, 178, 179, 182, 228

omophagia 21, 72, 81, 96, 151
onnagata 163, 179
opa 50, 66
Opera Elektrokandomblaika carnaval 87
orixá 80, 81

padam 193, 197

particularism xii, 218
perception 35, 41, 51, 53, 106, 108, 110, 111, 129, 131, 140, 158, 227
periodicity 77
phenomenality 20, 129, 130, 131
  phenomenal body 46, 130
polis 14, 19, 26, 45, 114, 133, 158
presence 2–4, 28, 29, 58, 59, 130, 174
propaganda 59, 63, 137

rasa 128, 191
realistic acting style 161, 162, 189
  realistic–psychological acting style 31, 160–162
Red Army Faction 5, 94
religion xi, xiv, 16, 18, 79, 142, 146, 150–153, 158, 169, 172–174, 176–178, 180, 187, 188
retheatricalization 110
rhythm 28, 36, 56, 60, 63–66, 76, 80–81, 83, 84, 97, 123, 125, 126, 165, 171, 180, 181, 193, 197, 213, 214, 226
rite of passage 31, 33, 34
ritual xi, 2, 11–21, 27, 28, 30–38, 40, 42, 43, 45, 48, 49, 51, 53–59, 64, 72, 73, 75, 79, 81–85, 87, 92, 95, 96, 98, 99, 112, 113, 117, 122, 123, 126–129, 131, 132, 143, 146, 150, 152, 153, 155, 166, 168, 170, 179, 197, 226
roda 81, 129

sacrifice 12–17, 20, 21, 35, 36, 42, 56–58, 96–98, 102, 103, 146–148, 150, 154, 189, 201, 216
sacrificial ritual 12–16, 18–21, 36, 96, 112, 143
samba 76
  sambista 74, 76
  sambódromo 74, 76
self-referentiality 110, 130
semioticity 129, 131
  semiotic body 46, 130
separation 11, 34, 72, 97, 166, 212
Shingeki 160–162, 165, 167, 207

shogekijo 160, 161
shuoshu 214
sloka 193
sparagmos 13, 21, 50, 72, 81, 85, 86, 96, 100, 112
Stasi 5
stylization 120
su lai bao 214

taboo 87, 88, 142
teatódromo 74, 78
temporality 81, 103, 118
terreiro 79
thyrsus 3, 10, 13, 50, 66, 85, 86, 130, 131, 149
topos 118
Tragicomédia Orgya 87
trance 79, 81, 122, 145, 146, 213
transformation 5–7, 10, 11, 16, 19, 21, 33, 34, 44, 45, 54–56, 58, 65, 75, 77, 78, 85, 87, 88, 91, 92, 105, 131, 132, 148, 181, 198, 200, 203, 225, 226, 230
transition 5, 10, 11, 16, 27, 50, 51, 53–57, 65, 131
tropicália 86

unity x, 15, 17, 26, 66, 179, 188, 189
universality 199, 214, 215, 218, 220

vagina dentata 45
Vietnam War 5, 6, 159, 163
violence 4–9, 11, 14–16, 27, 29, 32, 42–44, 56, 58, 63, 78, 170, 218, 226
visibility 118, 141

Westernization 6, 159, 167, 173
Woodstock Festival 27
wupo 213

xipi 206
xiqu 206, 208, 216–218, 220–223

Yakshagana 188